b 1760 646

D0843321

White Man's Paper Trail

White Man's Paper Trail

GRAND COUNCILS AND
TREATY-MAKING ON THE CENTRAL PLAINS

Stan Hoig

UNIVERSITY PRESS OF COLORADO

"We recognize them as nations; we pledge them our faith; we enter on solemn treaties, and these treaties are ratified as with all foreign Powers, by the highest authority in the nation. You know—every man who ever looked into our Indian affairs knows—it is a shameless lie."

—BISHOP H. B. WHIPPLE, *NEW YORK TIMES,* OCTOBER 3, 1868

"The old story of the Indians is, that the white men call them to councils, where they make promises that are broken, force them to sell their lands, and then send dishonest agents to cheat them out of their pay for it."

—JEROME A. GREENE, ED., "LT. PALMER WRITES FROM THE BOZEMAN TRAIL, 1867–68," *MONTANA MAGAZINE* 28 (JULY 1978), 26

© 2006 by the University Press of Colorado

Published by the University Press of Colorado
5589 Arapahoe Avenue, Suite 206C
Boulder, Colorado 80303

The University Press of Colorado is a proud member of
the Association of American University Presses.

The University Press of Colorado is a cooperative publishing enterprise supported, in part,
by Adams State College, Colorado State University, Fort Lewis College, Mesa State College,
Metropolitan State College of Denver, University of Colorado, University of Northern
Colorado, and Western State College of Colorado.

∞ The paper used in this publication meets the minimum requirements of the American
National Standard for Information Sciences—Permanence of Paper for Printed Library
Materials. ANSI Z39.48-1992

Library of Congress Cataloging-in-Publication Data

Hoig, Stan.
  White man's paper trail : grand councils and treaty-making on the Central Plains / Stan
Hoig.
       p. cm.
  Includes bibliographical references and index.
  ISBN-13: 978-0-87081-829-5 (hardcover : alk. paper)
  ISBN-10: 0-87081-829-5 (hardcover : alk. paper) 1. Indians of North America—Great
Plains—History—19th century—Sources. 2. Indians of North America—Great Plains—
Treaties. 3. Indians of North America—Great Plains—Government relations. 4. Treaties—
United States—History—19th century—Sources. 5. United States—Race relations—
Political aspects. 6. United States—Politics and government—19th century. I. Title.
  E78.G73H577 2006
  323.19707809'034—dc22
                                                                          2005034891

Design by Daniel Pratt

15   14   13   12   11   10   09   08   07   06   10   9   8   7   6   5   4   3   2   1

Contents

List of Illustrations / *ix*
Preface / *xi*

CHAPTER 1   U.S. Indian Treaties: An Essay / 1
CHAPTER 2   The Early Friendship Pacts / 14
CHAPTER 3   A Pathway to the Plains / 27
CHAPTER 4   Probing the Buffalo Prairie / 34
CHAPTER 5   Council on the Canadian / 47
CHAPTER 6   Sam Houston and the Indians / 57
CHAPTER 7   Expelling the Texas Tribes / 69
CHAPTER 8   Fort Laramie and the Road West / 85
CHAPTER 9   Protecting the Santa Fe Trade / 97
CHAPTER 10   For Colorado Gold / 106
CHAPTER 11   Redefining Indian Territory / 115
CHAPTER 12   The Cheyenne Resistance / 124
CHAPTER 13   War and Peace on the Platte / 133
CHAPTER 14   A "Manifest Falsehood" / 143
CHAPTER 15   Red Cloud's Demand / 154
CHAPTER 16   By a Sweep of the Sword / 164
CHAPTER 17   And the Stroke of a Pen / 172
CHAPTER 18   Conclusion: A Racial Parallel / 181

Appendix / 185
Notes / 194
Bibliography / 217
Index / 227

Illustrations

1.1. Lewis Cass and Thomas McKenney at Butte des Morts, 1827 / 12
2.1. Otoe chiefs in council, 1820 / 21
3.1. Pawnee Council, 1820 / 32
4.1. Leavenworth Expedition, 1834 / 39
6.1. Council Spring, 1843 / 67
7.1. Texas Rangers at the Alamo, 1861 / 83
9.1. Trade caravan on the prairie / 99
10.1. Indian delegation at Denver, 1864 / 111
11.1. Hancock at Fort Dodge, 1867 / 119
14.1. Satanta at Medicine Lodge, 1867 / 152
15.1. Red Cloud with President Grant, 1870 / 159
16.1. Crook's battle of the Rosebud, 1876 / 167
17.1. Carl Schurz addresses the Sioux, 1879 / 177

Preface

This book traces the history of treaty-making efforts by the United States (and the Republic of Texas) with the American native tribes that were active as prairie buffalo hunters and generally classed as Plains Indians. It provides a record of the many councils and treaties conducted with the Indian tribes of the Great Plains prior to 1871, when the U.S. Congress halted the practice of treaty making. This study ceases there and makes no attempt to examine either the complicated litigations that have afterward flowed from the initial treaties or the evolving character of U.S.-Indian relations.

Although the Plains tribes constitute only a portion of the larger picture of U.S.-Indian treaty making, the formal pacts made between them and the federal government bear heavily upon the Plains Indian wars during the second half of the nineteenth century. Whereas individual treaties are often discussed in the extensive literature of these wars, an interrelated overview is revealing of the continuum effects upon the various tribes.

Nor is there any intention here of fully examining U.S. Indian policy. That subject has been well attended by scholars such as Monroe E. Price, Felix S. Cohen, William R. Jacobs, Francis Paul Prucha, Vine Deloria Jr., and Raymond J. DeMallie, among others. Prucha's exhaustive studies led him to conclude that in the main, U.S. officials "sought to treat the Indians honorably, even though they acted within a set of circumstances that rested on the premise that white society would prevail."[1] Government officials who directed U.S. Indian policy, he contends, generally worked to ease the pain and suffering wrought upon Indians by white domination.

Although this may be true by intent, if often not carried out in practice, Prucha's premise—the impact of a prevailing white society—demands fuller consideration. Certainly, it was an attitude of white superiority that time and time again caused the bending of U.S. Indian policy to the benefit of white citizens and against that of Indian people. President Andrew Jackson, unwilling to honor solemn Indian treaties in the face of intense opposition from Georgia and other states, contended that the Cherokees would be better off west of the Mississippi River than remaining as neighbors to whites in their southern homeland. The Indians, he insisted, would be degraded and destroyed if they remained in contact with whites. "Humanity and national honor," he argued, "demand that every effort should be made to avert so great a calamity."[2]

One must suspect that behind his altruistic plea, Jackson nurtured an agenda that served whites far better than it did Indian people. Further, a sharp distinction existed between such pious rationalizations by policy makers and the often deceptive practices of those sent afield to arrange treaties with Indian tribes. No one understood this better than Jackson, who as an Indian commissioner had resorted to unadulterated bribery in securing a treaty with the Cherokees in September 1814 at the Chickasaw Council House and elsewhere.[3]

This is not to imply that Jackson was an Indian hater or that every commissioner, white official, and army officer was unsympathetic to tribal people. Indeed, there were honorable men who attempted to exercise judicious compassion in dealing with native peoples. Further, it would be unfair not to credit those who, however partisan their cause may have been, rode far beyond the pleasures and comforts of their own world—often at great risk—to meet with tribal leaders. Regardless, the impact of the agreements they wrought upon the tribes must be recognized.

In the main, this narrative presents a recounting of the formal relations and events of contact occurring between officials of the United States and the Republic of Texas with tribal leaders. It inevitably reflects upon legalities and ethics of Indian policy that lead to even deeper questions relating to national conquest and right of sovereignty. These matters in turn go to the basic question of who is the rightful owner of a given region and by what authority.

If it can be agreed that title to earthly lands was not and is not designated by a Divine Power, then it becomes a question as to what earthly privilege, other than brute force, establishes true title. In relation to U.S. conquest, the Indian claim was based upon prior occupancy and traditional inhabitation. Many of the tribes had only recently won sovereignty over their particular territory of residence on the Central Plains. Most, however, had done so prior to U.S. presence—a fact tacitly recognized in dealing with the tribes as separate, although dependent, nations in treaty making.

The principle of native sovereignty over regions in the New World was first established by Spain, which concluded that foreign discovery did not justify claim to title of lands already occupied. Nor could such properties be claimed by virtue of divine right by either church or crown. The Dutch and English held to this same legal rationale, setting a pattern that was essentially followed by the United States, which, although claiming broader proprietorship oversight in relation to other governments, recognized the right of Indian title to specific lands by virtue of occupancy.[4]

The United States based its proprietorship claim to the Central Plains upon arrangements between certain European powers. By dint of the Louisiana Purchase of 1803, the United States secured the Central Plains from the French (France had ceded it to Spain in 1762 but later regained it by treaty in 1800 and 1801), whose original claim rested upon the virtue of outside (European) discovery and initial exploration. Although this claim was constructed legalistically by men who had the formal education to do so—which thereby made it possible to claim ownership formally where others could not—an important element of its viability was military power. U.S. and Texas ownership of portions of the Louisiana Purchase, for instance, was challenged at one time or another by England, France, Spain, and Mexico and required a certain degree of military strength to resist. Rightly or wrongly, power generally triumphs.

From the beginning, however, this attitude of the United States toward Indian tribes was contradictory at best. It maintained that tribes residing on U.S. soil were subjects of the government as headed by the president, identified to them as their Great or White Father. At the same time, it recognized the tribes' resident rights to certain lands—but only so long as they peacefully acceded to U.S. demands. The penalty of not doing so was almost always forfeiture of territory.

Prior to the Civil War and during the after-surge of westward migration, U.S. officials looked to agriculture—then the mainstay of civilized nations—as the great hope of adaptation for the Indian tribes, some of which already practiced the growing of crops in addition to hunting and gathering. Following the war, herding cattle on the great prairies of the West emerged as another hope for altering Plains Indian culture.

Prucha defines the attitude of the United States as paternalism. That is about as close as U.S. Indian policy can be characterized in a single word, but operationally the U.S. government fostered a relationship seldom known between parent and offspring. Shame to say, but at its worst there was much of the master/thrall connection between the United States and its Indian tribes, which for many years had little or no capacity to defend themselves by law or even the freedom to do so. The United States of the nineteenth century was, after all, a world in which people of African descent and other minority groups, even white females, were denied basic rights of person.

Many American intellectuals promoted the concept of Anglo-Saxon superiority to justify expansionism during the Indian treaty-making period from 1800 to 1850. Reginald Horsman noted in his *Race and Manifest Destiny* that "[t]his was a superior race, and inferior races were doomed to subordinate status or extermination."[5]

Several factors influenced this sense of special right: race and diverse skin color, the piety of organized religion, commercial and social sophistication, the advantages of written communication, and a nationalism supported by a fervent belief in the United States as a great democracy. These factors all worked to make Anglo-Americans feel humanly advantaged and thereby more deserving than the tribal natives. White motivation in treaty making was essentially self-serving and activated by acquisitiveness.[6]

Continuing the European practice, the United States recognized tribal ownership of land; then, coincidental to its expanding military power, it used a variety of means by treaty and governmental edict to take away those lands. By and large, the United States failed badly in living up to the treaty conditions it worked upon the Indian. The ongoing contest between army officers and civilian humanitarians to control Indian policy centered largely on whether, in taking tribal lands and drastically altering native existence, the United States should exercise uncompromising force or act more humanely. By the reckoning of either course, the lands were going to go; and ultimately the Indian would have to take up the white man's mode of livelihood and godly—essentially Christian—beliefs.

These same impulses of U.S. Indian policy and techniques of treaty making east of the Mississippi River spread with U.S. expansion onto the Great Plains. The history of the American West has been couched all too often in terms of U.S. military conquest and Indian battles. Limited examination has been made of U.S. treaties in the context of the Indians' continual loss of land and self-determination.

This may stem from the fact that the shoddy record of U.S. Indian policies and operations is very difficult for many Americans to accept. There are opposing views. One can see the many things wrong with modern society and challenge the notion that the end justifies the means. Or one can find a just rationale in the value of the United States as the world's first modern great democracy and its world-altering precepts of human liberty and justice.

Still another view would assume it as inevitable that eventually tribal America would be overwhelmed by the growth of world population and the march of Western civilization. There is, in fact, throughout the chronology of world history, no satisfactory model for the conquest of lands and the resident peoples in them. *Arguably, if conducted fairly and with commitments fully honored, the treaty system may have been the only humanely plausible method of advancing one society over another. Even today, the treaties and agreements stand as the bedrock of the Indians' remaining rights and protection by law.* There still abides, however, the hard, uncompromising truth that American Indian tribes were victimized time and time again through the white man's treaty making.

Indian people were not long fooled by treaty documents, soon realizing the loss of land and freedom that resulted. They came to despise both the white man's paper and the surveyors who appeared on their lands following a treaty agreement. Unprotected surveying crews, sent afield with treaty documents to prove their right of entry, often discovered it was a dangerous practice to display the white man's paper before a band of angry warriors.

Beyond their legalities, the U.S. Indian treaty documents serve a valuable historical purpose for us today. They provide the names of those involved: the commissioners and their party, military officers who provided escort and bore witness to the agreements, interpreters who often held close ties with Indian people, and most important the tribal leaders, often identified with both an Anglicized version of their names and the English translation. Treaty documents normally list tribal leaders in order of importance, identifying the head chiefs and others in descending rank. Such records thus mark for them a much-deserved place in our recorded history.

The speeches made during the councils were usually recorded verbatim by commission secretaries. From this we receive the enormous benefit of learning the thoughts and opinions of Indian leaders that were often expressed with wisdom, eloquence, and untarnished honesty.

The scope of this book is limited to those pacts initiated through 1871, when the U.S. Congress abandoned the system of formal treaties. The U.S. government then turned to the practice of "Agreements" that no longer recognized the concept of tribal autonomy. Most of the old ratified treaties remain in effect.

Because of the use of "Sioux" as a tribal designation throughout the Indian treaty period, I have held to its use rather than the currently preferred "Lakota." Doing otherwise would create confusion in identifying treaty documents.

Once again, I thank my wife, Patricia Corbell Hoig, for her special help with this work.

White Man's
Paper Trail

U.S. Indian Treaties: An Essay

The winds of fifty-five winters have not blown my brains away.
—CHIPPEWA CHIEF

The British system of making formal treaties with the Indian tribes became the model for Colonial America. Incapable of protecting their early settlements militarily, the British Crown and its colonial governments sought to work out agreements leading to peaceful relations and friendly trade. A cost was always involved for the tribal native: the land on which he resided and hunted. For nearly a century, U.S. administrative officials followed a similar approach of instigating pacts with Indian tribes, considering the tribes as independent nations that legally possessed certain defined territories.[1]

"The United States were clearly the stronger party in every such case," Indian commissioner Francis A. Walker noted, "but the Indians were, in the great body of instances, still so formidable, that to wrest their lands from them by pure, brutal violence would have required an exertion of strength which the government was ill-prepared to make."[2]

Gradually, as the military and economic strength of the United States grew, the benevolence of this concept came into question. Even church humanitarians began to challenge the accepted policy of treaty making. Bishop Henry B. Whipple wrote:

We recognize a wandering tribe as an independent and sovereign nation. We send ambassadors to make a treaty as with our equals, knowing that every provision of the treaty will be our own, that those with whom we make it cannot compel us to observe it, that they are to live within our territory, yet [are] not subject to our laws, that they have no government of their own, and are to receive none from us; in a word, we treat as an independent nation a people whom we will not permit to exercise one single element of that sovereign power which is necessary to a nation's existence.[3]

Fellow churchman Felix Brunot concurred and concluded that often, when the United States entered into the intractable obligation of a treaty, "the fact of its non-performance becomes the occasion of disgraceful and expensive war to subdue their victims to the point of submission to another treaty. And so the tragedy of war and the farce of treaty have been enacted again and again, each time with increasing shame to the nation."[4]

In their *Documents of American Indian Diplomacy*, Vine Deloria Jr. and Raymond J. DeMallie explain how U.S. Indian treaties were developed:

In almost every instance in which treaties and agreements were made, Congress authorized a commission to be sent to a specific tribe or group of tribes to seek certain concessions and sales of particular lands, to establish peace on the frontiers, or even to settle intertribal quarrels. Sometimes the secretary of war (or later the secretary of the interior), the commissioner of Indian affairs, or federal territorial officials would request that the president ask Congress to authorize a treaty commission. Congress would respond and appropriate a fund that the president could use to support commissioners in their efforts to negotiate a treaty. Often specific limitations were placed on the kinds of expenditures that could be made.[5]

Treaty councils conducted with the Indian tribes of the Plains involved a unique intermingling of disassociated cultures and personalities of widely varied backgrounds who were, for the moment, brought together under the call of peace. In truth, however, "peace" was largely a pseudo-cliché used to disguise other agendas.[6] The government sought to extend U.S. influence and autonomy over tribal lands for right of passage, trade, and—as inevitably happened—white settlement. Tribal leaders saw the peace council in an opposite sense politically. To them, treaties offered a means of restricting outside influence over the lives of their people and, at the same time, a way to secure subsistence in an environment where the white man was threatening their traditional food supply.

For tribal members, the early treaty councils were often grand, colorful events much like county fairs. There the various bands could gather, meet old friends and even tribal enemies, sing and dance, flaunt themselves and their horses, conduct courtships, exchange presents, and—as was usually enticingly promised—receive gifts from the world of the white man. Foodstuff and other manufactured products constituted a potent magnet that drew tribal people forth from their native haunts and made them prey to other, often fallacious promises of protection and subsistence.

But as the tribes came to exercise less and less military and political power, as tribespeople became more and more starved (a word not used lightly), as their freedom of range constricted, and as their very tribal existence became direly threatened, the treaty council was much less celebratory. The hungry bands came to sign the white man's paper, collect their presents, and hurry back to their retreats.

Formal peace councils and treaty signings were vital elements of U.S. relations with the Indian tribes of America, bearing enormous effect upon both the course of the new nation and the lives of native people. In truth, the treaties created a backdrop for the drama of the Anglo-American advance across the North American continent, providing a legalistic and, by any consideration, moralistic screen against which the Indian wars were conducted. Few events of our Indian-related history— the opening of trade routes through Indian country, the establishment of forts and agencies, white settlement of Indian lands, the use of military force—can be rightly considered without reference to the treaty councils and the agreements thereupon entered into. These affairs, wherein U.S. peace commissioners persuaded chiefs of various tribes to sign formal pacts, bear directly upon the modern, breast-beating claim of "how the West was won."

Without exception, it was the United States that initiated treaties with the Indians, generally with ulterior motives that went well beyond mere peaceful relations. Most U.S. Indian treaties fall into one of four categories: (1) Military Support Treaties, initiated for the purpose of gaining fighting assistance in time of war; (2) Right of Passage Treaties, which sought acquiescence and protection from Indian tribes for white traders, explorers, immigrants, and others passing through Indian lands; (3) Assignment of Territory Treaties, effected generally to isolate Indian groups from the white population or to remove them to distant areas;

and (4) Restriction of Territory Treaties that resulted as white citizens demanded areas to which the Indians had been reassigned.

After Congress curtailed formal treaty making in 1871, the United States turned to enacting legal contracts with the Indian tribes that were called "Agreements." The Railroad Right-of-Way Agreement gave access to railroad construction across Indian reservations and served as a principal instrument in fulfilling the concept of a national Manifest Destiny. Railroads, in fact, accelerated the spread of whites across the Plains far beyond the speed achieved by covered wagons, creating depots or stations that soon became white town sites surrounded by ranches and farms.

Confiscation of Territory Agreements sounded the death knell to traditional tribal life by inducing tribal members to accept individual land allotments that severely disrupted and often destroyed their normal methods of self-governance.

During the early years of its existence, the United States of America was concerned with the native tribes located within its original Atlantic seaboard states. Generally, the newly formed nation followed the British pattern of holding grand councils and distributing presents—usually beads and trinkets—to work out formal pacts with the tribes. The essential issues at first were Indian support for military action against England, development of commerce, and safe passage for white traders who entered Indian lands. As settlers pushed ever forward onto tribal domains, the primary concern became protection for frontier settlements. Ever present was the white man's desire to occupy more and more Indian land.

The idea of removing the eastern tribes to beyond the Mississippi River emerged at the time of the Louisiana Purchase in 1803.[7] Madison's secretary of war, James Barbour, looked to pledge in "most solemn faith that it [the Western lands] shall be theirs forever."[8] Such was often promised either orally or by formal pact. Eventually, the United States sought treaty agreements to remove the Indians from white-invaded territory. Pacts were initiated whereby many northeastern tribes were removed to the Midwest and, eventually, on beyond the Mississippi River. Lands of the southern tribes—the Cherokees, Creeks, Choctaws, Chickasaws, and Seminoles—were reduced gradually by a series of treaties that followed military actions against them. Ultimately, these tribes were removed to the designated "Indian Territory" of present Oklahoma through the determined efforts of presidents Andrew Jackson and Martin Van Buren.

The original pattern of the Indian peace council involved a combination of English formality and native tradition. Representatives of the Crown sought to work out agreements and place them in writing with the validation of responsible signatories. In doing so, they found it convenient to utilize Indian protocol common to virtually all of the American tribes. This included the council circle, the ritual of smoking the calumet, exchange of gifts, oratory, and the presentation of peace symbols. A string or belt of white beads or shells known as "wampum" was commonly used by the eastern tribes.[9]

When a tribe gathered at an assigned locale, the chiefs and headmen would solemnly seat themselves cross-legged in a semicircle on the ground before the white representatives. A sacred calumet was passed around to all assembled to puff as a token of their willingness to meet in peace. The head commissioner would then address the gathering. On occasion a message would be delivered from the head of state, such as that from King George III read at a meeting with the Catawba Indians of Virginia in February 1756 to enlist their help against the French.

> Our common father, the Great King of England, has been pleased to direct your Brother, the Governor of Virginia, to send Commissioners hither, to assure you of his Affection, and to present you with as many Goods in Token thereof as it was convenient to send so far, at this Season of the Year. It was his Pleasure to appoint us to that charge, and at the same Time, to direct us to deliver you a Speech in his Name, with a belt of Wampum, which we are now ready to do, and hope you will be attentive thereto.[10]

The art of group discussion and debate was well developed among native peoples even before the influence of Europeans. The Cherokees maintained large council houses, some holding up to 500 people, and conducted regular sessions of governance. Moreover, they and other tribes traditionally designated a qualified person as their titled speaker.[11] In 1785, Nancy Ward, the famous Cherokee war-woman and tribal leader, addressed U.S. peace commissioners (who had come to make peace— and obtain land) at Hopewell, South Carolina:

> I am fond of hearing that there is a peace, and I hope you have now taken us by the hand in real friendship. I have a pipe and a little tobacco to give the commissioners to smoke in friendship. I look on you, and the red people as my children. Your having determined on peace is most pleasing to me, for I have seen much trouble during the late war. I am old, but I hope yet to bear children, who

will grow up and people our nation, as we are now to be under the protection of Congress, and shall have no more disturbances. [She then presented a string, a little pipe, and some tobacco to the commissioners.] The talk I have given, is from the young warriors I have raised in my town, as well as myself. They rejoice that we have peace, and we hope the chain of friendship will never more be broke.[12]

In dealing with Indian tribes, white commissioners generally initiated the talks by declaring the Indians' love of the "Great Father" and his people and their desire for peace and friendship. They would then outline their wishes or demands upon the tribe and the rewards that were promised in return.

Prominent chiefs responded in-kind with a welcoming talk. Many of their speeches as recorded by commission secretaries are heartfelt addresses drawing on symbols (often aped by white commissioners) from the natural world about them. In truth, many Indian leaders were great orators, an outstanding attribute of the American native revealing of his intellect. A Colonial journal, published in 1760, wrote of this communicative ability:

> Here it is that their orators employ, and display those talents which distinguish them for eloquence and knowledge of public business, in both of which some of them are admirable. . . . The chief skill of these orators [lies] in giving an artful turn to affairs, and in expressing their thoughts in a bold figurative manner, much stronger than we could bear in this part of the world, and with gestures equally violent, but often extremely natural and expressive.[13]

At the Treaty of Long Island, Tennessee, in 1877, wise old Cherokee chief Corn Tassel, an uncle of the renowned Sequoyah, lectured the commissioners on how the "great God of Nature" had placed the Indian and the white man in different situations:

> He has endowed you with many superior advantages; but he has not created us to be your slaves. We are a separate people! He has given each their lands, under distinct considerations and circumstances; he has stocked yours with cows, ours with buffaloe; yours with hogs, ours with bear; yours with sheep, ours with deer. He has, indeed, given you an advantage in this, that your cattle are tame and domestic while ours are wild and demand not only a larger space for range, but art [skill] to hunt and kill them. . . . Indeed much has been advanced on the want of what you term civilization among the Indians; and many proposals have been

made to us to adopt your laws, your religion, your manners and your customs. But, we confess that we do not yet see the propriety, or practicability of such a reformation, and should be better pleased with beholding the good effect of these doctrines in your own practices than with hearing you talk about them.[14]

Following the opening formalities of a council, chiefs normally retired to consult among themselves on the issues raised by the commissioners. Their views and arguments would be presented in forthcoming meetings. When verbal agreements had been reached, a treaty document was read and interpreted before being laid out on a table. By importance of rank, each chief then stepped forward, took the prepared quill pen in hand, and made an "x" where a commission aide indicated the chief's name was to be. The document might list both the chief's tribal name (as interpreted) and the English translation of it, or only one or the other.

When the signing had been completed, the distribution of presents—purposely withheld pending acceptance of the treaty stipulations—occurred. For the often impoverished tribes, this was a much anticipated event. Once the goods had been divided, the women quickly loaded their take aboard packhorses and broke camp. The assemblage then dissolved, ending the treaty council. On many occasions, in returning home or to Washington, D.C., the commissioners took with them a delegation of chiefs or headmen and at times their wives, whom they wished to impress with the magnitude and power of the white people.

Such visits to the white man's cities—particularly Washington but sometimes Philadelphia, Boston, or New York City—were a significant part of official U.S. strategy in influencing tribal leaders and enhancing their treaty commitments. Tours of the U.S. Capitol, the White House, army posts, shipyards, and other government institutions were designed to awe them with the U.S. military might. Visits to museums, theaters, marketplaces, and residential areas revealed a higher civilization and manner of livelihood that, it was thought, would cause the chiefs to return home and convince their people to alter their modes of existence and be less resistive to U.S. interests. Indeed, the visiting delegations were impressed, even though they were inevitably discomforted by the long, painful journeys and by being removed from their natural habitat. A number of such Indian delegates, in fact, died while in Washington, D.C., and are buried in the Congressional Cemetery.

But there was a negative reaction to such visits seldom foreseen by government officials. Those tribesmen who had remained at home were not easily convinced of the stories the chiefs told upon returning. It was often thought that the white men had placed "bad medicine" over the delegation's eyes to deceive them and make them see things that did not really exist.[15] After a group of Kiowa chiefs returned from Washington in 1873, they told their people of the many great sights and the endless white people they had seen. Their stories seemed so fanciful that the chiefs were believed to have fallen under a sorcerer's spell. At times they were derided as being "silly headed, like wolves running wild on the plains."[16]

Some treaty commissions dealt honestly and forthrightly with the Indians, and some were blatantly deceitful. But even when guided by the noblest of purposes, commissioners had the advantage in setting agendas, manipulating written language and the nuances of treaty commitments, and effecting agreements through the promise of reward, threat of punishment, or guise of deceptive misunderstanding. The commissioners, having been specifically instructed as to the wishes of the president, were well aware that they were to represent the interests of the United States.[17]

"I knew that the concessions the Indians were asked to make," one commissioner confessed, "were immensely more valuable than was indicated by the compensation proposed; that I was bound in good faith to the Indians of the agency to advise them for their good. Still, I was a member of the commission and could not counsel the Indians to reject the proposal."[18]

The overwhelming might of the United States, abetted in the main by its firearms and organized soldiery, in itself weighed heavily on the treaty conventions.

The debate on issues in any given treaty council provided the government with still another element of power: that of learned men pitted against unschooled tribal people. But commissioners often found that although the chiefs were deficient in their ability to read and write, their capacity to observe, reason, and express themselves was by no means limited. An English commissioner once commented that "[i]n their publick Treaties no People on earth are more open, explicit, and Direct. Nor are they excelled by any in the observance of them."[19]

Bishop H. B. Whipple recited the case of a treaty effort with the Chippewa Indians. Having seen the document in advance, Whipple told the U.S. agent: "The Indians will not sign this treaty, they are not fools. This is the poorest strip of land in Minnesota, and is unfit for cultivation. You propose to take their arable land, their best hunting ground, their rice fields, and their fisheries, and give them a country where they cannot live without the support of the government."

Nonetheless, the agent assembled the tribe to convince its members to sign the treaty, employing the figurative language of the Indian. "My red brothers," he said, "the winds of fifty-five winters have blown over my head and have silvered it with gray. In all that time I have not done wrong to a single human being. As the representative of the Great Father and as your friend, I advise you to sign this treaty at once."

After a moment of silence, a tribal elder rose to his feet.

"My father," he said, "look at me! The winds of fifty-five years have blown over my head, and have silvered it with gray. But—they haven't blown my brains away."[20]

Andrew Jackson played an active role in promoting fraudulent Indian treaties. Although his reputation as an "Indian hater" has been challenged, certain facts remain.[21] During the 1830s the Jackson administration supported the state of Georgia's overriding of solemn treaty agreements the United States made with the Cherokee Indians. Unrelentingly determined to remove the southern tribes from their native lands in 1830, Jackson pushed his Indian Removal Bill through Congress. Through Jackson's political pressure, it passed by one vote over strong congressional sympathy for Indian rights.

When the large and literately advanced tribes continued to resist, Jackson sent his emissaries to divide and conquer, pitting half-blood against less tutored full-blood elements. The tribes were finally forced from their homelands in Georgia, Tennessee, Alabama, and Mississippi and underwent often tragic travail in moving west and resettling there. By the 1835 Treaty of New Echota with the Cherokees, Jackson ignored the duly elected and popularly supported Cherokee leadership under Chief John Ross and instead accepted an ad hoc opposition group contrived by his commissioner, the Rev. John F. Schermerhorn.[22]

Bribery constituted another principal weapon in treaty making. Tribal leaders could be rewarded with special favors of various sorts: swords, peace medals, monetary supplements. Military uniforms of colonel or general rank were much-prized items. Chiefs normally had first choice from annuity allotments. At times, recognition of chieftain status for a compliant tribal member over a refractory leader could secure treaty conformity. Indeed, although many stalwart leaders worked diligently and forcefully against great odds to win the best agreements possible, some chiefs let themselves be seduced into betraying the welfare of their tribe.

Communication between U.S. commissioners and tribal leaders was conducted through interpreters—traders, tribal half bloods, or other frontier men or women, occasionally captives—who spoke both the native tongue and English or who could express ideas with the universal sign language or pidgin English. On occasion, it was necessary to translate through more than one language, as Jesse Chisholm did for Col. Henry Dodge in 1834: "[A] Toyash [Wichita] Indian who speaks the Caddo tongue communicated with Chisholm, one of our friends who speaks English and Caddo."[23] At times, when a tribesman who knew some Spanish or French was available, he was used to translate between English and native dialect.

Interpreters provided a critical service in exchanging thoughts across the chasm of unfamiliar languages. But flaws in interpretation could influence both meaning and understanding of these critical arrangements between conflicting societies. Although Indians knew the geography of their lands surprisingly well, descriptions of uncharted land to be ceded or assigned provided a major source of misunderstanding, and the language defining Indians' relationship to that land was often unclear.

"Even when there was no question regarding the good faith of the two parties," one authority noted, "there were great difficulties in drafting the intentions of both sides. As the Indians had no written language and few [i.e., practically none] of the chiefs even had a knowledge of English, the negotiations were carried on generally through interpreters, many of whom were inefficient."[24]

Henry Schoolcraft complained in 1838 that the Indian Department was "very much in the hands of ignorant and immoral interpreters, who frequently misconceive the point to be interpreted."[25] Additionally, treaty agreements sometimes held vested interests for interpreters who had married into a tribe or were offspring therefrom. There is no question, however, that frontiersmen such as William Bent, John Simpson Smith, Jesse Chisholm, and James Bridger rendered invaluable service to both the tribes and the government in serving as treaty council interpreters.

The agreement the Indians signed was not always what they got. Every treaty was subject to the approval of the U.S. Senate and the president. If revised, the modified version of the treaty had to be taken back for reacceptance by tribal leaders. Usually, it took a year or two for the revised pact to be returned to the tribe, and by that time both the tribal leadership and the situation on the prairie might have been altered.

Another enormous flaw in the system of Indian treaties lay in the government's reluctance to carry out its commitments. A large part of this resulted from the failure of a parsimonious Congress to enact measures called for by treaty, at times failing even to appropriate funds to adequately feed the tribes as their treaty had duly promised. Further, the system of providing Indian food and supplies through profiteering private contractors often opened the door to the poorest foodstuff and worthless goods being supplied.

John D. Miles, agent for the Southern Cheyennes and Arapahos, admitted to the pitiful quality of the beef he had issued to his charges. He complained about the matter to Texas beef contractors, yet he had little choice but to take what they drove to his agency. Had he done otherwise, the Indians would have gone without food.[26]

Although not written into the Treaty of Medicine Lodge in 1867, the Cheyennes and Arapahos were promised an issuance of guns and ammunition, which the tribes insisted were needed to feed themselves by the hunt through the winter as the government intended. But the commission had second thoughts about arming the Cheyenne Dog Soldiers and provided only a few defective cast-iron pistols that would not even snap a percussion cap. Further, to get the Dog Soldiers to sign the treaty, Commissioner John B. Henderson orally assured them that they would still be free to range in western Kansas so long as the buffalo remained, a nonbinding verbal concession that essentially contradicted the central purpose of the treaty.[27]

Men assigned as agents for political reasons often proved either incompetent or corrupt. It was the dire condition of the agency system that led President Ulysses S. Grant to place the Indian Bureau in the hands of the Quakers in 1869. Further, the much repeated promise of U.S. protection for the tribes was a sham both in its intent and its potential. Seldom did the United States have the military ability or the true desire to safeguard Indian tribes from either their tribal enemies or white Americans. Further, in many instances the U.S. military proved to be more a violator than a protector of tribal interests.

Although manipulation and deceit were in play throughout the making of U.S. Indian treaties, on occasion the welfare and rights of Indians were duly considered and protected by competent commissioners, concerned agents, honest interpreters, and conscientious military officers. Lewis Cass, when governor of Michigan and ex officio superintendent of Indian affairs for the region, wrote to Secretary of War John Calhoun in regard to a purchase of Indian lands: "I should badly discharge the trust reposed in me, and fail altogether in carrying into effect the views of the government, had I endeavored to procure the land at the low-

Commissioners Lewis Cass and Col. Thomas L. McKenney arrive at the Butte des Morts council grounds (J. O. Lewis, Aboriginal Port Folio).

est possible price which their necessities might have induced them to accept."[28]

U.S. exploration of the lands beyond the Mississippi River began with the Louisiana Purchase of 1803, even as treaties of relocation were being worked out with the sedentary tribes of the East and South. Although essentially the same format of treaty making was followed with the migrant tribes of the Central Plains, the greater distances from supply centers and the logistics of contacting and bringing together the Plains Indians created special problems.

These tribes' warring traditions presented still another obstacle. Chiefs of the Plains tribes had limited control over war societies and no regulatory body to restrict the activities of war parties that chose to ignore treaty commitments. A fallacious but pervasive notion to the contrary existed among officials who initiated treaties on the basis that the signatory chiefs held strict command authority over the entirety of their tribes. Seldom was that the case. This serious problem was two-sided, for many times the federal government exercised little control over its citizens or military forces on the distant prairie.

The United States was not the only body engaged in seeking accommodations with the Plains tribes. Before it became a state of the Union in 1845, the Republic of Texas dealt with Indian problems relating to its region. After being relocated in the Indian Territory, the Cherokees and Creeks also worked to help the United States resolve conflicts with the prairie tribes in their difficult adjustment to America's rush for empire.

The treaty system had begun during the time when the military and political posture of the Indian tribes was a force to be reckoned with. Tribes were considered separate nations that, although dependent upon the United States, were deserving of legal proprietorship of their native domain. But over the years that concept eroded as the United States grew stronger and the tribes weaker. Eventually, the government was able to break up the tribal system altogether, forcing native people to accept individual allotments and, by spurious methods, sell much of their tribal properties.[29] The citizenship role thrust upon Indians proved to be a direly second-class status from which many have not escaped even today.

CHAPTER TWO

The Early Friendship Pacts

Your great father has not sent us here to ask any thing from you; we want nothing— not the smallest piece of your land—not a single article of your property.
—TREATY COMMISSIONER WILLIAM CLARK

The Meriwether Lewis and William Clark Expedition of 1804–1806 constituted the first official U.S. contact with tribes of the American Central Plains. The explorers made no attempt, however, to conduct any formal peace treaties with the Indians they met. During the summer of 1806, Lt. Zebulon Pike and his "Damn'd set of rascels" visited a Kitkehahki Pawnee village on the Republican River of present Nebraska. They found that an army from Mexico had only recently visited the village, which was flying the Spanish flag. The Pawnees received Pike and his men in friendship but strongly objected to their continuing on to the country of their enemies in the Southwest.[1]

"You are a brave young warrior," Chief White Wolf (Sharitarish, Characterish) told Pike. "I respect you. I love brave men. Do not oblige me to hurt you. You have only twenty-five men while I can command a thousand."[2]

Undeterred, Pike led his men through the mass of armed, hooting warriors who were restrained by White Wolf. "Were I to stop you now," the chief told the explorer, "I should forever after feel myself a coward."[3]

Relations with Indian tribes along the Missouri River, however, deteriorated badly in the years following these initial explorations. The growing fur trade and the competition between U.S. and British/Canadian concerns for the game-rich Northwest contributed to a fierce rivalry for the allegiance and support of the Indians along the crucial water route of the Missouri River. As Indian depredations against U.S. fur traders increased, western newspapers raised a loud cry of British instigation. The cry was heeded in Washington, D.C.[4]

James Madison was president during the summer of 1815 when a treaty-making party traveled up the Mississippi River to the Portage des Sioux near St. Louis, Missouri (then Indian Territory). The group was led by William Clark (now governor and superintendent of Indian affairs for Missouri Territory), Illinois governor Ninian Edwards, and St. Louis pioneer Auguste Chouteau. They were accompanied by Missouri militia leader Henry Dodge (later governor of Wisconsin Territory) and fur trader Manuel Lisa, among others. Talks were conducted with chiefs of the Pottawatomie, Piankeshaw, Teton Sioux, Sioux of the Lakes, Sioux of St. Peter's River, Omaha, Kickapoo, Osage, Sac, Fox, Iowa, and Kansa (Kaw) tribes. With each of these groups, the commissioners arranged treaties of peace and friendship "on the same footing upon which they stood before the late war between the United States and Great Britain."[5] Several of these tribes would be active on the buffalo prairies in the years ahead.

In common, the treaties stipulated that all past injuries or acts of hostility committed by either party would be forgiven. The chiefs and warriors acknowledged themselves and their tribe to be under the protection of the United States of America and that nation alone. Still other treaties were signed at St. Louis during the spring of 1816 with the Sac of the Rock River, Eastern Sioux, and Winnebago tribes.[6]

To counter the British fur-trade competition in the Northwest, in 1818, Secretary of War John C. Calhoun ordered the building of a fort at the mouth of the Yellowstone, as well as other posts on the Missouri River. Calhoun and President Monroe hoped not only to quell the Indian troubles along the river and drive British traders from the region but also to open a trade route to the Pacific and possibly on to China.

To do so, Col. Henry Atkinson was chosen to carry out the military-scientific effort, which became known as the Yellowstone Expedition. By October 1819, Atkinson, a North Carolinian whose military experience had been largely administrative, had moved his Sixth Infantry troops to a site three miles above present Council Bluffs, Iowa.[7] There he erected a small military redoubt that he named Cantonment Missouri.

This done, he sent runners to contact the Pawnee Indians, whom he held responsible for an attack on an army paymaster detachment and theft of its horses and guns. During the previous year at St. Louis, Clark and Chouteau, representing the United States, had signed friendship treaties with four bands of Pawnees designated as the Grand Pawnees, Noisy Pawnees, Pawnee Republic, and Pawnee Marhar (Maha). The United States had promised them protection, and the Pawnees agreed to turn over anyone who violated their accord. Commitments by both soon proved unrealistic.[8]

Atkinson had no previous experience dealing with Indians. Unaware of impassioned tribal enmities, when the Pawnee delegation arrived he rewarded the chiefs with sabers and feasted them with a ceremonial dinner. This action angered an Omaha chief, who accused Atkinson of treating with his enemies.[9] Still, Atkinson realized the value of pomp and ceremony in negotiating with the Indians. He paraded his troops before them and conducted military maneuvers in a show of U.S. military strength even as he demonstrated his friendship.

On September 30, Atkinson and Maj. Benjamin O'Fallon concluded a treaty with the Pawnees. By its terms the Pawnees were to accept the supremacy of the United States, in whose territorial limits they resided. The United States would take them under its protection and establish sites for trade, which would be conducted only with authorized U.S. citizens. The Pawnee chiefs bound themselves to protect the traders and their property, as well as any American citizen traveling through their country. Any tribal member guilty of offending a white man would be delivered to U.S. authorities. Further, the tribe would not trade or supply any other nation with guns or other implements of war. Eshcatarpa (The Bad Chief) and twenty-four other Pawnee chiefs x-ed the document.

With winter close at hand, Atkinson was forced to hold the Yellowstone Expedition at Cantonment Missouri until the next spring before moving on to the Mandan villages at the bend of the Missouri and to the Yellowstone River. The great financial panic of 1819 and ensuing national depression, however, brought severe reductions in army appropriations. Congress rejected any further funds for the Yellowstone Expedition, and in April Calhoun cancelled it. He did, however, call for Cantonment Missouri to be strengthened. During the winter of 1819 and 1820, the isolated post suffered a severe outbreak of scurvy. Nonetheless, its importance as an advance up the Missouri caused it to become the largest of all U.S. military posts for a time. In 1821 the army renamed it Fort Atkinson.

Troubles along the river persisted, however. The most violent of these involved the Arikara, who resided above the Moreau River in present South Dakota. During 1822 a large Arikara war party raided a Missouri Fur Company post. The loss of two of their men on this occasion caused them to seek revenge against the fur traders. Arikaras' feelings were still high when William Ashley arrived at their villages the following year. The Indians attacked his party and drove it downstream, with a loss of much property and fourteen men killed. Col. Henry Leavenworth, with a combined force of 226 troops, hurried forth from St. Louis to punish the Indians. They were joined by some fur company employees and several hundred allied Sioux warriors to form a so-called Missouri Legion.

The Sioux reached the Arikara village first and attacked it unsuccessfully. When Leavenworth arrived, he bombarded the village with his four small artillery pieces. The Indians fled their homes, leaving Leavenworth without a victory and the issue of transportation safety on the Missouri still unresolved.[10]

Simultaneous to the Arikara difficulty, word arrived in St. Louis of an attack on a party of Missouri Fur Company men by the Blackfoot Indians of Montana. Seven employees had been killed and $15,000 worth of furs taken. These and other incidents ignited a public clamor for the government to act. Recognizing the army's inability to forcibly intimidate the Indians along the Missouri River or to provide adequate protection for the fur trade, Congress approved an Indian Peace Commission by which a new effort could be made to initiate treaties with tribes along the river.

Atkinson was again placed in command of a new Yellowstone Expedition, and he and O'Fallon were appointed as commissioners to treat with the Indians. Although Atkinson was military and O'Fallon—a nephew of Governor Clark—represented the Indian Department, their attitudes in dealing with the Indians were the opposite of the expected. Whereas O'Fallon was harsh and less compromising, Atkinson was more humane and flexible. Their disagreement on how to deal with Indians arose during the Pawnee affair and continued to haunt them throughout their relationship. On one occasion, it brought them to the point of physical combat.

Supporting the two men was a military escort of 476 First and Sixth Infantry troops, which, it was hoped, would impress the Indians with the importance and military power of the United States. Fort Atkinson would serve as a base from which to launch the expedition, but reaching it with the equipment and other encumbrance of the expedition was not easy. Having found in 1819 that steamboats often ran aground and were undependable for river use, Atkinson made use of shallow-draft keelboats equipped with paddle wheels to transport men and supplies. The paddle wheels were operated by an inventive system whereby a crew seated on either side of the boat exerted power through a system of shafts and cogwheels. This method was supplemented by oars, poles, and sails when the wind was favorable and at times by the cordelling method whereby men on shore pulled the boats upstream by rope, sometimes over banks 120 feet high. To test the boats, Maj. Stephen W. Kearny was sent ahead from St. Louis to Fort Atkinson in September 1824 in four of the keelboats with four companies of troops.[11]

The transportation experiment was a success, and on March 17, 1825, the Atkinson-O'Fallon Expedition set forth up the Missouri River from St. Louis in nine keelboats: the *Buffalo, Elk, White Bear, Otter, Raccoon, Beaver, Mink, Muskrat,* and the sutler's transport *Lafayette*.[12] Kearny and Leavenworth, both of whom became famous in the West, were members of the party. Another was Capt. Richard Barnes Mason, later the first military governor of California. It took a month and two days for the expedition to reach Fort Atkinson at Council Bluffs, arriving on April 19. There it rested, repaired equipment, and waited for supplies to arrive.

Finally, early on the morning of May 16, the remaining garrison and families waved goodbye from the river bluffs as the expedition began its voyage upstream. Forty horsemen under Capt. William Armstrong followed the expedition by land. They reached the Ponca villages in present northeastern Nebraska several days ahead of the flotilla, which seldom made over twenty miles on a good day and halted occasionally to make repairs. On June 8 the expedition disembarked at the mouth of White Paint Creek and began clearing ground for a tent encampment in preparation for the first U.S. experience in conducting treaties with the tribes of the Central Plains.

That same day the Ponca chiefs and headmen were received, the object of the expedition was explained, and a time was set for a council the following day. Early the next morning, Atkinson paraded his brigade of troops in full uniform before the crowd of curious Ponca onlookers. With other troops in full dress lining the perimeter of the council area at noon, the brigade band performed several musical airs. O'Fallon made an opening address and passed out medals and a few presents to the leading men. Atkinson then rose to explain that his mission was one of peace and friendship and to offer a treaty to that effect. He had, in fact, brought the treaty already drawn up and printed. Its provisions would be explained, but there would be no negotiating. The Poncas were expected to simply agree. They did so unanimously and were then awarded more presents that included a few guns, cloth, blankets, knives, and tobacco.

Each of the treaties concluded by Atkinson and O'Fallon with the tribes along the Missouri River contained several basic agreements, all weighing heavily in favor of the United States. The tribes would acknowledge the supremacy of the United States, they would trade only with the United States and at places designated by the president, traders not authorized by the United States would be apprehended and turned over to U.S. officials, the Indians would not sell or trade guns and ammunition with tribes unfriendly to the United States, and they would deliver to authorities for punishment any Indian having committed an injury on a U.S. citizen. Any U.S. citizen guilty of crimes against the Indians, the treaties solemnly promised, would be punished in a like manner.[13]

As a reward for doing these things, the tribes were promised the protection and friendship of the United States. The treaties did not say from whom the tribes would be protected: a foreign power, U.S. citizens, or other tribes that presented their principal threat. In any sense, the promise was an empty one at best; the United States had little capacity to provide the tribes with protection. And in many respects, the vows of friendship made by either side would prove equally as hollow.

After repairing machinery on the keelboats, on June 10 the expedition made ready to push on. As it did so, a group of Ponca warriors wearing skins and eagle feathers and their bodies daubed with paint appeared before the boats and performed a parting war dance.[14] Still fighting sandbars, snags, and breakdowns but enjoying a good buffalo kill en route, the expedition headed on up the Missouri, reaching the mouth of the White River on the sixteenth. There they were signaled from the bank by two Indians who proved to be a Sioux father and son. The Indians carried a message and a half dozen buffalo tongues sent by subagent Peter Wilson at Fort Kiowa (or Kioway, as it was then called), an American Fur Company post located a few miles upriver.[15]

On the following day the expedition arrived at Fort Lookout, a Columbia Fur Company post located just below Fort Kiowa on the right (west) bank of the Missouri River. Wilson, who met them there, said the main bands of Sioux camped up the Teton River (now Bad River) were out on a buffalo hunt. Runners were sent to bring them in, and others were dispatched to look for the Cheyennes.[16] The Teton, Yankton, and Yanktonai bands of the Sioux soon arrived. On the morning of June 21, following a showy parade of the uniformed troops under arms, talks got under way. The expedition's journalist described the Sioux:

> These Tribes deport themselves with gravity & dignity. They dress well in long leggins of dressed skin, shirts, or rather a close hunting shirt with sleeves & highly ornamented with fringe & porcupine quills. Robes of Dressed Buffalo & coverings of various sorts for the head such as skins of fured (sic) animals & some curiously formed with ears of animals attached in an upright manner.[17]

The first day was consumed mostly in determining which chiefs and headmen would represent each band. A Yankton captive girl whom O'Fallon had purchased from the Otoes was returned to her people as a token of goodwill. That night Atkinson ordered twelve or more rockets fired across the river to impress the Indians.

On the following day, as with the Poncas, Atkinson and O'Fallon explained the treaty, and the chiefs and leading warriors accepted it without question or discussion. Gifts, a few guns, and other goods were distributed to the top men. In return, the Sioux presented Atkinson and O'Fallon with Indian clothing of dressed leather, robes, two eagle feather caps, and a half dozen pipes.

The flotilla pushed slowly past Fort Kiowa while members of the commission party conducted hunting excursions ashore. On June 30 the expedition camped a short distance above the mouth of the Teton River (Pierre, South Dakota). There they were met by the Oglala Sioux, Saone Sioux, and Cheyennes. The Oglala, whose lodges were reckoned at 110 and warriors at 250, arrived first, led by their principal chief Standing Buffalo, a "dignified & well behaved man of great influence."[18] The Saones and Cheyennes appeared soon after and were present to share in a special event of hospitality, a dog feast, that the Oglalas held for the commissioners and army officers on July 4.

The guests were seated on buffalo robes, beaver skins, and domestic cloth around the outer rim of a lodge, the same being provided to the commissioners. A charged pipe rested on a pedestal of buffalo dung before them. Standing Buffalo lit the pipe and passed it to Atkinson who, after taking a few puffs, handed it on to O'Fallon. Once the pipe had made the rounds, Standing Buffalo emptied the ashes and presented it to the general. The commission party then bravely partook of a meal consisting of the flesh of thirteen dogs well boiled in kettles. Further, the drinking water brought up from the Missouri River in buffalo paunches held a disagreeable taste. The affair lasted an hour and a half, after which

An Otoe chief expresses his desire for peace to officers of the 1819 Yellowstone Expedition (James, Account of an Expedition to the Rocky Mountains).

the commission party returned to their camp to top their Indian meal with wine and fruit.[19]

The next morning, Atkinson put the military on display for the Indians, with the brigade marching in review. The cavalry escort dashed handsomely across the prairie with the artillery caissons bouncing along behind. That night Atkinson invited the chiefs to witness the firing of twenty rockets into the night sky. A council with chiefs of the Oglalas, Saones, and Cheyennes followed the next day, and treaties were readily signed. Then followed the gift presentations: three horses, pistols, and, to the headmen, swords. That evening the Cheyenne principal chief, High-backed Wolf, returned to camp with a handsome mule, which he presented to Atkinson. An officer observed of the chief, "He is one of the most dignified & elegant looking men I ever saw."[20]

Another treaty was made with a band of Saones under Fire Heart above the mouth of the Cheyenne River. Although gifts were issued as usual, O'Fallon spied a British medal on a young brave in the band and demanded that it be given up. The treaty council ended at half past twelve, whereupon Atkinson and O'Fallon mounted Indian ponies and rode a short distance into the hills to investigate an intriguing discovery.

Several footprints of a medium-sized man were clearly distinguishable in a solid eleven-by-nine-foot rock on a hillside.[21]

On July 15 the commission party went into camp a half mile below the Arikara village, located on the west bank of the Missouri two miles below the mouth of Grand River. A group of Hunkpapa Sioux, on a peace mission to the Arikaras with whom they had been at war, visited them there. After initiating a treaty with the Hunkpapas under Little White Bear, Atkinson and O'Fallon accepted an invitation to a feast at the Arikara village. Finding a number of the Indians reeling about drunk, they returned to their camp in disgust. The Arikaras sent word asking them to come back. Atkinson declined, but O'Fallon did return to admonish the Arikaras for their past behavior with the traders. In repentance, they offered him seven horses, a pile of buffalo meat, and some pots.

The next morning the villagers massed atop a rise to watch Atkinson's men perform their military drills and fire artillery across the river. A council was held on July 18, and a treaty was concluded. Atkinson presented a medal to Chief Handful of Blood, but because of the Arikaras' recent depredations, only armbands and plugs of tobacco were given to others.[22]

Thus far the hunters had supplemented the expedition's food supply with a variety of wild game: an occasional elk, buffalo, deer, rabbit, and prairie dogs that were eaten despite their bad smell when cooked. The troops had also harvested large black currants along the banks and an abundance of fish from the Teton River. The expedition noted an increase in the number of buffalo as it progressed up the river. Numerous dead animals floated by on the river. In approaching the Mandan villages on July 22, the troops witnessed a buffalo herd of around 10,000 head, as well as large wolves, on the nearby hills. The countryside had changed into wider bottoms covered with cottonwood, elm, and ash.

The treaty party passed a deserted Mandan village on the twenty-third and another, on the east bank nearly twelve miles above present Bismarck, North Dakota, on the twenty-fifth. This last site, once fortified with an earth breastwork, stood on a perpendicular cliff, the face of which was covered with bones, many of them human. The village site was also strewn with bones, arrow points, stone axes, broken pottery, and other artifacts. On Atkinson's order, a soldier lowered himself down the cliff by rope to secure a human skull that faced out onto the river.[23]

Fifteen miles farther on, the flotilla halted and made camp below a sixty-foot bluff upon which an occupied Mandan village was situated.

The commission learned that another Mandan village was located four miles above and three Gros Ventre villages at intervals three miles beyond. Treaties were conducted on July 30 with the Mandans and Gros Ventres jointly. Both tribes denied that they harbored any intentional hostility toward whites and were given a large number of presents. That night the military conducted rocket and artillery demonstrations.

A long-standing clash of personalities came to a head in camp that evening. Although they had shown a face of unity to the Indians, Atkinson and O'Fallon had long been at odds over how to deal with them. At dinner that evening an argument erupted when O'Fallon, who held the Mandans and Gros Ventres guilty of depredations, objected to the amount of presents Atkinson had given them. The confrontation became so heated that the two commissioners seized cutlery from the table to use as weapons. Sutler George F. Kennerly, who managed to separate the men, later held O'Fallon to blame for the incident. The Indian agent, Kennerly said, "provoked the Genl. to this line of conduct, by his continual bad humor, and unnecessary interference with his duties as a military officer."[24] O'Fallon threatened to report Atkinson to the War Department, and from that point on the two men did not speak to one another. O'Fallon's temper soon contributed to another incident, this one involving a Crow Indian.

Villagers reported that a band of Rocky Mountain Crows, who periodically came to the Missouri River villages to trade, were camped nearby. Capt. Bennett Riley rode out to invite them in. The Crows, who arrived in camp on August 3 somewhat reluctantly, were found to be "fine looking Indians, and well mounted."[25] Their 3,000 tribespeople and 600 warriors strongly outnumbered Atkinson's forces.

The next morning the brigade once again donned its dress uniforms and paraded under arms. The Crow leaders, headed by Chief Long Hair, were taken into council. After some discussion, a treaty was signed before noon. After the signing, however, an argument developed when Atkinson demanded that two Iroquois captives, whom the Crows had taken from the Blackfoot, be released. The Crows resisted and became more and more hostile. O'Fallon then spied some of the Crows attempting to take their presents before they were invited to do so.

In a fury he brandished his musket, hitting three or four of the chiefs on the head, severely gashing one. The tent erupted into a near melee that was prevented only when Atkinson ordered his troops under arms and calmed the Indians. He persuaded the chiefs that the trouble had resulted from a misunderstanding and invited them to accept presents that would "cover their wounds."[26] The Crows thereafter remained friendly, and Atkinson's timely action prevented a deadly altercation.

Atkinson still hoped to reach the Yellowstone River and, if possible, to consummate treaties with the Assiniboine and Blackfoot tribes. For the next twelve days the expedition made its way up the river, passing the site of Lewis and Clark's Fort Mandan, of which little tangible evidence remained. The buffalo became scarcer, but elk and deer abounded. The hunters also killed bears, among them some special white ones, the meat of which the men enjoyed as a change from their usual fare. An abundance of mosquitoes troubled the expedition considerably.

The flotilla reached the mouth of the Yellowstone on August 17. There, Atkinson established Cantonment (or Camp) Barbour, naming it for James Barbour, the current secretary of war. A deserted post constructed by Ashley in 1822 stood in ruins on the south bank of the Missouri. Two days later, Ashley arrived at the head of his twenty-four-man party. The men carried a hundred packs of beaver pelts. Atkinson welcomed the men aboard his boats and offered Ashley transportation back down the river. Before returning, however, he wished to travel farther up the Missouri in hopes of contacting the Assiniboine or Blackfoot tribes.

Taking five of the keelboats, 330 soldiers, and one piece of ordnance, Atkinson and O'Fallon, accompanied by Ashley, continued up the river for four and a half days to what was known as Two Thousand Mile Creek.[27] Having found no Indians and with the season growing late, Atkinson turned about at midday on August 24. Three days later at Cantonment Barbour, the horses and beaver packs were loaded aboard the keelboats, and the downriver journey commenced. Treaties were conducted with the Otoe, Missouri, Pawnee, and Omaha at Council Bluffs on September 26, 1825.[28] The expedition arrived at St. Louis on October 20. Not a man or a boat, Atkinson proudly noted, had been lost on the long, difficult journey.

On November 7, 1825, Atkinson and O'Fallon jointly made their report to Barbour. They cited the treaties that had been concluded and gave a general estimate of the various tribes they had encountered or learned of. They especially debunked rumors that British traders of the Northwest Fur Company held an "injurious influence" over the Missouri River Indians. The hostile Blackfoot tribe, however, was an exception.[29]

With the Atkinson-O'Fallon Expedition, the United States had made its first official pacts with the tribes of the Upper Missouri based on its concerns of British intrusion and protecting the fur trade. During August 1825, at the same time Atkinson and O'Fallon were moving up the Missouri, another major treaty-making effort was in process with tribes of the Upper Mississippi River. A commission headed jointly by William Clark and Lewis Cass, governor of Michigan, tendered treaties to other tribes at Prairie du Chien, then Michigan Territory but now Wisconsin. For the most part, these tribes were from the Midwest and Great Lakes region—the Chippewa, Sac and Fox, Menominee, Iowa, Winnebago, Ottawa, and Pottawatomie—but there were also some Yankton Sioux from the prairie.[30] An observer described the gathering of 3,000 Indians:

> They all arrived at the council ground, clothed in their war dress and armed with bows and arrows, war clubs and other Indian implements of warfare, very few having fire-arms, and encamped, separately, under their respective chiefs. The Sacs and Foxes were the last to arrive, and are represented as making a very warlike and imposing appearance. They came up the Mississippi in a fleet of canoes, and, as they approached the Prairie, they lashed their canoes together, and passed and repassed the town in a connected squadron, standing erect, singing their war songs and dancing after their custom. On landing they drew up in martial order, as if in warlike defiance of their enemies, the Sioux, who were encamped on the opposite side of the town, and shot back the fierce look of defiance upon their ancient foes.[31]

The council convened beneath a large arbor on August 5. Among those present was Indian agent Henry Schoolcraft, later a noted ethnologist and explorer. Artist J. O. Lewis made more than fifty drawings of the principal chiefs and various aspects of Indian life. Clark opened the council, saying: "Your great father has not sent us here to ask any thing from you; we want nothing—not the smallest piece of your land—not a single article of your property. We have come a long way to meet you for your own good, and not for our benefit."[32]

The commission's purpose, he said, was to persuade the tribes to cease their warring on one another by agreeing on fixed boundaries. This said, the council adjourned until the next morning, at which time the chiefs responded. In doing so, some expressed strong doubts that their young men could be controlled. Clark replied angrily that the old men of the tribes would have to take the tomahawks from the warriors and throw them in the fire. Further, he said, no more whiskey would be issued until the council was finished. After a break for the Sabbath, the council resumed, the chiefs outlining their claims to territory. The Chippewas presented a map drawn on a shake of birch bark. Sioux chief Wabasha (the Leaf) spoke: "I will relinquish some of my lands for the sake of peace. I formerly owned the land on which we now are, but I do not claim it now, because it belongs to the whites."[33]

Another Yankton, Wap-pe-ton (the Little), added: "The bands of the lake have been speaking. I am of the prairie. I claim the land up the river Corbeau to its source, and from there to Otter-tail Lake. I can show the marks of my lodges there, and they will remain as long as the world lasts."[34]

The talks continued several more days, with the chiefs unable to reconcile the boundary lines between them. Finally, an agreement was reached among them and with the commission, and treaties were prepared. On August 19 the documents were explained to the chiefs in council, and a belt of wampum was passed around the circle for all to touch. The following morning, copies of the treaty were distributed to the bands, the pipes of one another were smoked, and the commissioners held a great feast. The council ended with Clark declaring that the war tomahawk would never be raised again "as long as the trees grow, or the waters of this river [the Mississippi] continue to run."[35]

Cass and Thomas McKenney met again and made new treaties with the Menominee, Winnebago, and Chippewa tribes at Butte des Mort on the Fox River of Michigan Territory on August 11, 1827.

By these initial treaties, the United States established formal contact with the northern tribes west of the Great Lakes. It had asked only for friendship with and safe passage of U.S. citizens. But the dynamics of a young nation exploding forth would bring critical new concerns and conflicts with the tribes who had so complyingly signed their first treaties with the white man. Much more, especially land, would be wanted of the Indian.

CHAPTER THREE

A Pathway to the Plains

*Our great father owes us for hogs, cattle and chickens due us
by the Treaty [of 1825], but which we have never received.
Father, what I have said is the truth. I don't lie.*
—KANSA FOOL CHIEF, 1836

The purchase of the Louisiana Territory gave great importance to the area that is now essentially the state of Missouri. Having an established population, principally French, and being located centrally at the leading edge of the country's new wilderness empire made the region a matter of special consideration for the Jefferson administration. National interests required that the United States establish its proprietary rights over the vast land areas along and beyond the Mississippi River. Exerting its influence over the European-descended citizens, who reluctantly but willingly accepted their new role as citizens of the United States, was far simpler, however, than doing so over Missouri's Indian population.

Especially troublesome were the Osage Indians. Their tall, athletic warriors had won a reputation for fierceness and savagery. Not only were they notorious horse thieves, but their battle habit of decapitating their victims made them a dreaded force on the Missouri frontier.[1]

The Osages resided in permanent villages and were not purely a Plains Indian tribe that depended entirely upon the buffalo and moved with the great herds. Their war parties, however, ranged over a vast territory that included large portions of present Missouri, Arkansas, Kansas, Oklahoma, and Texas. They had for years been a threatening force against the control of both French and Spanish regimes and an enemy much feared by other tribes. Governor of Louisiana-Missouri Territory Meriwether Lewis wrote to Secretary of War Henry Dearborn on July 14, 1808, saying:

> The band of the Great Osages, on the Osage river, have cast off all allegiance to the United States, and with but few exceptions no longer acknowledge the authority of their former leader White Hair [Pawhuska]. They have threatened the lives of the inhabitants of the territory; have taken several prisoners and after retaining them some days, insulting and otherwise maltreating them, dismissed them destitute of provisions and nearly so of clothes at a considerable distance from the inhabitants.[2]

At that moment, Lewis reported, the Osages were far off at the great saline (on the Cimarron River of present Woodward County, Oklahoma) holding a council with the Spaniards, who still contested the legitimacy of the Louisiana Purchase.[3] William Clark, former coleader of the Lewis and Clark Expedition and now acting both as military commander and Indian agent for the Upper Mississippi, sought to distinguish between the "friendly and well disposed Little Osages" and the aggressive Great Osages.[4] He hoped that by building a trading establishment among them—actually, and more important, a U.S. fort—and initiating a new treaty, he could alleviate the Osage problem. President Jefferson expressed his thoughts on the matter: "If we use forbearance, & open commerce with them, they will come to, and give us time to attach them to us."[5]

Even as Fort Osage (originally known as Fort Clark) was being constructed at Fire Prairie on the Missouri River east of present Kansas City, Clark met with the assembled chiefs. He presented them with a treaty proposal he himself had conceived:

> I drew up some Articles of a Treaty which I red [sic] and had explained to the Great and Little [Osages] on the morning of the 13th. On those different articles we had frequent Conversations. During the day, they declared their emplicit [sic] Confidence in me and their perfect Satisfaction and approbation to every article and would at any time Sign those articles; I had three Copies made of those articles and on the 14th we again met in Council and red [sic] over and explained every article of the Treaty to them.[6]

By this Clark-initiated pact, the Osages agreed to give up their claim to a huge body of land between the Missouri and Arkansas rivers. Clark declared it "some 200 square miles of the finest country in Louisiana."[7] In return, the Big Osages would receive an annual annuity of $1,000 and the Little Osages an annuity of $800, a mill, a blacksmith shop and the aid of a smith, ploughs, a house for each of two head chiefs, availability of a government trading house, and cancellation of some minor debts the tribes owed from depredation claims.[8]

After the Osage leaders had inked the treaty at Fort Osage, cannons were fired and Clark issued presents. The two head chiefs were awarded a gun and ammunition, and the tribespeople were given vermillion, tobacco, and blankets—a total of $317.74 worth. The delighted Osages, apparently oblivious to what they had signed away by the treaty, celebrated the night away with dancing and singing. Clark felt he had achieved a coup, writing the secretary of war that if the treaty was not confirmed, "it will require five times the amount to effect a purchase of the same tract of country."[9]

Not long after the treaty had been consummated, a party of seventy-four Osages arrived at St. Louis to turn over some horses their warriors had stolen. While there, they voiced strong opposition to the treaty, saying they had no intention of giving up title to their lands. Lewis met with them, reading the treaty and explaining it to the group. The chiefs declared that White Hair and the other chiefs who had signed the treaty had no right to sell their lands without the general consent of the tribe.[10]

Lewis was undeterred. He personally revised the treaty, boosting the annual annuity to each Osage group to $1,500 and adding Osage title to some lands along the river. He then turned to the Osage agent (Jean) Pierre Chouteau, one of the founding fathers of the city of St. Louis, who was intimately acquainted with the Osages. Lewis instructed Chouteau to go to Fort Osage, taking the strict new guidelines he had outlined in writing. Lewis's instructions read in part:

> Those of the Great and Little Osages who refuse to sanction this treaty, can have no future hopes, that their pretensions to those lands now claimed by them, will ever be respected by the United States; for, it is our unalterable determination, that, if they are to be considered our friends and allies, they must *sign* that instrument, *conform* to its *stipulations*, and establish their permanent villages, near the fort erected a little above the Fire Prairie [original emphasis].[11]

As a Louisiana Frenchman who had led an Osage delegation to Washington and had met with President Jefferson, Chouteau held a strong desire to prove his fidelity to the United States. He firmly issued Lewis's demands when he met with the Osages on November 10 and secured the signatures of all the Great and Little Osage chiefs, along with a large number of warriors. Whereas Clark and others lauded the American success, a much different view of the affair was given by George C. Sibley, factor at Fort Osage, who had witnessed the event:

> Having briefly explained to them the purport of the treaty, he [Chouteau] addressed them to this effect, in my hearing, and very nearly in the following words: "You have heard this treaty ex- plained to you. Those who now come forward and sign it, shall be considered the friends of the United States, and treated accordingly. Those who refuse to come forward and sign it, shall be considered enemies of the United States, and treated accordingly." So much were the Osages awed by the threat of Mr. Chouteau that a very unusual number of them touched the pen, many of whom knew no more the purport of the act than if they had been a hundred miles off; and I here assert it to be a fact, that to this day the treaty is not fairly understood by a single Osage."[12]

Clearly, however, it was Lewis who set the harsh demands of the United States for the Osage lands. However threatening Chouteau may have been, he was in fact acting as an agent for Lewis, who was in direct contact with President Jefferson on the matter. Clark insisted that the treaty had been fully explained to the Indians, and Lewis concurred: "I well know that General Clark would not have deceived the Indians."[13] And he was confident that the treaty interpreter (Paul Lous or Loise, commonly thought to be Pierre Chouteau's half-blood son, Paul[14]) had translated it faithfully.

The Osages, already divided between Great and Little Osage groups, split again, with one group still residing in villages on the Osage River of southwestern Missouri and the other, known as La Chaniers, living on the Verdigris River of present northeastern Oklahoma. The latter had been encouraged to move there by Pierre Chouteau, when in 1802 he temporarily lost his Osage River trading monopoly to the noted Spanish trader Manuel Lisa. The two groups of Osages maintained an active relationship, and the United States continued to deal with them as one by treaty.

In 1815 the Osages, along with other Mississippi River tribes, signed a peace and friendship treaty with the United States at the small village of Portage des Sioux on the west bank of the Missouri a short distance above St. Louis. Although the Osage pact was inconsequential in terms of territory, it constituted a portion of a major treaty undertaking by the United States with tribes of the Upper Mississippi River.

The Portage des Sioux pacts of 1815 and others loosened a tide of white immigration into Missouri and ultimately onto lands occupied by the Plains Indians. This tide was soon joined by the forced removal of eastern tribes west of the Mississippi. New treaties would soon be needed to adjust the conflicts created with white settlers and newly arrived Indians such as the Cherokees on the Arkansas River in Arkansas.

The Cherokees and Osages became enmeshed in a fierce war, each tribe committing brutal assaults against the other. In 1818 an adjunct to the Treaty of Fort Osage was entered into at St. Louis. By it the Osages ceded to the United States a large tract of land along the Arkansas River from Frog Bayou in western Arkansas to the Verdigris River. This action cleared the way for Cherokee settlement of the region.[15]

By still another pact, in 1822 the United States was released from its 1808 obligation of maintaining a well-stocked store where the Osages could barter their furs and pelts. In exchange, the tribe was freed from the $2,309.40 debt it owed at the Fort Osage U.S. factory store.[16]

The Osage warrior, nonetheless, remained a haunting threat to the ballooning citizenry of Missouri Territory when it was admitted to the Union in 1821. Calls were heard demanding that the new state "be freed from the nuisance of an Indian population [and] place it beyond the dread of Indian wars."[17] To this purpose, the U.S. government made ready to remove the remaining Osage and Kansa (Kaw) Indians from Missouri permanently.

Newly appointed Osage agent Alexander McNair, a former governor of Missouri Territory, was assigned the task of working out a new treaty with the tribe. A delegation of sixty tribesmen from the Osage villages on the Lower Verdigris and the Upper Neosho River in Kansas were recruited to make the long trip by horseback and foot (the Osages were notorious walkers) to St. Louis. They were led by White Hair and Clermont (the town builder). During May 1825, they met with William Clark, now superintendent of Indian affairs; Edward Coles, governor of Illinois; and McNair, agreeing to terms of the new treaty as proposed by the United States.

By the treaty of 1825, the Osages ceded all claim to lands in Missouri, Arkansas Territory, and regions that are now part of Kansas and Oklahoma. Thomas McKenney of the Office of Indian Affairs wrote that the treaty "extinguished Indian title to three or four million acres of land

The Long Expedition holds council with the Pawnees (James, Account of an Expedition to the Mountains).

in the state of Missouri and Arkansas territory, and to nearly 100,000,000 acres west of Missouri and Arkansas."[18]

As recompense for this large body of land, the Osages accepted a strip of reservation, fifty miles deep, extending westward across southern Kansas from a north-south line twenty-five miles west of the Missouri border.[19] Both the Great and Little Osages would be rewarded with an annuity of $7,000 per annum for twenty years, payable in money, merchandise, provisions, or domestic animals, as they chose. Additionally, the United States would furnish 600 head of cattle, 600 hogs, 1,000 domestic fowls, 10 yoke of oxen, 6 carts, and farming utensils as thought necessary. A blacksmith would be provided and supported to repair utensils, tools, and arms. And for each of the four principal chiefs, the government would build a "comfortable and commodious dwelling house."[20]

The government further agreed to liquidate several small debts the Osages owed to traders, and the Osages would compensate white citizens for all horses and property their warriors had stolen since their last treaty.[21] But the main import of the 1825 treaty was to relocate both the Osage River Osages and the Verdigris River Osages together on the Kansas reservation.

On the day following the Osage signing, a similar pact was consummated with the Kansa Indians. The Kansa had long held to the northeastern portion of present Kansas, residing in villages along the Kansas River north of present Manhattan. By the treaty signed on June 3, the tribe was persuaded to cede approximately 1.5 million acres of land, essentially the top two-fifths of present Kansas, to the United States in exchange for a reservation 30 miles wide by 200 miles long running west from near present Topeka.[22]

The treaty marked a sharp point of decline in the history of the Kansa tribe. Not only did it cause bitter dissension among the tribe, but a great flood in May 1826 and another the following spring wiped out the Kansas' corn crop. On top of this, a decimating epidemic of smallpox, brought to the region by white traders, swept their villages, as it did those of the neighboring Osages. It was reported in 1827 that nearly two-thirds of the Kansa tribe had been infected. All this misfortune was further exacerbated when Indian superintendent Thomas H. Harvey callously recommended "less annuities and more Christian teaching" for the hapless tribe—this while the government had not yet fulfilled the basic rewards it had promised the Kansa in the 1825 treaty.[23]

Poorly housed, sick, and starving, increasing numbers of Kansas resorted to raiding the Santa Fe caravans or stealing from the settlements near the mouth of the Kansas River, where unscrupulous white men operated "whiskey shops in their place, using every stratagem in their power to get the Indians to drink."[24]

Even as the situation of the Kansa continued to deteriorate, the government was seeking to crowd more removed tribes into Kansas Territory. The lands assigned to the Kansa in 1825 offered an inviting solution to the problem. Taking advantage of the tribe's poor bargaining position, in January 1846 the government arranged a new treaty council at Mission Creek, Kansas. By it the Kansa Indians were relocated southward from the 2 million-acre reservation to a 256,000-acre tract just below the Santa Fe Trail on the headwaters of the Neosho River.[25] There, white squatters, timber thieves, and attacks by Santa Fe traders emerged as new threats to the tribe. Their removal did not end there. Ultimately, the press of white advancement would require that both the Kansa and the Osages be removed to Indian Territory.

Still other tribes had been conveniently removed to the region beyond Missouri. The Iowas, Sacs, Foxes, Kickapoos, Delawares, Shawnees, Menominees, Peorias, Kaskaskias, New York Indians, Pottawatomies, Weas, Otoes, and Piankeshaws were tribes the government had relocated in the region and now stood in the path of westward migration across the Central Plains. They, too, would have to go—again.

CHAPTER FOUR

Probing the Buffalo Prairie

The words of the white man fall pleasantly on our ears.
—OSAGE CHIEF CLERMONT

In removing eastern tribes to beyond the Mississippi River, U.S. officials had ignored the fact that other tribes were already occupying much of the land on which they were being placed. It soon became clear that the prairie tribes, most of which regularly warred with one another, were not amenable to either sharing their hunting grounds or accepting their new neighbors in friendship. To rectify the situation it had created, the United States sought to work out treaties with the resident tribes for concessions and peaceful compliance.

First, however, it was necessary to locate these nomadic tribes that moved with the buffalo herds within a general range of safety from other tribes. In 1820 a party under Lt. Stephen H. Long conducted talks with the Pawnee on the Loup River but failed to make friendly contact with the Comanches. Jesse Bean's 1832 expedition from Fort Gibson into central Indian Territory, accompanied by the noted writer Washington Irving, likewise failed. A stronger force of U.S. Mounted Rangers under Col. James B. Many marched from Fort Gibson to the Wichita Mountains the following spring. Many took medals and flags with which to lure tribal chiefs to Fort Gibson for talks. This effort, however, produced no amicable meeting with the Indians and suffered the loss of trooper George G. Abbay, who was carried off by an unidentified band of Indians.[1]

The government had other reasons for addressing the problem of the Plains tribes. By 1825 an important avenue of commerce and travel, the Santa Fe Trail, had developed between Westport in Missouri and Santa Fe in New Mexico. Pierre Vial, a Frenchman who served the Spanish crown, was the first person known to have traveled the route from New Mexico to Missouri, in 1787. During the early 1800s American merchants began traversing the famous route, one of the first being Missourian William Becknell, who took the first trade wagons over the trail in 1822. Soon after, enterprising American and Mexican merchants alike were plying the road with trading caravans. Fur traders working the South Park region of the Upper Arkansas also used the trail. In 1828 Bent's Fort was established near the mouth of the Purgatoire River in present southeastern Colorado, serving as a vital resting place for travelers.[2]

In its course through present Kansas and Colorado, the Santa Fe Trail followed an indefinite dividing line along the Arkansas River between the ranges of the Cheyennes and Arapahos to the north and the Comanches, Kiowas, and Plains Apaches to the south. To war parties from these tribes as well as those of the Loup River Pawnees, Kansa, and other bands, the plodding, ox-drawn caravans laden with goods offered great temptation. The year 1828 was severe. One caravan had three of its men killed by the Indians; another lost nearly a thousand head of stock; and another all of its horses and mules. These drovers were forced to leave their wagons and walk back to Missouri.[3]

As had happened when the fur trade was threatened, the incidents caused great excitement among white citizens. The Missouri legislature issued a memorial to the U.S. Congress listing trail-related injuries and demanding that federal military protection be provided. In March 1829, Maj. Bennett Riley, who had been a member of the Atkinson-O'Fallon Expedition, was sent to provide escort for the traders.[4]

The U.S. Army, however, was ill equipped to patrol the long, precarious road, and the traders were usually forced to provide their own protection. They were not always able to do so, and during the 1830s a number of offenses against Santa Fe transportation occurred. Mountain-man explorer Jedediah Smith was killed by unknown Indians on the Cimarron Cutoff of the trail during the summer of 1831.[5]

Other incidents occurred as well. In late 1832, a company of traders returning from Santa Fe along the Canadian River of the Texas Panhandle was attacked by Kiowas. After a fight, during which two of the traders were killed, the remainder escaped in the night, leaving behind $10,000 or more in bullion. The men, some wounded and all nearly starved, finally reached St. Louis after forty-two days on the trail.[6]

Even immigrant Indian and white settlers along the Red River of eastern Indian Territory were victimized by raiders from the prairie. One such party killed planter Judge Gabriel Martin and carried off his nine-year-old son, Matthew, and a male slave during May 1834.[7] These depredations, along with the capture of ranger Abbay, caused the government much concern. Some frontiersmen, however, could see the Indian view.

"For this [their infractions]," one observer noted, "I cannot so much blame them, for the Spaniards are gradually advancing upon them on one side, and the Americans on the other, and fast destroying the furs and game of their country, which God gave them as their only wealth and means of subsistence."[8]

To counter Spanish influence and protect its interests in the region, the U.S. government authorized an imposing military expedition designed to meet and establish friendly relations with the Comanches and Wichitas, the latter generally known as the Pawnee Picts, Toyash, or Taovaya. Because of his experience with the Arikara in the north, Gen. Henry Leavenworth was placed in command of the expedition. It consisted of the First Regiment of Dragoons, organized at Jefferson Barracks, Missouri, during the spring of 1834, and the Seventh Regiment, U.S. Infantry. New recruits were mustered in and drilled preparatory to marching to Indian Territory.[9]

When assembled at Gibson, Leavenworth's officer corps included several of the former Atkinson Expedition command plus other notable military men. Col. Henry Dodge was second in command, followed in rank by Lt. Col. Stephen W. Kearny and Major Richard B. Mason. Company commanders included Capt. Edwin V. Sumner; Lt. Nathan Boone, son of Daniel Boone; and First Lt. Jefferson Davis, future U.S. secretary of war and eventual president of the Southern Confederacy.[10] On April 30, Leavenworth reviewed both regiments as they made a number of charge and repulse battle maneuvers before the Fort Gibson garrison and a throng of curious Indian visitors. The dragoons were particularly striking, their companies arranged by color of their mounts.

"Each company of horses has been selected of one color entire[ly]," a witness noted. "There is a company of blacks, one of whites, one of sorrels, one of grey, one of cream color, &c., &c., &c. which render the companies distinct, and the effect exceedingly pleasing."[11]

Units of the Seventh Infantry were sent to the field first with orders to lay out and mark a road to the mouth of the Washita at the Red River, following the most direct and best route possible. Lieutenants Enoch Steen and Lucius Northrop led a detachment of twenty dragoons to scout the Washita country in advance. Recruiting, equipping, and training new recruits, however, delayed the departure of the expedition into mid-June, much later than preferred. It was necessary, also, to wait for the arrival of several nonmilitary members.

Although treaty commissioner Montford Stokes, former governor of North Carolina, and Choctaw agent F. W. Armstrong accompanied the expedition, both remained in the background. No treaties were planned, but it was intended that such would result from the visit. There were hopes, likewise, of improving relations between the prairie tribes and the more domesticated tribes that had been removed from the East and the South to eastern Indian Territory. The principal of these were the Cherokees, Choctaws, Chickasaws, Creeks, and Seminoles, all of which were anxious to work out peaceful relationships with the prairie tribes.

The Osages were likewise concerned. They had long been at war with the Wichitas, Comanches, and Kiowas in particular. Only the year before, an Osage war party had massacred a Kiowa village near the Wichita Mountains, decapitating their victims and taking a Kiowa boy and girl captive. Although the boy was killed by a belligerent ram while at Fort Gibson, officials purchased the Kiowa girl and a Wichita girl to return to their respective tribes as peace offerings.[12]

In hopes of further defusing these tribal conflicts, certain leading men were invited to accompany the Leavenworth Expedition. They included the Cherokee war leader and chief known as Dutch; George Bullet, principal leader of the Delawares; and French-Osage half blood Pierre Beatte (Beatie), who was highly regarded by the Osages and had figured prominently in Washington Irving's *Tour of the Prairies*. Cherokee half blood Jesse Chisholm also served as a guide and interpreter. A civilian member of the expedition, artist George Catlin, sought to enlarge upon his recent experience of painting Indian life along the Upper Missouri. He also proved an able chronicler of the difficult and death-ridden march.

With a total of around 500 members accompanied by a train of supply wagons, the expedition departed Fort Gibson on June 17 and moved up the west bank of the Arkansas River a few miles before going into camp. Leavenworth paused there to consolidate and make final arrangements before pushing off southward. Four days' march took them to the mouth of Little River on the Canadian, where Lt. T. H. Holmes and troops of the Seventh Infantry were erecting a blockhouse and barracks for a military post.[13]

Even before departing, the expedition had begun to suffer a mysterious depletion of men and horses from a debilitating illness that struck troops and animals alike. An officer and twenty-seven men, too sick to continue, were left behind at the Canadian. By the time the command reached the Washita River, three more officers and forty-five men had been stricken and seventy-five horses and mules disabled. The expedition's surgeon blamed the heat and rapid march. There would be many more such casualties among both men and stock.[14]

Leavenworth was among them. While taking part in a buffalo hunt on the Blue River with his officers and Catlin, the general had been thrown from his horse and suffered a bad fall. The fall may not have been as injurious as having a vein in his arm opened by Catlin, who was exercising the then-popular method of "bleeding" a wounded or ill person.[15] In addition to his wound, Leavenworth was hit by the illness that continued to plague the march.

At the confluence of the Washita and Red rivers, the expedition found troops of the Third Infantry from Fort Towson erecting Camp Washita. Four horses drowned as the command forded the narrow, steep-banked Washita on July 4, then marched eight miles beyond to establish Camp Leavenworth. The new camp, with good grazing for the stock, raised the hope for improved health of the command. But the sickness continued. The seriously ill Leavenworth became so incapacitated that he was forced to turn command of the expedition over to Dodge. On July 7 the decimated dragoon regiment was reorganized as six companies of forty-two men each. Wagons were abandoned, baggage was reduced to a minimum, and with only six days of provisions the expedition pushed west in search of the Wichita Indians. After they had departed, Leavenworth struggled up from his sickbed and tried to rejoin the command. But he could not catch up with his troops before dying on the trail.[16]

Now divided into three columns under Major Mason, Capt. David Hunter, and Captain Sumner, the command became increasingly impeded with litters of sick men as the dragoons passed over rolling prairie cut by brushy ravines and spotted with clumps of scrub oak. Immense herds of buffalo darkened the distant hillsides, and droves of wild horses flitted across the landscape.

On the morning of July 14, the dragoons had their first encounter with Indians, a band of thirty Comanches out on a hunting expedition. A Mexican captive who had become a Comanche warrior rode forward to

Dragoons of the Leavenworth Expedition meet the Comanches in 1834 (Catlin, North American Indians).

parley. His comrades sat their horses in the distance, with bows, arrows, lances, quivers, and shields in a style that reminded one member of the expedition of "the more chivalrous days of ancient Britain when the knight templars laid lance in rest."[17]

To the surprise of the expedition, which had feared the worst in invading this unknown land of the Plains Indian, the Comanches proved both friendly and hospitable. They invited the dragoons to follow them the two miles to their camp. Dodge and his men cautiously did so, welcomed there by around 200 horsemen. The Comanche camp, backdropped by the barren peaks of the Wichita Mountains, sat looking like "a great meadow with the small cocks of hay scattered promiscuously over it."[18] The fields surrounding the village of 340 lodges were covered with the band's vast horse herds—no fewer than 3,000 head, it was judged.[19]

The dragoons were further surprised to see an American flag flying over the Comanche village. Just how it got there was puzzling until later, when a Wichita chief was asked about it. The Pawnees from the Platte River, Dodge was told, had sent two—one for the Comanches and one for the Wacos.[20]

Cautiously, Dodge went into camp with a small brook before him. He placed a strong guard around a rectangle that included the dragoon mounts and issued orders that no one should venture into the village without special permission. To the Mexican captive-warrior, who became known to the dragoons as the Spaniard, he presented a gun and a weapon box. From him, Dodge learned that the chief of the village, away on a hunt, would be back the next day.

Rather than wait for the chief, however, Dodge preferred to move on in search of the Wichita village, which he had learned was to the west beyond the Wichita Mountains. After marching seven miles, the command stopped near a cool stream to build a breastwork and an arbor for a sick camp. There he left thirty-five ill men, including Catlin, under the protection of seventy-five dragoons.

A Pawnee, who said he had been to the Wichita village, guided the command over a mountainous route studded with sharp rocks that severely injured the dragoon mounts' unshod hooves. Finally, on the fourth day from the sick camp, the dragoons found the Wichitas in a high-walled gorge of the Red River's North Fork. Their village of 400 thatched huts, nestled on the riverbank beneath a towering granite bluff, stood surrounded by large fenced plots of corn, melons, pumpkins, beans, peas, squash, and other common vegetables.

At first, the village inhabitants appeared alarmed at the sudden appearance of the dragoon force. Fearing trouble, Dodge ordered bayonets fixed and all preparations made for a conflict. But the Wichita girl was brought forward, and the Indians' demeanor soon changed. An uncle embraced the girl with tears running down his face. After Dodge had gone into camp near the village, the tribeswomen began bringing much-welcomed dishes of corn, beans, watermelon, and wild plums to the troops, who for some time had eaten only meat.[21]

The chief, We-ter-ra-shah-ro, told Dodge he thought Abbay may have been captured and killed by Indians who lived near San Antonio. He was, however, able to produce both young Matthew Martin and the slave captured with him. A Wichita man who had protected the boy when others wished to kill him was rewarded with both a rifle and a pistol. Other firearms were presented to the Wichita leading men.[22]

During their second day of talks with the Wichitas, brief conciliatory speeches were made by Dutch for the Cherokees, by Beatte, by an Osage boy who was the son of a chief, and by the Delaware chief Bullet—all speaking for peace between their tribes.

"We wish much to make peace with the Osages," We-ter-ra-shah-ro told them. "We have long been at war with them. We wish to see the lands of the Creeks and the Cherokees also, to shake hands with them."[23]

During that day, a large band of Comanche Indians under Chief Ta-we-que-nah (Big Eagle) arrived at the Wichita village. Dodge met with him and two other chiefs in his tent. After complimenting the chief for flying the U.S. flag, he inquired about Abbay's disappearance. Ta-we-que-nah replied that a Comanche band from Texas had carried Abbay across the Red River and killed him. When the chief asked that Dodge turn the captive Kiowa girl over to him, the officer refused. He would give her back to her people himself without price, he said, to show his friendship. He had barely said those words when the meeting was interrupted by a great commotion outside his tent.

A band of twenty or more Kiowa warriors had dashed headlong into camp ready for battle, their bows strung and quivers filled with arrows. The Kiowas had learned that there were Osages with the expedition and remembered well the massacre of their people the year before. As the "bold and warlike-looking" Kiowas pulled up before Dodge's tent, the women and children who were visiting the camp fled in terror, and the dragoons quickly took up their arms.[24]

Dodge, however, was able to calm the Kiowas with reassurances that his visit was a peaceful one and that he intended to restore the captive Kiowa girl to her family. The Kiowas were invited to attend a general council along with the Wichitas and Comanches the next day, at which time the girl would be turned over to them. She was, it was learned, related to a Kiowa chief. When the council assembled in the woods near the dragoon camp the next morning, the grounds swarmed with over 2,000 Indians: Wichitas, Comanches, Kiowas, and some Wacos who resided near the Wichita village. Many were armed with war clubs or battle-axes and some with rifles. The dragoons were kept on high alert. Dodge seated the captive girl among the circle of chiefs, and Kiowa women came forth to embrace her joyfully. An uncle threw his arms around Dodge and thanked him tearfully.[25]

Once the council circle had smoked the pipes, Dodge addressed the assembly, expressing the wish of the Great Father that the tribes be at peace with one another. He promised that traders would be sent to provide the guns, blankets, and other items of the white man that they desired. But, he said, he was not a big enough chief to make a treaty with them, and he would like for them to send representatives with him when he returned to Fort Gibson.

The Indians were willing to make peace—but they were very skeptical and concerned about traveling through the Cross Timbers, a belt of scrub oak and brush that separated their range from the woodland east. Dodge promised them safe escort. On the day before the dragoons were to depart, fifteen Kiowas led by Tiche-toche-cha arrived ready to ride. The Comanches were more cautious, but finally four Comanche men and one woman, along with the Spaniard, joined the group, and soon thereafter We-ter-ra-shah-ro and two of his Wichita warriors came forth and with them We-ta-ta-yah, a Waco chief.

Two days brought the party back to the sick camp, where a number of men were still very ill. Catlin and others required litters upon which to travel. A servant of the expedition's chronicler, Lieutenant Wheelock, died. When the Comanche woman, too, became ill, the party turned back. The Spaniard, however, continued on.[26] The return march to Fort Gibson was horrendous. Catlin, who rode much of the way in a baggage wagon with several sick soldiers, described the ordeal:

> We sometimes rode from day to day, without a tree to shade us from the burning rays of a vertical sun, or a breath of wind to regale us, or cheer our hearts—and with mouths continually parched with thirst, we dipped our drink from stagnant pools that were heated by the sun and kept in fermentation by the wallowing herds of buffalo that resort to them. . . . The sickness and distress continually about us, spread a gloom over the camp.[27]

Even after reaching Fort Gibson, men continued to die. Recuperating in his quarters there, Catlin could hear the mournful beat of a muffled drum several times a day as burial processions made their way to the post graveyard.[28] But after a few days' rest and improved diet, the still-mysterious plague subsided among the dragoons, and Dodge arranged for a council to be held among the representatives of the prairie tribes and the immigrant nations of eastern Indian Territory. The council would provide Catlin with his opportunity to make sketches of the Indian personalities present.

The council got under way at Fort Gibson on September 2, 1834. Dodge, Armstrong, and Stokes represented the United States; Civil John and To-to-lis the Senecas; Moosh-o-la-tu-bee (Musha-la-Tabbee—the Man Killer) the Choctaws; Thomas Chisholm and John Rogers the Cherokees; Roly McIntosh and his nephew Chilly McIntosh the Creeks; Clermont the Osages; Tiche-toche-cha the Kiowas; We-ter-ra-sharro the Pawnee Picts (Wichitas); and We-ta-ta-yah the Wacos. As the only

Comanche present, the Spaniard stood in for Chief Ta-we-que-nah. With other members of the various nations included, the meeting was composed of around 150 persons.[29]

The Fort Gibson meeting was devoted to working out peaceful relations between the various tribes that had been warring with one another. Agent Armstrong set the agenda at the start. "The object of this meeting," he said, "is peace between you."[30] Dodge added to this after pointing out that he and the others had no power to make treaties at present.

"It is the wish of your Great Father," he told the woodland tribes, "that you shake hands with the Pawnee Picts, and Kiowas, & other wild tribes—that you forget the past now behind you, every thing that was done in war. Let your hands be clean, and be not stained with each others blood."[31]

The prairie tribes were greatly concerned that Osage chief Clermont had shown a noticeable lack of cordiality. On the second day, Armstrong forced the issue by bringing the Osage chief face-to-face with the Kiowa Tiche-toche-cha and urging them to "bury the Tomahawk." The two inveterate enemies embraced one another, although Clermont remained cold and reluctant.

"Why are there not more Osages here?" We-ter-ra-sharro asked. "It is they we wish most to see. . . . They have one of my people: my sister's child. I want them to restore the girl."[32]

Armstrong promised to do all he could to have the girl returned, as well as the sacred Taime medicine bag the Osages had taken from the Kiowas in 1833. The Western Cherokee war with the Osages was addressed as well. Thomas Chisholm, a Western Cherokee chief and an uncle of Jesse Chisholm, was also concerned about the Osages' intentions. But Clermont stepped forward to explain that his people had been held back by an outbreak of cholera. He addressed the prairie tribes: "The words of the white man fall pleasantly on our ears. Our Father tells us well: he says to us, we should come together and live like friends. You must listen to our Father. Our children will not grow if we shut our ears to his words. Our race will be no more. It will vanish away."[33]

On September 4, Chisholm opened the council by deferring talk until the white beads of peace had been presented to the prairie tribes and the pipe of friendship had been smoked. But the question arose as to who would be honored to fill the pipe. Cherokee chief Rogers decided the issue by recommending the Senecas, "eldest of all the Red men present."[34]

"Our custom," Chisholm explained, "is to give beads and tobacco; the white beads are emblems of `peace and purity.' When you smoke the tobacco of friendship, all evil will go off with the smoke."[35]

The procedure was delayed when Tiche-toche-cha would not permit the tobacco in the pipe to be touched; nor would he allow it to be lit with the right hand—only the left. When the pipe had finally been passed about, Seneca chief Civil John addressed the prairie tribes.

"Forget not what we say," he said. "Let your children hear it. It is only by being thus, friends, that our children can flourish."[36]

"I am pleased with all that I have seen," the Kiowa replied. "I am not young, but my word will live forever; my children will be your friends as I am since I came to make peace with all the Red men here. The road to my country is open. You can travel in safety. I have seen the houses of the white man, but I have not seen many horses. When you come to my country you shall see vast numbers of horses."[37]

More speeches committed to peace and friendship among the tribes were made by Roly and Chilly McIntosh and Benjamin Perryman for the Creeks, by Clermont, and by Moosh-o-la-tu-bee for the Choctaws. The latter concluded: "We have been long talking. You are wearied; few words are always best. I am an old man and may not live long on the Earth. May what has been done [here] remain bright and strong with my children. We will now shake hands and part."[38]

At this point, Commissioner Stokes handed three silver peace medals and a U.S. flag to Colonel Dodge, who presented them to the prairie tribes. Armstrong made a concluding speech, praising the tribes for their promises of peace and admonishing them not to take each other's horses, as "this brings war on the offending party."[39]

The council was adjourned, and hands were shaken all around. The participants departed with anticipation of attending a big treaty-making assembly the government planned to hold on the prairie "when the grass next grows."[40]

Before this could take place, however, Colonel Dodge received orders to lead a dragoon expedition north to quell the rampant intertribal warring of the Central Plains region that imperiled both the Santa Fe trade and frontier settlements.[41] The expedition was organized at Fort Leavenworth and marched from there on May 29, 1835, with three companies of mounted dragoons (120 men), two swivels, two wagonloads of flour and other rations, and twenty-five beeves.

Upon reaching the Platte River, Dodge held talks with chiefs and warriors of the Otoes, stressing that they remain at peace with their neighbors. He told them their Great Father was doing "everything in his power to make his red children happy" and advised them to cultivate the soil and raise cattle. Head chief Jutan replied that they would do so, and the tribe was given blankets, knives, tobacco, and cloth. The Otoes celebrated the event with a dance.[42]

Moving on up the Platte, Dodge conducted a similar affair with head-men of an Omaha village and, on June 23, with an assembly of chiefs and warriors representing the four divisions of the Pawnee tribe. Two years earlier, on October 9, 1833, the Pawnees had conducted treaty talks here at the Grand Pawnee village with a U.S. delegation headed by Commissioner Henry W. Ellsworth and Indian agent John Dougherty. By the resulting treaty, the Pawnees made their first cession of land in exchange for annual annuities and assistance with schools, agricultural implements, and blacksmithing.

Each of the four confederated bands ceded and relinquished claim to all land lying south of the Platte River. The Pawnees would, however, be free "at the pleasure of the President" to hunt the ceded land along with other friendly Indians. By this, the United States could conclude that "all of their rights and interest of the Pawnees to lands lying south of the Platte river was extinguished."[43]

With the four divisions again assembled, Dodge met with them in council. After speeches were made and presents distributed, the chiefs expressed a strong desire to make peace with the Cheyennes and Arapahos. To this aim, they agreed to send three envoys to accompany the expedition.[44]

Dodge's expedition pushed on up the river, meeting at the forks of the Platte with the Arikaras, whom the Sioux had driven from the Missouri. After admonishing the Indians for depredations along the Platte, Dodge led his dragoons on to the Rocky Mountains and southward to Pike's Peak and the Arkansas River. There, on July 31, the expedition found an assembly of Arapaho, Gros Ventre, and Blackfoot Indians who were anticipating the arrival of Cheyennes, Comanches, Pawnees, Creeks, and Kiowas. The tribes planned to meet "for the purpose of a friendly understanding between themselves & the government."[45]

With his supplies wanting, Dodge continued on down the Arkansas to Bent's Fort, there meeting with chiefs of the bands gathered to conduct trade. He found the Cheyennes badly debauched by whiskey secured from Mexican traders. Only recently, they had killed their principal chief, High-backed Wolf. Councils were held with the Pawnee emissaries and the Cheyennes. They agreed to be friends and to live in peace.[46]

This amnesty was reinforced when a large party of Pawnees, under Pawnee Loup chief Axe, and Arikaras appeared on a hill near the Cheyenne village, fired their guns, and raised a flag indicating their desire to make peace. The Cheyennes led them to their village and initiated a ceremony of smoking the peace pipe (a member of the expedition observed that "smoking is above everything else with them in peace making."[47]) The tribes exchanged presents and feasted. The Cheyennes presented the Pawnees and Arikaras with over a hundred horses, and the Pawnees responded with a number of guns.[48]

Dodge concluded that "[t]he good effects of the expedition are thus becoming apparent, and it will probably have the effect to establish peace among all the different tribes between the Arkansas and the Platte . . . they will thereby have an extensive country opened to them, covered with innumerable buffalo, where they can hunt in safety without the fear of being attacked by their enemies."[49] That, unfortunately, was not to be the case.

Council on the Canadian

There is one thing I have to ask of you. I do not want any one
to settle here. If they do they will drive off the game.
—WICHITA CHIEF KOSHAROKA
(the Man Who Marries His Wife Twice)

The powerful Osage nation had once dominated a vast territory that included a large part of southern Missouri, northern Arkansas, eastern Kansas, and eastern Indian Territory extending to the Red River. By 1835 portions of these lands had been ceded to the United States to permit the relocation of eastern tribes, the Osages being moved to a far less favorable reservation in southern Kansas. In a letter to the secretary of war, Col. Auguste Chouteau passionately addressed the matter:

> If any Nation has been heretofore deceived and oppressed it is the Osages. . . . Look at the immense value of country that they ceded to the Government in their former treaties. The land now occupied by the Choctaws, Cherokees, Creeks, Senecas, and a number of other tribes to the north, was once owned by the Osages; and what have they received for that immense country? Few presents and a small annuity, of which the great part will cease in a few years.[1]

In an effort to gain even further cessions, Commissioner F. W. Armstrong met the tribe in council and signed a lengthy new treaty at Fort Gibson in January 1835. As he touched his pen to the paper, Chief Clermont expressed his doubts that "my Great Father will give me all in that Treaty."[2] His elder brother, Ki-he-kay-tungah, was likewise pessimistic about receiving the awards, saying, "I am tired of making treaties. The red people who have advanced in civilization do not appear to be as happy as the whites."[3] The U.S. Senate failed to ratify the treaty.

The treaty council that had been proposed with the prairie tribes for the coming spring was slow to develop, and its success suffered because of its extension into the searing heat of July and August. Congress had allocated $10,000 for a new treaty effort, but arranging a meeting with the prairie tribes was not easy for several reasons. Habitually, the tribes followed the grazing migration of the buffalo, which during the early spring drew them south into Texas. Normally, the Comanches, Kiowas, and Plains Apaches did not return north until the summer when the Wichitas harvested their green corn.[4]

Furthermore, the problems of selecting a site, organizing the treaty commission, and procuring treaty presents caused delay on the government's end. The commissioners' health was also an impediment to the commission's progress. Montford Stokes, who joined Agent Armstrong and Gen. Matthew Arbuckle—commander at Fort Gibson—on the treaty commission, was late arriving from Washington and soon became so ill he could not sit up. Also, word came from the Choctaw agency that Armstrong was too sick to risk the trip. He, in fact, died and never made it to Fort Gibson to join the other commissioners.

With the buffalo scarce and the hunting poor, the Indians were anxious to know when and where the council was to be held. Trader Holland Coffee arrived at Fort Gibson from his trading post on the Red River to report Indian interest in the affair. Further, two Wichitas and a Waco Indian appeared at Fort Gibson to inquire about the council, but lack of an interpreter prevented any communication with them for several weeks.[5]

With both Stokes and Armstrong incapacitated, Arbuckle attempted to change the plan for meeting on the prairie, hoping to bring the Indians to Fort Gibson again. Maj. Richard B. Mason was ordered to select a campsite on the Little River branch of the Canadian River in territory then assigned to the Creek Indians by U.S. treaty. From there he was to contact the Comanches and other tribes and persuade them to come in. Traveling with him and two troops of dragoons were Chouteau, who operated a trading post in eastern Indian Territory; four Osage guides and hunters; the three Indian visitors to Fort Gibson; and a Wichita captive woman named Ascimke who had been retrieved from the Osages to serve as an interpreter.

Departing from Fort Gibson on May 18, Mason reached the Little River and advanced to the head of the stream at the western edge of the Cross Timbers to select his campsite. From there he established contact with Coffee and his traders and through them with the various bands of prairie Indians. The chiefs, he found, were anxious for the council but adamant in their refusal to go to Fort Gibson. The commission relented and agreed to meet them at Mason's camp, a "beautiful and healthy place" near present Norman, Oklahoma. It had timber to the east and a level prairie to the west, a number of springs, and a fine running stream. Mason named the site "Camp Holmes."[6]

By the first of July, the Comanches, Kiowas, and Wichitas had assembled at the site in large number. But with them came rumors of possible trouble. On July 2, Mason sent an Osage galloping to Arbuckle at Fort Gibson with word that a Comanche chief still camped at Coffee's place was threatening an attack on the camp. The chief was telling others that the whites had called the meeting to betray them to the Creeks, Cherokees, and other woodland tribes. He was being held back from making an attack, however, by another Comanche chief.[7] Arbuckle responded by rushing Capt. Francis Lee and two companies of the Seventh Infantry, guided by Beatte, to support Mason. The threatened attack proved to be mostly talk and never materialized.[8]

The Comanches, who were busy afield killing buffalo and drying meat to live on during the council, had indicated that they wanted to meet with the treaty commissioners by July 22. Mason so informed Arbuckle, assuring him that the prairie tribes would be present then. Arbuckle wrote back that he felt there was too much uncertainty regarding the prairie tribes to make plans with the others so early. He set August 20 as the day for holding the treaty council.[9] Mason replied to Arbuckle on July 8, saying that had the tribes not been ready as he had indicated, he would certainly have said so.

"I doubt exceedingly whether I shall be able to keep them here until the middle of August," Mason complained. "They are restless and impatient to be off. I made an effort today to prevail on them to send a delegation to Fort Gibson, but they most positively refused."[10]

Comanche chief Tabaqueena, the man who had talked of wiping out Mason's dragoons, had become more amenable after the arrival of the infantry troops. When they fired their cannon, he moved his camp farther away from the troops. Another Comanche chief, who wore a dragoon jacket with a pair of infantry epaulets, was well liked. His pretty daughter was the belle of the camp. She wore a red blanket over a deerskin capote fringed with elk teeth, and the part in her hair was streaked red with vermillion to match her eyelids and lips.[11]

Assistant Surgeon Leonard McPhail arrived on June 30 with a military detachment that had laid out a road from Fort Gibson. His diary provides interesting insight to camp events and activities as the dragoons and Indians waited through the hot days of July and early August for the treaty commission to arrive. McPhail described an Indian who was in mourning for a child who had died. The Indian's body was painted black, and suspended from his neck was a doll, the head of which was covered with a lock of the infant's hair. A great wailing that awoke McPhail one night proved to be coming from a Wichita lodge. The family there had received word that a son had been killed in an attack on a Mexican settlement. On one occasion, a Comanche man and the wife of another man were caught after they had run off together. As punishment, their faces were gashed and charcoal rubbed in the wounds.[12]

McPhail was forced to amputate the hand of a soldier who suffered an accidental gunshot wound when he attempted to stop a warrior from washing his feet in the spring. The body of another soldier, who had become separated from his infantry unit, was found dead on the prairie two weeks later about three miles from camp. McPhail was kept busy tending to sickness among both whites and Indians at the camp. Swarming flies pestered the horses so much that fires were kept burning to smoke the insects away.

On a happier note, the soldiers and Indians engaged in friendly wrestling bouts and foot races. Entertainment was provided one evening by the Comanches who, fully painted and decked in feathered costume, performed a dance for the camp audience.[13] These matters, however, could not erase the Indians' impatience for the council to begin. With buffalo scarce, the chiefs complained that their people were starving. They began moving their camps away onto the prairie. The council should have been held when the grass was in the *blade*, they said, not in the *leaf*.[14]

The Osages, who had long conducted war with the prairie tribes, were important factors in this attempt to bring peace to the region. Osage chief Black Dog (Shone-ta-sah-ba) arrived at the council site early.[15] He was reportedly incensed when word came that his fellow chief Clermont had sent word to the Comanches that Mason and his officers were not chiefs of importance but were "dead as the prairie grass— good for nothing." Black Dog hoped Arbuckle would come and make Clermont out to be a "crooked talker."[16] Even Black Dog, who had waited patiently for the commission to arrive, grew weary by August 7 and prepared to leave. He and his band, however, would return to attend the treaty council. Clermont would not, but his younger brother, also a chief, was present.[17]

Stokes recovered enough from his illness to make the long trip to Camp Holmes. Finally, on August 9—as the Dodge Expedition was meeting with the Cheyennes and other bands at Bent's Fort—the two commissioners departed from Fort Gibson. They were accompanied by a large retinue of Creeks, Choctaws, Senecas, and Quapaws; various traders; a large wagon train of treaty gifts; and two additional companies of Seventh Infantry. Ten days later the entourage arrived at the council grounds to be greeted by a salute from Lee's artillery. Only a few Comanches and Wichitas remained at the site, and the Kiowas had disappeared. A detachment of dragoons had been sent to find them and extend an invitation to attend the council, but it returned after a week without success. Later, a Kiowa man and his wife appeared in camp, but they did not stay.[18]

Disturbed at the tribe's absence, the commissioners asked the Comanche and Wichita chiefs if the Kiowa chiefs could be brought back within ten days. No, they were told, the Kiowas were like wolves, so difficult were they to find on the prairie. No chiefs and headmen of other missing bands would return either. They had waited a long time at the council site, but their children were starving. They were gone for good, and some speculated that the Kiowa people still feared the Osages who had destroyed their village two years before. But, the chiefs still present insisted, the Kiowas would agree to any treaty that was made.[19]

A large brush arbor was erected for the council, with seats made of split logs. The arbor gave little protection, however, from the spell of rainy and sometimes stormy weather that set in. When the council got under way on August 22, the commissioners sat before a body composed of Comanche, Wichita, Cherokee, Creek, Choctaw, Seneca, Quapaw, and Osage Indians. Lt. Washington Seawell, aide-de-camp to the commissioners, was appointed secretary and assigned to record the meeting. Speeches by the commissioners were interpreted to the Comanches and Wichitas by the captive girl, Ascimke.[20]

Stokes made a brief opening address, saying that nothing more would be asked of the tribes than to be at peace with the United States and with Indian nations that had treaties with the United States. Then, noting that he had just risen from a sickbed, he deferred to Arbuckle, who repeated the call for peace and friendship. The commission, Arbuckle said, had brought a prepared treaty and would read and explain it to those present. After the treaty had been signed, presents would be given out to show the goodwill of their Great Father.[21]

The treaty document called for perpetual peace and friendship among all, forgiveness of previous acts of hostility, and friendly intercourse between the signatory tribes. A promise, essentially a futile one, that the United States would pay for stock stolen from the Indians by whites was included. But other clauses of the treaty went well beyond the mere friendship of which Stokes and Arbuckle spoke. The treaty stipulated that the Comanches and Wichitas, as well as any associated bands, would freely permit U.S. citizens to pass through their settlements or hunting grounds and would, in fact, pay indemnification for any injury or loss of property that they incurred. Moreover, all nonprairie tribes west of Missouri and south of the Missouri River would have total freedom to hunt and trap west of the Cross Timbers. These were significant concessions for a people who depended principally upon wild game for subsistence and whose way of life would be seriously threatened by outside intrusion.[22]

These stipulations were followed by Article 8, which reasserted that the United States was asking nothing in return from the Comanches and Wichitas except to remain at peace with them. Even more curious, Article 9 declared that signing the treaty would in no way interrupt the "friendly relations" of the Comanches, Wichitas, and their "Associated Bands" (the Kiowas and Plains Apache, by implication) with the Republic of Mexico—where the prairie tribes traditionally raided. This was the clause Wichita second chief Kosharoka objected to most. He feared it bound the Wichitas to keeping peace with the Republic of Mexico.

"The Spaniards have attacked us three times," he said. "They have killed three of my children, and two of my warriors."[23]

Stokes and Arbuckle assured both the Wichitas and the Comanches that their warring with Mexico would not cause the United States to make war on them. Chief Kosharoka declared his commitment to peace with the other tribes. He said, however, "There is one thing I have to ask of you. I do not want any one to settle here. If they do they will drive off the game."[24]

Ichacoly (the Wolf), who avowed that he was the one and only head chief of the Comanches, made a similar declaration. The day's meeting concluded with a letter from Cherokee chief John Rogers (Chief Thomas Chisholm having died of typhoid the previous winter) designating Dutch, John Brown, and David Melton to represent the Cherokee nation.[25]

August 24 was spent obtaining signatures on the treaty document. A thunderstorm with heavy rain interrupted the procedure, and the signing was continued the following day. When completed, the treaty document bore the names and marks of nineteen Comanches, fifteen Wichitas, two Cherokees, forty-two Creeks, thirty Choctaws, thirty seven Osages, eighteen Senecas, and twenty-two Quapaws. Stokes and Arbuckle signed for the United States. Mason, Lee, Seawell, McPhail, and Chouteau, who would soon erect a small trading post near the Camp Holmes site, were among the witnesses listed on the document.[26]

After the signing, chiefs of the woodland tribes were given their opportunity to be heard. Roly McIntosh spoke for the Creeks and presented white beads to the prairie chiefs. Choctaw chief Musha-la-Tabbee noted that his people now lived in towns and had houses like the white man. "If there be any killing," he said, "let it be by the falling of the limbs of trees."[27]

Chief Black Dog told the prairie chiefs: "Look at all my brothers here. My Great Father is the cause that I have shaken hands with them. Our Fathers want to have a big open road, and it is my wish that we should have one between your country and mine."[28]

He was followed by Thomas Brant, chief of the Seneca nation. "Here are you Red Brothers," Brant told the assembly. "We have all made peace. Do not break it. We want to raise our children in peace."

Brant then presented the prairie chiefs with tobacco, saying, "When you get home, let all your people smoke it, and when they do they must think of us [the Senecas]."[29]

He-ka-too (Hi-ka-toa, or the Dry Man) of the Quapaws made a final address. "My Brothers, the Muscogees [Creeks], Choctaws, Osages, and Senecas," he told the Comanches and Wichitas, "have made you a white road, and have given you beads. There must not be any blood on that road unless it be the blood of the buffalo."[30]

August 26 was spent distributing presents to members of the two prairie tribes. On the following day, the Indians began breaking camp to leave for their homes, and the commission departed from Camp Holmes for Fort Gibson.

The Comanches soon realized they had come off badly by the Treaty of Camp Holmes. They were particularly angered by the realization that the pact gave eastern tribes the freedom to enter their country. They ripped their copy of the agreement to shreds and threatened to attack Camp Mason, a military post recently established near the site of the former Camp Holmes.[31] But government officials were undeterred; a treaty with the Kiowas was still needed. During the spring of 1836, Maj. Paul Liguest Chouteau, Osage subagent and brother of Colonel Chouteau, was sent to locate the tribe and bring them in. He traveled as far south as the Colorado River of Texas before he eventually found a combined encampment of Kiowas, Comanches, and Plains Apaches. Reluctantly, the Kiowa chiefs finally agreed to send some of their men to Fort Gibson.[32]

The Kiowas did not appear as promised, and a new initiative was undertaken the following winter by Edward Chouteau, son of Paul Liguest, and four other men. They, too, were unsuccessful and returned home to report that the Comanches were very angry and hostile.[33] During the spring of 1837, however, a delegation of twenty-four Kiowas under Ta-ka-ta-couche (the Black Bird) came to Chouteau's trading post and expressed a willingness to make a peace treaty. With them were seven Katakas and two Wichitas. Paul Chouteau escorted the group on to Fort Gibson, overtaken on the way by four Tawakaros.

On May 26, Stokes and A. P. Chouteau, now a treaty commissioner, initiated a pact with the Kiowas, Katakas, and Tawakaros that was essentially the same as the 1835 pact. The woodland tribes were represented by the Creeks under Roly McIntosh and the Osages, this time with Clermont present. After the signing, goods remaining from the 1835 council plus other supplies were given out.[34]

"It secures from further molestation," Stokes said of the treaty in writing to Secretary of War Joel R. Poinsett, "the Traders that travel the St. Fe. road as well as all our licensed Traders on the South Western Frontier . . . perfect peace and friendship now exists between the United States and all the Nations and Tribes with the Superintendency of the South Western Frontier; and between all these Nations and Tribes among themselves."[35]

In the same letter, however, Stokes admitted to serious disturbances among the southern tribes. The horse herds of the Kiowas, Comanches, Wichitas, Wacos, and even the Osages were being severely ravaged by Pawnee Maha raiders from the Platte River and Cheyennes from the Upper Arkansas River. Although the Pawnees had made a treaty with the United States in 1833, they were not party to any agreements with the southern tribes. In some instances, the southern Indians said, whole villages had nearly been destroyed, with several men killed and women and children taken captive. The Kiowas complained that one of their principal chiefs had not been able to accompany the treaty delegation because the Pawnees had stolen all his horses.[36]

"They had the audacity," Chouteau reported, "to take about twenty head out of a lot adjoining the fort [Holmes], which I had sent to this place packed with merchandize and provisions intended as presents at the contemplated treaty."[37]

Still another problem was being realized. The Republic of Mexico, which had suffered the loss of its large Texas province in 1836, had agents working among the southern tribes, urging them to make war against the Texans. These activities had excited the young men's marauding blood and created turmoil in Texas. Women and children were regularly taken captive on the Texas frontiers. To calm the situation and strengthen their allegiance to the United States, government officials prepared to take a tribal delegation to Washington, D.C.[38]

The idea had been broached with the Wichitas and Comanches at Camp Mason in 1835. Because the various bands were so scattered on the Texas prairie and were so predatory, however, Chouteau felt he could not arrange a satisfactory interview with them until the coming spring of 1838. At that time, he hoped to secure one chief from each band for a deputation to Washington. Chouteau suggested that to include the Osages would "substantiate and continue the existing friendship" between the tribes.[39]

Chouteau, whose health was bad, prevailed on Tabaqueena to visit the various tribes relative to the Washington visit. The chief returned in late May with a large delegation representing eight tribal groups: the Kiowas, Katakas, Padoucas, Yamparika Comanches, Shoshones, Hoish, Cochetaka Comanches, and Wichitas. They included twenty-two chiefs and a number of warriors. Present also were some Osages and Piankeshaws. Chouteau was forced to tell them that the government wished to postpone their visit. By issuing them presents, he managed to allay their displeasure and reassure them that the trip would only be delayed.[40]

During the council, the Indians informed Chouteau that they were going to war against the Pawnee Mahas and Cheyennes. War parties of the latter tribe had also been coming south to steal horses. The Kiowas had recently caught and killed a sizable party of Cheyenne horse thieves. The chiefs agreed to hold off on their war plans until the government had looked into the horse-stealing raids. They requested also that Chouteau relay word to a Comanche camp located to the northwest regarding the arrangement they had made with him.

Chouteau did so, sending his nephew Edward with Maj. Lucius B. Northrop, Tabaqueena, and another Comanche chief, along with eight warriors and twelve dragoons, up the North Canadian to Wolf Creek in northwest Indian Territory. There, the men came onto the scene of a terrible massacre. A joint force of Cheyennes and Arapahos had conducted a revenge raid on a Comanche camp from which the men were absent on a buffalo hunt, killing a large number of its occupants and horses and burning the village. The attackers left thirteen of their own warriors on the field.[41]

Chouteau's continuing illness prevented him from meeting with the tribes in October as planned. He died on December 25, 1838, and was buried with military honors at Fort Gibson. His death left a large vacuum in the government's relationship with the prairie tribes. Acting superintendent of the Southwestern Territory William Armstrong was unsure where affairs stood regarding the visit to Washington.[42]

In early May 1839 a Comanche-Kiowa delegation of seventeen men and seven women, all riding good mules, arrived at Camp Mason expecting to be taken to Washington. Only then did they learn of Chouteau's death. Delaware leader John Connor took charge of the Indians and escorted them to Fort Gibson, being fed en route by Jesse Chisholm at his home at the mouth of Little River and by his brother George Chisholm at Webbers Falls on the Arkansas.[43]

From Fort Gibson the Indians were taken to meet with Superintendent Armstrong at the Choctaw agency at Skullyville. Armstrong left it up to them as to whether they would continue on, but he pointed out that in doing so, they would be confined in steamboats and stages and would suffer a severe change of diet and climate. Not surprisingly, they chose not to do so. Armstrong presented them with a large number of blankets, bolts of cloth, and other articles. Before they began their return home, the prairie Indians watched with great interest as the Choctaws and Chickasaws conducted a game of stickball.[44]

Even as the United States was attempting to protect its interests on the Southern Plains, similar efforts were being made by the Republic of Texas, whose expansion northward and westward from San Antonio brought it into sharp conflict with bands native to the area, as well as with those who came to hunt or pass through to raid in Mexico. The promotion of white settlement into north and west Texas included immigrant European groups, principally of German nationality, who would be severely victimized by Indian raids and kidnappings.

CHAPTER SIX

Sam Houston and the Indians

The Land I now stand on was once mine, the Whiteman now
owns it. . . . What our white brothers have said about giving us land
and permission to hunt the Buffalo in peace, I believe to be true.
—WACO CHIEF ACAQUASH
(Short Tail)

Prior to becoming a republic, the region that is now Texas had experienced a long and tumultuous relationship with its Indian population under both Spanish and Mexican rule. In particular, the large Comanche nation, whose bands migrated down from the upper Rockies during the eighteenth century, pressed hard against both the Spanish settlements and the Lipan Apaches who were native to southwestern Texas. During July 1785, Pierre Vial, a Frenchman working for the Spanish in Texas, met with the Comanches along the Red River and persuaded them to send a peace delegation to Bexar. There, during October, the Spanish authorities and Comanches signed a formal treaty arranging for peace and trade between them. Silver-headed canes, Spanish uniforms, guns, and white flags bearing the Burgundian cross were presented to the chiefs.[1]

Despite this peace arrangement, bloody conflicts still persisted by the time of Texas independence in 1836, and Comanche warriors held dominance over much of Texas north and west of San Antonio.[2]

"The Comanches are a numerous tribe," a person on the frontier noted, "and according to our Indian notions are wealthy, with no permanent abodes. They pride themselves in their patriotism, and of having fought and kept the Spaniards, whom they enslave, at bay for a series of three hundred years."[3]

Concurrent with the historic events of the spring of 1836—the Alamo disaster, the slaughter of James W. Fannin's men at Goliad, and Sam Houston's victory at San Jacinto—a large band of Comanche and Kiowa Indians appeared at Parker's Fort near present Groesbeck, Texas. After a brief parley, the Indians attacked the post, killing many inhabitants, raping women, and carrying off nine-year-old Cynthia Ann Parker and her six-year-old brother, John, into captivity.[4] This and other Indian depredations, such as the Cherokee County massacre of the twelve-member Killough family in October 1838, emphasized the vulnerability of the newly founded republic.

Sam Houston, who had been raised among the Cherokees in Tennessee and rejoined them in Indian Territory in 1829, was sympathetic to native people and sought to work out alliances with the various tribes. Even while he was still residing near Fort Gibson on the Arkansas River, Houston had worked to make peace among the warring Osages, Pawnees, and Comanches. Although his offer in 1830 to serve as a peace commissioner was not accepted, during 1832–1833 he journeyed via Fort Towson on the Red River to Bexar, Texas, where he met with Comanche leaders. Although he hoped to take a delegation back to Fort Gibson for a treaty council with Col. Matthew Arbuckle and other U.S. commissioners, Mexican officials resisted.[5]

Under Houston's administration as the first president of the Republic of Texas, treaties were consummated with the Cherokees of northeast Texas in February 1836, the Tonkawas in November 1837, the Lipan Apaches in April 1838, the Comanches in May 1838, the Kichais (Keechis) and other tribes in September 1838, and the Shawnees in August 1839.[6]

The Comanche treaty was conducted at Houston, Texas. The visiting hundred or so tribespeople were witnessed en route at Austin by a touring Frenchman who described the elderly Comanche chieftain as wearing the uniform of a French soldier, with epaulets and metal buttons. Remarkably, some of the Comanche children bore vaccination scars.[7] The *Houston Telegraph and Texas Register* told how the impoverished band had scoured the alleys of Houston to salvage discarded—but to them extremely valuable—tin plates, iron hoops, metal scraps, glass bottles, and the like.[8]

Houston himself conducted the treaty talks. The final agreement was predicated on the idea that "The Comanche Tribe of Indians, through their several Chiefs being desirous of enjoying their hunting grounds and homes in peace, and also [wishes] that their white Brothers may be more fully assured that they sincerely wish to love them as brothers."[9] By the pact, Texas promised to appoint an agent for the tribe who would superintend its business, protect its rights, and see that its agreement was complied with by all. In turn, the Comanches would trade with no one other than persons authorized by Texas, restore stolen property, hand over tribal members guilty of crimes against Texas citizens, make war on tribes making war against Texas, and—important in view of Mexican efforts to incite the tribes against Texas rule—stand by the republic against all its enemies. Signing for the Comanches were three chiefs whose names have otherwise been lost to record: Muguara, Muestyah, and Muhy.[10]

The fragile nature of these agreements, however, soon became apparent by actions of both Texas and the Indians. Houston had ridden to the village of his good friend Chief Bowles, leader of the Cherokees, who had settled along the Upper Neches and Trinity rivers in northeast Texas. There, he initiated a treaty that recognized the Cherokees' claim to a large segment of territory in east Texas and their autonomy of self-governance so long as their laws were not contrary to Texas laws. The pact also contained the usual commitments to peace, trade, and legal behavior. The Texas legislature, however, did not share Houston's sympathy for the Indians and failed to ratify the treaty. When Mirabeau Lamar, an ardent opponent of the Indians, succeeded Houston as president of the Republic of Texas, he sent the newly formed Texas army under Gen. Thomas Rusk to drive Bowles and his Cherokees into Indian Territory. In a hard-fought battle on July 16, 1839, Bowles was killed and the Cherokees were evicted.[11]

Lamar was determined to punish the Comanches, whose raiding and captive taking had continued. In hopes of rescuing whites taken by the tribe, a punitive expedition of sixty-three Texas Rangers, along with sixteen Lipan and Tonkawa scouts, under Col. John H. Moore was launched in early 1839. Scouring the country northwestward from San Antonio, the force discovered a Comanche village on the Spring Creek tributary of the San Saba River. In a surprise predawn attack, the camp was overwhelmed, and many of its occupants were killed. Still, the Comanche warriors managed to counterattack, driving off a number of Moore's horses and putting many of the Rangers afoot. Any hope of rescuing the captives was ruined when Moore's Lipan scouts killed their captive Comanches.[12]

The strike on their camp caused the Comanches to sue for peace. During the spring of 1840, three of their chiefs arrived at San Antonio to arrange a peace council. The Texans agreed to such. Early on the morning of March 19, a large body of mounted and well-armed Comanches, led by Chief Moo-war-ruh (the Spirit Talker), rode into the city's courthouse plaza and set up their camp. The Texans invited them into the courthouse. Once inside, the Comanches were told to lay aside their arms. They refused, keeping their bows and arrows and knives with them as they seated themselves in a circle on the courthouse floor.

When the Texans asked the Comanches to bring forth their captives, they produced only sixteen-year-old Matilda Lockhart, whose scarred face and body showed evidence of abuse. The enraged Texans had concluded that they would take the twelve chiefs hostage if the captives were not produced. When the guards moved in to do so, pandemonium erupted and the peace council quickly turned into a bloody massacre. The entrapped Comanches fought back with great fury. When the melee had ended, the chiefs were among forty Comanche men who, along with seven Texans, lay dead. Many other Comanches were taken captive.[13]

One of these, a Comanche woman, was placed on a horse and sent back to warn her people that if the white captives were not returned within twelve days, the prisoners at San Antonio would be hanged. That was a serious miscalculation. Instead of releasing their captives, the Comanches tortured them to death. Under the command of Buffalo Hump (Po-cha-na-quar-hip), they then organized a force of around 300 warriors and appeared before the walls of the Alamo where the Texans had taken refuge. The Comanches screamed insults and threats, but charging a fortified position was not their style of fighting. Instead, they rode back to their camps and laid plans for a massive invasion of the white settlements along the Texas Gulf Coast.

Bypassing San Antonio at night, Buffalo Hump's warrior army swept through the area. Totally unopposed, they ravaged the unprotected towns of Victoria, Port Lavaca, and Linnville—killing anyone before them, burning homes and barns, looting, and slaying or driving off stock. With their revenge satisfied, Buffalo Hump's warriors headed home by a route north of San Antonio. They were unaware that a force of Texas Rangers and Tonkawa Indians under Capt. Ben McCulloch had set up an ambush for them at Plum Creek. In the resulting conflict, the Comanches lost eighty-plus warriors to McCulloch and his men.[14]

The war continued, with Moore and his Rangers making another foray into Comanche-held country along the Colorado River. After searching for three weeks, he discovered a village in a bend of the river 300 miles west of Austin. Once again his men launched a surprise attack at daybreak. When it was over, forty-eight tribespeople had been killed, and an estimated eighty more had either been drowned or shot while fleeing across the river. Moore returned to Austin with a herd of 500 captured horses.[15]

Other search-and-destroy forays were conducted under Ranger captain Jack Hayes. During 1841 he and his men killed ten Indians near Uvalde Canyon west of San Antonio; later, on the Llano River, he attacked a Comanche village on the move, killing several more in a running battle.[16] But with the reelection of Sam Houston as president, the Republic of Texas again made a drastic reversal of Indian policy, turning from aggressive war action to peacemaking efforts.

Houston had been severely angered over the killing of his friend Bowles, whom he openly declared "was a better man than his murderers."[17] Once back in office, he set out to make new peace arrangements with the Indian tribes of Texas. He believed a regulated trade with the Indians was vital to keeping the tribes at peace. Accordingly, he hoped to separate them from white settlements with a line of trading houses along the frontier.[18]

Any success at this venture depended largely upon making peace with the sizable Comanche nation, whose 1845 population was estimated at about 14,300. The Comanches then existed as six separate bands: the Yam-pa-ric-coes (Yamparikas), or Root Diggers; the Hoo-ish (Hoish or Pentekas), or Honey Eaters; the Cochetakas (Kotsotekas), or Buffalo Eaters; the Noon-ah, or People of the Desert; the No-coo-nees (Nokonis), or People in a Circle; and the Te-nay-wash, or People in the Timber. These bands—with their own independent societal and organizational structures of head chiefs, medicine men, war chiefs, and captains—were linked together loosely by a common language. No one chief represented all of the Comanche divisions at this point in their history.[19]

During August 1842 a three-man commission appointed by Houston visited a Caddo village in Indian Territory, where it initiated a preliminary treaty with the chiefs of four tribes. The chiefs agreed to send emissaries with presents to twenty hostile tribes, calling them to a council on the Brazos River the following October. It would be the ensuing spring, however, before the meeting could be arranged.[20]

Houston called on old friends he had known in Indian Territory to help "talk in" the tribes. Delawares John Connor, Jim Secondeye, and Jim Shaw and Cherokee Jesse Chisholm were among those sent afield to contact the various chiefs and act as interpreters. Finally, on March 28,

1843, the chiefs assembled on Tehuacana Creek, eight miles above Torrey's Trading House No. 2, located just east of present Waco, Texas. To the dismay of Houston's commissioner Gen. G. W. Terrell, the Comanches were not among them. The fear and hatred they held for the Texans was still too strong.

Many of the tribes in attendance had once been large and powerful but were now mostly small, splintered bands. They were the Delaware, Shawnee, Caddo, Ioni, Anadarko, Tawakoni, Waco, Wichita, and Kichai. Terrell was joined on the Texas commission party by J. S. Black and Thomas J. Smith. Cherokee agent Pierce M. Butler, former governor of South Carolina and a veteran of the Florida Seminole wars, came down from his agency near Fort Gibson in Indian Territory, escorted by an officer and fifteen soldiers, to represent the United States.[21]

Butler's party also included artist John Mix Stanley, who sketched Indian life and produced a painting of the treaty council as it convened on the bank of Tehuacana Creek.[22] The council began with the reading of a letter from Houston to Shawnee chief Linney. Terrell then spoke.

"Our business is to remove all cause of War, and establish peace between us," he said. "The path between us has long been red with the blood of the white and the red man. The bones of our brothers and kindred have been strewed along the path we have traveled. Clouds and darkness have rested upon it."[23]

He went on to promise that trading houses would be built in the Indians' country for them to trade their horses, mules, skins, and other items for the white man's goods. President Houston, he said, had sent for 300 fine lances to give the chiefs as presents. Butler supported Terrell, saying, "I believe the Govt. of Texas will act in good faith with the friendly Indians with whom they may treat."[24] Both men insisted on an end to warring on both sides.

Concurring speeches were made by Delaware chief Roasting Ear, Shawnee chief Linney, Caddo chief Bintah, and Anadarko chief Jose Maria. Waco chief Acaquash, whose tribe had once been a powerful force on the Brazos River, recalled the time of his youth: "The Land I now stand on was once mine, the Whiteman now owns it. . . . When I was a little boy, I attended the Councils of Old men where the white flag waved in peace. . . . What our white brothers have said about giving us land and permission to hunt the Buffalo in peace, I believe to be true."[25]

Each of the chiefs duly placed his mark on the treaty document that promised a cessation of war, release of captives by both Texas and the Indians, and, importantly, another grand council that included all the other tribes—namely the Comanches—residing on or near the Texas frontier.[26]

In May, Houston directed his superintendent of Indian affairs, J. C. Eldredge, at Washington-on-the-Brazos to go to the Comanches and persuade them to attend a council to take place at Bird's Fort on the Trinity River just north of present Arlington, Texas. In addition to pack-horses carrying gifts, Eldredge took with him a captive Comanche girl he had purchased from a Texas citizen for $100. At the Tehuacana Creek council grounds, he was joined by trader Thomas Torrey; Connor, Shaw, Secondeye, and four Delaware hunters; Waco chief Acaquash; two Waco girls being returned to the Wacos after ten years among the Texans; and a captive Comanche boy who had been given the name William Hockley.[27]

Although making peace with the Comanches was Eldredge's goal, in traveling up the Brazos and across north Texas he was forced to deal with bands of the smaller tribes represented at the Tehuacana council—Kichai, Tawakoni, Waco, and Anadarko. These tribes, Eldredge said, were "friendly with each other, intermarry, join each other's war and hunting parties and act generally in concert."[28] He also encountered Nah-ish-to-wah (Lame Arm), head chief of the Wacos. The chief outranked Acaquash, who had attended the treaty council merely to see what the Texans would offer. When Eldredge prepared to turn the two girls over to Nah-ish-to-wah, they wept piteously. Only when the chief threatened to tie them on their horses did they consent to go with him, although they were still "shrieking distressingly."[29]

On the west branch of the Trinity River eight miles from its mouth, Eldredge and his party visited the Anadarko village of Jose Maria.[30] There they met in council with several chiefs of the smaller tribes and distributed some of the presents intended for the Comanches. While with the Anadarkos, he received a report that the Comanches had just returned from Matamoras where they had concluded a peace treaty with the Mexicans.[31]

From the Anadarko village, Eldredge's party pushed on to a Tawakoni village. He found it to be a large one, with well-built lodges sitting atop a high hill and surrounded below by 100 acres cultivated with corn, beans, melons, and pumpkins. Approaching the site on June 6, the group was met by 150 warriors who rode their horses at full speed about them, simultaneously beating drums and blowing whistles before pulling up in a line in front of their visitors. Elderly chief Ke-chi-ka-rogue (Stubborn), who was at their lead, and his subchiefs dismounted and embraced Eldredge, Torrey, and the others affectionately.[32]

Eldredge presented a white flag and tobacco to the chief, after which a feast was held. Ke-chi-ka-rogue opened the ensuing council with a speech. The ground on which they sat, he declared, was his; the water they drank was his; and the meat they had eaten was his. But, he said, his guests had been welcome. He had made a treaty of peace with the United States, and he wanted to do the same with Texas.

"Not many times have the leaves come and gone," he said, "since I and my people lived near the white man in peace. Had I wished[,] I could have slain them all. They were weak and we were strong, then he killed my people, took away our lands and blood was in our path. Treaties of peace were then made but were broken by bad men."[33]

Word arrived from the Wichitas that the Comanches were now on the Big Salt River (probably the Cimarron) 250–300 miles distant where they were gathering salt, hunting buffalo, and waiting for a trade-and-peace visit from the Osages. Afterward, they were expected to go to the Wichita village in time for the corn to be roasted.

Dissension had now arisen between Eldredge and his Delaware guides, who had become uncooperative. On June 11, Connor and Shaw left to take their personal packhorses and goods obtained at the Tehuacana council to trade at Warren's trading post at the conflux of Cache Creek and the Red River. Much to his dismay, Eldredge was left without guides or interpreters and was unable to proceed at the Tawakoni village for sixteen days until they returned on June 27. He later learned that while at Warren's, the Delawares had dispatched a letter by runner to Cherokee agent Butler. Eldredge suspected it related to his expedition.[34]

Finally, on July 6, Eldredge was able to continue, pushing through a wide stretch of cross timbers (scrub oaks), then north across the Big Wichita River and the Red River before moving up Cache Creek to a Wichita village east of the Wichita Mountains. The Texas expedition remained there for nearly a month waiting for the Comanches to arrive. When they did not appear, Eldredge decided to move west of the Wichita Mountains in search of the tribe. On August 5 the expedition reached a Comanche camp beyond the North Fork of the Red River.

The camp was under Comanche chief Pahaucah (variously Pah-hah-u-ca, Pah-hah-yuco, the Amorous Man), who had replaced the deceased Tabaqueena as head of the Hoish band. A large, portly man with a pleasant disposition, jovial nature, and courteous manners, he received the delegation in good spirits. This was not the case, however, with many of his chiefs and warriors, who were still angry and burning with a desire for revenge over the San Antonio courthouse massacre. Eldredge became very apprehensive. But Pahaucah mounted his horse and rode through the camp issuing orders in a loud voice that no one should molest the Texas party or bother its property.[35]

When Eldredge, with the two captives at his side, met in council with the Comanche chiefs and warriors, he stressed that he represented a different Texas chief than the one who was chief when the Comanches were slain at San Antonio: "Houston the great chief of Texas has always been the friend of the Red man. He grew up from a Child among them. He has sat by their side and eaten bread with them since he became a man. He has never told the red man a lie nor has he ever turned away from his friends."[36]

As proof of Houston's sincerity, Eldredge presented the two captives to Pahaucah. A grandfather of the girl came forward and expressed his thanks with flowing tears. A letter from Houston to Pahaucah was produced and interpreted, and presents were distributed. Eldredge implored the Comanche head chiefs to attend "a great council on the Trinity [River] this moon" and to bring all their white prisoners. Pahaucah indicated that he would have to meet with his chiefs before he could answer.[37]

In the next council with Eldredge, the chief agreed to visit the different Comanche bands and bring them in to a council "four Moons from this present full moon" on the Clear Fork of the Brazos River. With this assurance, Eldredge drew up an armistice agreement, which both he and Pahaucah signed. As he was departing on August 10, the Comanche leader requested that Chief Houston be asked to send him a silver medal, a spear, and a uniform coat. He also asked for and received the sword carried by Eldredge.[38]

Despite Pahaucah's good intentions, the Comanches were not present at Bird's Fort on September 29 when a treaty council was held between a Texas commission headed by Terrell and E. H. Tarrant and representatives of ten tribes. Thomas Torrey, who was also present, died during the council. The tribes attending were the Delawares, Chickasaws, Wacos, Tawakonis, Kichais, Caddos, Anadarkos, Ionies, Biloxies, and Cherokees. The Bird's Fort treaty contained twenty-four stipulations whereby the Indians declared allegiance to Texas in conflicts, committed themselves to Texas laws, and agreed to the conduct of trade. Texas promised to assign agents to the tribes and to send blacksmiths, teachers, and missionaries among them.[39]

Probably because communication between Texas and Indian Territory was difficult and slow, Eldredge had not known that Agent Butler was planning a treaty-making visit to the Cache Creek area in support of the Texas effort. Marching from Fort Gibson to Fort Washita and up the Red River, Butler went into camp opposite the mouth of Cache Creek on December 3. The Comanches, led by Buffalo Hump, were there to meet him. Pahaucah was absent, Butler was told, because his only son had been killed in a fight with the Mexicans. By Comanche custom, he would conduct no business until the following spring. The mournful chief had burned five of his six magnificent lodges and killed nearly all of his horses and mules. He had gone off to the Salt Plains to build new lodges and make a new home.[40]

Artist Stanley was present to paint portraits of several Comanches, including Buffalo Hump, and various scenes of Comanche life. He also produced a badge that Indian participants wore with great pride.[41]

Butler was surprised to find that the Texas commission was not at Cache Creek. Although he felt that without them the object of his mission could not be achieved, he proceeded to meet with the Comanche chiefs, smoke the peace pipe with them, and reaffirm the 1835 Camp Holmes agreement. The chiefs insisted that they had no white captives except a boy who had been with them from infancy and was on a war party into Mexico.

Houston's efforts to bring the Comanches in for a treaty council continued during the spring of 1844. In February, emissaries Daniel G. Watson and John Connor left from Washington-on-the-Brazos and rode up the river, going from one tribal village to another until finally the Comanches were found on a branch of the Colorado River. The chiefs said it would be impossible for them to meet at the time set, as their young men were out in all directions and could not be called together quickly enough.[42]

Watson and Connor returned to the council ground, meeting Jesse Chisholm en route. Also arriving at Tehuacana Creek was Waco chief Acaquash, who said he had been to see Houston and had then talked with other tribes. Everyone greatly wanted Houston to attend the council as he had promised to do. A secretary to the Texas peace commission wrote to Houston: "The young men wish to see and know what sort of man you are; could they see you and hear you speak, there would be no trouble then in getting the Comanche to come in."[43]

In June, Indian trader Col. L. H. Williams and Chisholm were commissioned to make another effort at bringing the Comanches in to a treaty council at Council Springs with the promise that Houston would attend.[44] They were successful. On October 7, 1844, the Comanches un-

Texas commissioners meet with the Plains tribes at Council Springs, 1843 (Courtesy, Oklahoma Historical Society).

der Buffalo Hump, Old Owl (Mo-pe-chu-co-pe), and Chom-o-pard-u-a met in council with chiefs of the Kichais, Wacos, Caddos, Anadarkos, Ionis, Delawares, Shawnees, Tawakonis, and Lipan Apaches. And, true to his word, Sam Houston rode in, accompanied by commissioners, agents, military men, Indian traders, and various frontiersmen. After greeting one another with an embrace, Houston and the Indians seated themselves in the usual circle and took turns puffing on the long-stemmed pipe Houston had supplied.[45]

An observer noted: "His excellency arose from his seat, and requested Ecoquash [Acaquash] to rise also; when he bound around his brow a silk handkerchief with a large pin in front and proclaimed him chief of the Wacos."[46]

Houston explained that he did this because Acaquash was a good man and walked straight, putting his men aside when they were bad, and also because the chief remembered his treaties.[47] To the remaining chiefs, Houston distributed gorgeous robes and other gifts, apologizing because he could not offer more.

"Six years ago," he said, "I made a peace with the Comanche: that peace was kept until a bad chief took my place. That Chief made war on the Comanche and murdered them at San Antonio: he made war, too, on the Cherokee, and drove them from the country. Now this had to be mended; war can do us no good."[48]

Houston said that if his people should injure Indian people, he would punish them. He offered an exchange of prisoners. And, he told the Comanches, when they became convinced that they would not be harmed, he would invite them to Galveston where they could see the ships with their big guns and the wide waters "where the ships go out from the sight of land."[49]

In addition to the usual declarations of peace and nonaggression, the 1844 treaty made several stipulations in regard to a "line" between the Indians' hunting grounds and the trading houses and forts that Texas would establish. In general, the line would run from the mouth of Cache Creek past Comanche Peak, near present Hillsboro, Texas, to the old San Saba mission and on southwesterly to the Rio Grande. The tribes would trade with Texas traders only. Texas would not permit "bad men" or unauthorized traders to cross the line into Indian country and would appoint only "good" agents. But the Indians, in particular the Comanches, objected to the line, and no definition of it was made in the treaty document.[50]

Although the three Comanche leaders signed the treaty, Texas officials were much concerned that neither chief Santa Anna nor Pahaucah had come in or accepted the pact. Also absent had been the Wichitas and certain headmen of the smaller tribes. The 1844 treaty called for annual councils, and another was held at Council Springs on November 16, 1845. At that time the Wacos, Tawakonis, and Kichais signed a new pact that endorsed the agreements of the 1844 accord. Still absent, however, were the Comanches under Santa Anna and Pahaucah.

On December 29, 1845, Texas ceased to be an independent republic and became the twenty-eighth state of the Union. Now the United States bore the principal responsibility for Indian affairs in the new state. Accordingly, the United States prepared to make its own effort to resolve the Indian problems in Texas.

CHAPTER SEVEN

Expelling the Texas Tribes

This is the Country of Captives: the weeping Camanche girls, held in duress by the Texans, the silvan face of anglo Saxon Sons & daughters and the Sons of the Montezumas & Guatimozin cursed and driven, traded as slaves by the roving & haughty Camanchee. O, what a country of freedom in name, a nation's birthright to two miles [million] of African Slaves.

—CHEROKEE JURIST ELIJAH HICKS

Even as the politics of Texas statehood were being played out during 1845, federal officials looked to a major new treaty-making effort with the Comanches and other tribes that resided in Texas and western Indian Territory. By doing so, they hoped to develop consistent and uniform agreements to replace the conflicting ones initiated with those tribes previously—in particular, where the Texas pacts had precluded Indian allegiance to the United States. Further need for reaffirming peaceful relations with the tribes stemmed from Mexico's efforts to reclaim Texas and the tensions presaging the 1847 U.S.-Mexican War. An Indian war could seriously impede military efforts on the prairies and endanger settlements, particularly in areas where men of the Texas Republic had gone off to fight the Mexicans.[1]

Former Cherokee agent Pierce M. Butler and Col. M. G. Lewis were appointed as commissioners to conduct a council and effect new agreements with the tribes. While in Washington, Butler had reported information received from a rescued white boy named Gillis Doyle that the Comanches were still holding about twenty white American boys and four girls captive. This led to the former bank president, governor, military officer, and Indian agent's appointment to the commission.[2]

Butler met with Lewis in New Orleans, then went on ahead to Fort Gibson to make preliminary arrangements for the treaty venture into central Texas, which was, for the moment, still solidly "Indian country."[3] To help negotiate with the Plains tribes, he secured the services of two learned Cherokee nationals: William Shorey Coodey, scholarly speaker of the Cherokee National Council, and Elijah Hicks, Cherokee judge and former editor of the *Cherokee Phoenix*.[4]

When Gen. Matthew Arbuckle at Fort Gibson refused to provide a dragoon escort, Butler recruited guides from the Cherokees, Chickasaws, Creeks, and Seminoles of eastern Indian Territory for protection as well as guidance. Runners were sent out to contact the Plains bands. Some of these emissaries met with hostility to the point of having their lives threatened. One Comanche chief, who was on his way to the Salt Plains of northern Indian Territory where he said he hoped to kill some Osages, refused to turn back.[5]

Although disappointed in being unable to effect a January meeting, Butler dispatched two new sets of runners, one to scour the Colorado River country and the other the Brazos and headwaters of the Trinity River. In late December 1845, at the lead of around thirty people including Josiah H. Washbourne, editor of the *Arkansas Intelligencer*, Butler rode south down the Texas Road for Coffee's trading house on the Red River. En route, at Edwards's store on the Canadian, he was joined by Seminole chief Wild Cat and several of his warriors. The chief, who had fought Butler in Florida before being removed to the west, had many interesting tales to tell.

Lewis and his English-born wife traveled overland by wagon by way of Shreveport,[6] meeting the party at Coffee's trading house on the Red River. Now with fifty members, the treaty expedition set out for Comanche Peak, an early landmark on the west bank of the Brazos fifty miles below present Dallas, where the tribes had been asked to gather. Chickasaw and Seminole scouts rode in advance. Pack mules carried presents valued at $1,200. A herd of beef cattle for Indian consumption during the council had been driven ahead of the expedition on a different route.[7]

On reaching the Red Fork of the Brazos above present Dallas, the expedition divided into four separate parties to better contact the prairie bands. The commissioners continued more directly south, but no one in their group had ever been to Comanche Peak. Their guide, a Cherokee named Doublehead (son of the infamous Alabama chief of that name), who did not know the country as well as he claimed, led them beyond the Brazos to the Colorado River over a hundred miles beyond Comanche Peak. The date originally set for the council, the full moon of February, was thus impossible to meet. Fortunately, the runners who contacted the Indians realized that the swollen condition of many Texas streams would delay the Indians and had postponed the meeting until the March full moon.[8]

Upon discovering that they were lost, the commission party turned back east to the Brazos, reaching it below present Waco. It was learned that Buffalo Hump and a small party of Comanches were waiting for them at Comanche Peak two days' ride—an estimated eighty miles—above them on the river.[9] With the two Cherokee leaders, Delaware Jim Shaw who could speak both English and Comanche, and a few others, Butler hurried to the peak. There, he met with the Comanches and some Lipan Apaches with whom the Comanches were now friendly. Hicks recorded the council in his journal:

> Thursday March 5th. This day Govr had his first Conference with the Comanches Buffalow [Hump] Princpl Chief. A party of Chiefs, Wares [warriors], women & children (150) in number appeared and seated themselves in a half moon. Young men fantastically dressed painted with full heads of hair, well dressed in Comanche dress and trinketted and appeared well, tho somewhat effeminate.[10]

Through Shaw, Butler explained his purpose in coming. The talks went well until Butler indicated that the treaty council would be held at Council Springs. The Comanches, not wanting to go that far south, balked and began striking their lodges preparatory to joining their band on the Colorado. Faced with an early defeat of his mission, Butler persuaded Hicks and Coodey to talk with Buffalo Hump, described by Hicks as "an excellent looking man of 50 years over the middle size & has a graceful address."[11] Both Cherokees delivered speeches in an effort to persuade the Comanches to change their minds.

"The hands of the Cherokees and Comanches are white [clean]," Hicks said. "We have never done each other any wrong. To us, we care not where the meeting is held; if you shall choose it elsewhere, then at this point, we are willing to acquiesce."[12]

Coodey stressed the good that would come from a peace council. He vouched that the president was able to fulfill his promises and assured the Comanches that both the Cherokees and the Creeks had benefited by listening to the Great Chief's talk. This claim was endorsed by Creek chief Chilly McIntosh, who had recently reached the camp with some of his men.

"We have listened to your talks," Buffalo Hump replied. "We now reply and say that we have decided to meet them [the commissioners] at Barnard's trading house on the appearance of the second new moon (calculated to be on April 25) and promise to bring the Camanches [*sic*] to the meeting."[13]

Soon after this, the Wichitas, Wacos, Tawakonis, and Kichais made their appearance. During another council, these tribes also accepted the new meeting place and date. Then, on March 15, Pahaucah and his people arrived. He, too, was amenable, promising to bring his band and others to the council. Messengers were sent to contact other bands still in the field.

As the commission party prepared to return to Barnard's, a dispute arose between Butler and chiefs Cah-ser-oo-cah of the Tawakonis and Na-as-to-wa of the Wacos, who complained about the promise of extra beef and other goods. Butler said he could not make any further issuance until they reached Barnard's post. Na-as-to-wa angrily replied that he would not return the horses his men had stolen from the dragoons. Butler threatened to send soldiers to take the horses. Tempers flared, whereupon Hicks conciliated the chiefs: "This is a small matter to create a great wrong; and I ask that we pass over the goods for the peace and friendship of the Whites and the Indians, that brought us to this place."[14]

Returning south, the commission made camp at Council Springs eight miles up from Barnard's and began erecting a large council arbor and a small stock house for storing the treaty goods that were to arrive. Commissioner Lewis, who had planned to join Butler at Comanche Peak, had been ill for some time and was taken to Galveston for medical care. He would be absent from the council proceedings until late March, at which time he took over from Butler, who had become so sick that he was confined to his tent.[15]

On April 1, word was received from Austin that a large party of German immigrants was on its way to occupy a grant the Texas government had issued to the group. Alarmed at the effect this would have on the treaty negotiations, Hicks contacted the commissioners, who immediately dispatched Jack Harry with some other Delawares and Lipan Apaches to contact the Comanche band still on the Colorado. The group returned on the nineteenth, bringing a Comanche captive, a German boy four to five years of age for whom they had paid a ransom. They also reported that the band had murdered two white families on the frontier.

Because of these infractions, the Comanches were reluctant to attend the meeting.[16]

Harry and his men were sent back with assurances of friendship for the Comanches, requesting that they meet with the commissioners. On the same day, a party consisting of trader L. H. Williams, Jesse Chisholm, Doublehead, and others, which had been sent out on February 22, returned from the head of the Washita River in Indian Territory to announce that three bands from that region were on their way.[17]

More disquieting news reached the camp when it was reported that a Texas Ranger force had recently killed a number of Lipan Apaches on the Colorado River. The report produced heart-rending wailing among the Lipan women at the council site.[18] This disturbance frightened the commission party, which realized that it was far distant from military protection. Two representatives from the state of Texas stressed the urgent need for the commission to prevent any uprising among the tribes.[19] Gen. Zachary Taylor had earlier stationed army and Texas Ranger units in position to protect Austin and San Antonio against Comanche raids. But many of these units had recently been withdrawn to the Rio Grande where Taylor was engaged with Mexican forces prior to the Battle of Palo Alto on May 8.[20]

The Comanches, under chiefs Old Owl and Santa Anna, arrived on May 9 after being delayed by a driving rain. It took some time for the band, around 200 strong, to float its baggage in canoes and swim the horses across the Brazos before pitching its lodges near the commission camp. The cadence of the group's drums and dancing continued until sunrise.[21]

Other persons of interest began to accumulate at Council Springs. A number of Comanche girls and others whom the Texans had taken prisoner at San Antonio in 1840 were brought to the site, causing the Cherokee jurist to lament: "This is the Country of Captives: the weeping Camanche girls, held in duress by the Texans, the silvan face of anglo Saxon Sons & daughters and the Sons of the Montezumas & Guatimozin cursed and driven, traded as slaves by the roving & haughty Camanchee. O, what a country of freedom in name, a nation's birthright to two miles [million] of African Slaves."[22]

Another figure of note, journalist George W. Kendall of the *New Orleans Picayune,* rode up from the small Brazos River town of Bucksnort. In 1841, Kendall had been a member of the ill-fated Texas Santa Fe Expedition whose members had been captured and imprisoned in Mexico's leper colonies. Indian agents Robert S. Neighbors and John H. Rollins, both prominent players in Texas Indian affairs, were also present. On May 12, the Comanches under Pahaucah, along with the Wichitas, Kichais, Wacos, and Tawakonis, arrived, about 200 in all. They pitched their lodges around those of the commission party to produce a huge assemblage from which arose a hubbub of many different tongues.

Reporter Kendall estimated the gathering to contain 12,500 Comanches, 150 Wichitas, 150 Tow-y-ash, 140 Kichais, 130 Wacos, 160 Tawakonis, 250 Ionis, 350 Anadarkos, 300 Caddos, 120 Lipan Apaches, 750 Tonkawas, 4,000 Essequeta and Muscalero Apaches, 300 Kickapoos, 60 Cherokees, 30 Delawares, 20 Shawnees, and 10 Biloxis.[23] As had been demanded of them, the Comanches delivered some white captives, an American and four Mexican boys who were ransomed from them. Kendall commented on the sale of a Mexican prisoner to trader George Barnard: "The price of the lad—who was a smart, intelligent little fellow, about ten years of age—was one hundred dollars in goods, and it was a study to watch his countenance as the good-hearted trader and the Comanche chief chattered about the price of his freedom."[24]

Jesse Chisholm reported that while serving as emissaries, his party had spotted Cynthia Ann and John Parker, but efforts to retrieve them had been unsuccessful.[25] The commissioners stated:

> They were in captivity of the Yam-pr-ric-coes, and were on the head of the Wash-e-taw, where our runners saw them last. The young woman [Cynthia Ann] is claimed by one of the Comanches as his wife. From the influence of her alleged husband, or from her own inclinations she is unwilling to leave the people with whom she associates. The head men seemed to acquiesce in the propriety of her being surrendered, on an adequate sum, in the way of ransom being paid. A large amount of goods, and four or five hundred dollars were offered, but the offer was unavailing, as she would run off and hide her self to avoid those who went to ransom her.[26]

The four months in the field had been a long, fatiguing, and painful effort for both Butler and Lewis. Once the tribes were finally assembled, the commissioners lost no time initiating the treaty talks. On the same day Pahaucah arrived, the commissioners held a gathering beneath the arbor to say that a meeting would be convened at nine on the following morning to deliver the talk of the president of the United States. That evening a supper was held for all. The fare consisted of 200 pounds of boiled beef spread over a tent cloth on the ground, large pones of cornbread, and three kettles of coffee. The offering was soon exhausted.[27]

At the council on May 13, a new treaty of permanent friendship was proposed to set boundary lines between Texas settlements and Indian lands. Jim Shaw, John Connor, and Jesse Chisholm interpreted for the Comanches; Lewis Sanchez for the Caddos, Tonkawas, and Lipans; and Nancy, the Wichita girl, for the Wichitas, Wacos, and Kichais. The chiefs were asked to return with a definite answer to the various proposals at the next meeting.[28]

It had been suggested also that a delegation of Indian leaders from the various tribes be taken to visit the Great Father in Washington. The chiefs returned to council on the fifteenth, and Pahaucah announced that the Comanches would sign the treaty document. The Comanche chief led the signing, followed by Old Owl—a "little old man with a cunning, diplomatic face,"[29]—and twenty-two others, including Buffalo Hump and Santa Anna. Pahaucah indicated that he and his chiefs wished to defer the important boundary line question until they talked with the president. Buffalo Hump and Santa Anna were chosen to represent the Comanches at Washington, but Buffalo Hump refused the offer.

The U.S.-crafted treaty specified the usual commitments to peace and friendship and acknowledgment of U.S. sovereignty by the tribes. By the pact, the United States was given the sole and exclusive right to regulate trade, white prisoners would be given up, tribal members guilty of crimes against whites and stolen stock would be turned in, and offenders would be punished. The United States would have full discretion to establish agencies, military posts, and trading houses on the borders of Indian land. In return, it would reward the tribes with goods to the value of $10,000 and send among them blacksmiths, schoolteachers, and preachers.[30]

Two clauses of the treaty were later struck out by the U.S. Senate. One, inserted by Buffalo Hump, restricted any citizen from entering Indian country except by permission of the president; another permitted the Indians to send representatives to Washington.[31]

Kendall, who hurried off to Matamoras, Mexico, to become America's first war correspondent, described the treaty signing: "The ceremonies of the treaty were solemn and imposing. The pipe of peace with the tobacco wampum, the usual emblems of such ceremonies, were handled and interchanged, as indicating a long white road of peace. As each chief would sign the treaty, he would approach the Commissioners and they would embrace."[32]

With the pact consummated, the tribespeople began striking their tents and arranging their treaty goods aboard packhorses before moving off into the boundless expanse of prairie land. Forty-one chiefs, warriors, and interpreters remained behind with Commissioner Lewis as delegates to Washington.

For most of the delegation it was an awesome, sight-filled journey overland by horseback from Council Springs to Fort Caddo, Louisiana, then by steam-belching paddle wheeler down the Red River to New Orleans and up the Mississippi and Ohio rivers to Wheeling, West Virginia. There, they boarded back-jolting stagecoaches for the trip over the Cumberland Road to Cumberland, Maryland, and on to Washington, D.C. The blanketed and buckskin-clad visitors from the Plains arrived at Washington's Globe Hotel on June 26, immediately drawing a large crowd of curious onlookers.[33] On July 1, President James Polk received the delegation in the White House. He recorded the event in his diary:

> At 5 O/Clock P.M. Between 40 and 50 chiefs and braves of the Comanche and other bands and tribes of wild Indians from the prairies in the North of Texas, were presented to me by M. G. Lewis, Esq'r., who had been sent with Gov. Butler last fall to visit these tribes. I received them in the Ladies Parlour above stairs, in the presence of a few ladies and other persons. I held a friendly talk with them through an interpreter [Jesse Chisholm]. . . . After the reception and talk were over Miss Pleaston performed for them on the Piano. They were afterwards conducted to the East Room and through all parlours below stairs.[34]

In his short speech, Polk assured the Indians that they could rely on the friendship and protection of the United States. In his diary, Polk described Santa Anna as "a fine looking man of good size and middle age, evidently a man of talents. He has an honest face, and looks like a bold and daring leader."[35] The Comanche told the president that he had once thought his people could outfight any nation in the world, but he found that the whites were more numerous than the stars.[36]

The delegation was entertained lavishly in Washington. The members were taken on tours of the U.S. Naval Yard, the Armory, Center Market, and the City of Washington. At the Congressional Library they viewed an exhibition of Indian paintings by George Catlin, whom some of them had met with Dodge in 1834. Another old acquaintance, Sam Houston, now in Washington as a U.S. senator from Texas, took them on a personal tour of the Capitol building. There, they saw portraits of American dignitaries, including to their great delight one of Houston himself.[37]

After more than two weeks in Washington, however, many of the tribesmen became homesick and anxious to return home. On July 17 they complained about this to President Polk at the White House. A week later, when they returned to take their leave, Polk presented silver medals to eighteen of the chiefs. Polk noted the event in his diary, concluding that when the Indians left they were apparently well pleased, promising to remain friendly and keep the peace.[38]

After the chiefs had returned home and rejoined their bands, however, it was learned that the U.S. Senate had adjourned without ratifying the treaty or appropriating funds for the rewards promised. The angry tribes threatened to raid Torrey's and take what the government owed them. Sam Houston came to the rescue, authorizing Torrey's to issue $10,000 worth of goods to the tribes.[39]

Nothing was achieved in Washington regarding an agreement on a boundary line between whites and Indians in Texas. It was, in truth, an issue neither the tribes nor the Texans could or would have faithfully abided by. An equally serious problem was created by Article 3 of the Butler/Lewis treaty, which placed the Texas Indians solely under the protection of the U.S. government. In recognition that Texas retained exclusive jurisdiction over its public domain, however, the Senate struck out the clause. As a result, U.S. trade and intercourse laws did not apply to Texas.[40]

This further left the frontiers of Texas essentially unprotected by the U.S. Army and subject to Indian raiding from north Texas to the Rio Grande. Nonetheless, the state of Texas continued to promote immigrant settlements westward along the Llano River even as Comanches and other bands roamed the region to hunt and war parties conducted forays southward into Mexico. During the spring of 1847, Buffalo Hump led a raid into Mexico, bringing back a thousand horses along with prisoners.[41]

Such incursions by the Comanches and others required passage across west Texas and presented a threat to white settlement of the region. One such colonization was that promoted by the Society of German Noblemen, the *Adelsverein*, which secured a grant of 3 million acres of land between the Llano and Colorado rivers—an area on which the Comanches resided and considered as their range. Although relations were amicable at first, the German settlers soon began to suffer depredations: two German officers were murdered and scalped, settlers were shot at in their fields, children were taken captive, and stock was stolen.[42]

To prevent a new war on the Plains, the governor of Texas appointed Neighbors, a member of the Washington delegation, as a special agent for the Indians of Texas in March 1847. A determined man with much courage and energy, he arranged a council between the Germans and the Comanches and helped work out a treaty permitting the colony's occupation of the tract for $3,000 in goods. The Comanches agreed not to harm the colonists, to report thefts of stock, and to permit survey-ors—"men with the things that steal the land (compasses),"—to deter-mine the boundary line.[43]

Neighbors met the chiefs again in May to obtain their approval of the U.S. Senate's revision of the Treaty of Comanche Peak. Old Owl and Santa Anna were amenable, but Buffalo Hump objected to deleting the requirement of white people having to secure permission of the presi-dent to enter their country. Although angered by the presence of sur-veyors on Comanche lands, he eventually signed the revision. Three surveyors had recently been killed and scalped, and Neighbors feared the issue might ignite another war.[44]

Comanche leaders still sought some definition of a boundary line separating them from Texas settlers. During 1847, the state of Texas es-tablished a line of Ranger camps along the frontier, but this only created more discontent. Old Owl complained that Rangers stopped his war-riors while en route to raid in Mexico. The Treaty of Guadalupe Hidalgo, which concluded the war between the United States and Mexico, had called for such interceptions, even though the Treaty of Comanche Peak had not.[45]

Texas, meanwhile, advanced its line of frontier protection, establish-ing Fort Martin Scott near present Fredericksburg, Fort Gates near present Gatesville, Fort Graham near present Hillsboro, and Fort Worth on the Trinity River, along with others to the south and west of San Antonio.[46] Neighbors, who had worked closely with the tribes and visited them often, was relieved of his position in June 1849 for political reasons. He was replaced by John H. Rollins, an older man who suffered from tuber-culosis. Despite his illness, Rollins made difficult trips into the Indian country of central and west Texas to locate and talk with the scattered bands. In May 1850 on the Llano River, he met the Seminole leader Wild Cat, who was on his way to seek accommodations with Mexican offi-cials.[47] Again that fall, with a small escort of troops and Delaware Indians, Rollins ventured beyond forts Graham and Gates to eventually contact Buffalo Hump, with whom he conducted "very good" talks.[48]

A major blow to harmony on the Texas frontier occurred during the California Gold Rush of 1849, when a scourge of smallpox and the dreaded cholera swept through the southern tribes. Both Old Owl and Santa

Anna, leading peacemakers among the Penetekas, were among the hundreds of Comanches who perished. Their demise left the more belligerent Buffalo Hump as the dominant leader of the southern bands. Despite his promise to stop them, small bands continued to raid frontier settlements and take captives.[49]

Pressed by Congress to act, Rollins, with twenty soldiers and eleven Delaware Indians, made the long ride from San Antonio to the Clear Fork of the Brazos 125 miles northwest of Fort Graham to meet with the Comanches during September 1850. Buffalo Hump and the other chiefs denied any role in Texas depredations but defended their right to raid Mexican settlements. Rollins managed to elicit their promise not to travel south of the Llano River in return for his offer to provide trading houses and an agency where they could receive goods of the white man. The old issue of a boundary line still persisted, however, and Rollins felt a new treaty agreement was needed to resolve it and other issues.[50]

To accomplish this, Rollins was sent forth from Fort Martin Scott with a wagon train of treaty goods, escorted by soldiers of the Second Dragoons and Texas Mounted Volunteers plus some Delaware guides. John Connor and Jesse Chisholm accompanied the expedition to serve as advisers and interpreters.[51] The entourage joined the Comanches along with bands of the Caddos, Lipans, Quapaws, Tawakonis, and Wacos at the head of Spring Creek just south of its juncture with the San Saba.

The beef herd needed to feed the Indians did not arrive until December 1, and on the fourth a violent norther and snowstorm struck, causing great suffering for whites and Indians alike. When the council got under way, Rollins reiterated the principal arrangements of the Comanche Peak treaty, then he heard from the Indians. The tribesmen complained strongly that the white man had taken their country away from them, leaving them in great poverty. Although they had no love for the white man, they said, they now had no choice but to rely upon the kindness of the government.[52]

During the council, a scout was sent north to the Red River to retrieve a young German girl who had been taken captive by the Northern Comanches. He returned twelve days later with the girl, having purchased her at the price of a gun and a silver bridle.[53]

With Rollins's poor health limiting his participation in the treaty process, much of the council was conducted by Neighbors and John S. Ford through Connor and Chisholm.[54] The instrument signed on December 10, 1850, contained pledges regarding maintaining peace, regulating trade, delivering tribal predators to the military, returning white captives—neither Rollins nor the Indians took this to include Mexican prisoners—and surrendering slaves who had been taken as they attempted to escape across Texas to Mexico. The boundary issue was addressed in part by limiting the Indians from going below the line of military posts on the east side of the Colorado River or below the Llano River and a line running west from its head without written permission of the military. Nothing was included to restrict white intrusion into Indian country.[55]

One further treaty with the Comanches and the Lipan and Mescalero Apaches was initiated on the San Saba on September 28, 1851, by Indian agent John Rogers. Rogers replaced Rollins, who had died the previous fall. By this pact, which was signed by obscure Comanche chiefs, the tribes reaffirmed the agreement of Comanche Peak and reiterated their promise to return captured slaves. Additionally, they agreed to accept the restrictions of the Treaty of Guadalupe Hidalgo whereby they were required to turn Mexican captives over to U.S. authorities for return to Mexico.[56]

The U.S.-sponsored treaties in Texas were successful in pacifying the Peneteka division of the Comanches and other tribes to the south. Following the September 1851 treaty on the San Saba, Texas enjoyed a period of tranquility on its frontier, with no Indian engagements of consequence during the ensuing two years. In part, this was because the Southern Comanche bands and Lipan Apaches were raiding into Mexico rather than Texas. Although the treaty commitments of 1850 and 1851 undoubtedly influenced the tribes, their activities in Texas were also contained by an aggressive Indian campaign by the U.S. Second Dragoons and Texas Mounted Volunteers.[57]

With some Comanche bands bound by treaty and some not and rogue war parties of the various tribes operating from north of the Red River, it was impossible to know who was guilty when crimes were committed. Further, the strong anti-Indian climate in Texas led to unfounded rumor and accusations. During September 1852, both Texas Indian officials and U.S. military officers gave lie to a newspaper report that the Comanches had descended on Fort Graham, killed a few officers and men, and driven off a herd of mules. Agent Jesse Stem reported instead that other than a few small thefts, the entire line of the Texas frontier had been exempt from Indian depredations. From his camp in Indian Territory near the Wichita Mountains, Chief Pahaucah sent assurances that his people desired to be at peace and that he would gladly meet in council.[58]

This, however, did not speak to the woeful conditions of the Comanches and other tribes in north and west Texas. Agent Horace Capron found a large band of Comanches under Sanaco and Katumse residing on the Concho River, suffering from extreme hunger bordering on starvation, with their young men severely debauched by the wares of unscrupulous white whiskey traders. A chief asked, "What encouragement have we to attempt the cultivation of the soil, or raising of cattle, so long as we have no permanent home, and in every attempt we have ever made to raise a crop, we have been driven from them before they could mature by the encroachment of the white man."[59]

The condition of the smaller bands of Caddos, Anadarkos, Kichais, Tawakonis, Tonkawas, and others scattered along the Brazos River was even more pitiable. The state of Texas now contended that its Indians were not its responsibility but that of the U.S. government. During the spring of 1853, at the same time Thomas Fitzpatrick was initiating a treaty with the Northern Comanches, Texas hired Delaware guide John Connor to gather up all of the remnant bands of Delawares, Shawnees, Quapaws, Cherokees, and Seminoles considered foreign to Texas. He was then to lead them to their previous homes in Indian Territory north of the Red River. With the exception of a few stragglers, Connor completed the assignment that fall.[60]

Although it stoutly maintained that neither the Indians nor the United States possessed any property rights in Texas, the state legislature, by its act of February 6, 1854, authorized the federal government to select a reservation site for the Comanches and other tribes native to Texas. During 1854 two tracts were chosen on the Upper Brazos River northwest of present Fort Worth.[61]

Even as efforts by Agent Robert Neighbors were under way to move the Comanches to the new reservation, word of a forthcoming military expedition from Fort Chadbourne caused Comanche bands under Sanaco and Buffalo Hump to flee north. Many of them united with Comanche bands along the Red River that had never committed themselves by treaty to the United States. Only 180 Comanches under Katumse joined Neighbors on the Lower Brazos reservation.[62]

During the months that followed, white immigration into northern and western Texas increased dramatically and with it a sharp escalation of Indian depredations. The regions west and south of Fort Worth were hit particularly hard. The undermanned U.S. forces stationed along the line of Texas frontier forts were ineffective in defending settlers from the marauding tribes. The situation became so severe during 1858 that both state and federal authorities determined that a punitive military offensive would be required to drive the hostile Indian Territory tribes to the reservation. Accordingly, in the spring of 1858 a Texas Ranger force led by Capt. John S. Ford and supplemented with a band of Anadarko, Tonkawa, and other Indian scouts from the Brazos reservations crossed the Red River in search of Comanches.

Marching north along the 100th meridian that separated Indian Territory and the Texas Panhandle, the command found a buffalo hunt under way near Antelope Hills. Ford and his men took cover in a ravine overnight, and on the morning of May 12 they launched an attack on the unsuspecting Kotsoteka Comanche camp of Chief Buffalo Hump, located northeast of the hills on Little Robe Creek. Seventy-six Comanches were killed and eighteen captured. Among the dead was Chief Pohebits Quasho, or Iron Jacket. When the rangers peeled back the buffalo robe from his body, they were amazed to find a coat of mail. This was divided among the command for souvenirs. The Rangers also captured over 300 horses and mules, none of which were identified as having been stolen.[63]

Fearing a counterassault against frontier settlements, Texas officials requested U.S. troops to wage "a military campaign against the savages."[64] Gen. David Twiggs, commanding the Department of Texas, responded by ordering Maj. Earl Van Dorn into Indian Territory with a command of U.S. troops. After establishing Camp Radziminski west of the Wichita Mountains, Van Dorn learned from his Tonkawa spies that a large entourage of Comanches was camped near a Wichita village on the east side of the mountains. The Comanches, headed by Buffalo Hump, had been persuaded by the Wichitas that the whites sincerely desired peace and were on their way to a peace council with Indian Bureau authorities at Fort Arbuckle. Making an overnight forced march around the Wichita Mountains, Van Dorn reached the Wichita village at daybreak and attacked indiscriminately. Once again the Comanches suffered heavy losses. Van Dorn claimed nearly sixty victims while losing only five of his men. Among them was Lt. Cornelius Van Camp, who had taken a Comanche arrow in his heart. The Wichitas also suffered severely. After the fight, Van Dorn torched 120 lodges.[65]

Still other incursions into Indian Territory occurred during 1859, with military strikes from Fort Arbuckle and south from Fort Leavenworth. In April, Van Dorn marched north to Ford County, Kansas, where he once again found the unfortunate Buffalo Hump. His attack resulted in forty-nine tribespeople being killed and thirty-six captured.[66]

Texas Rangers celebrate before General Twigg's headquarters at the Alamo (Harper's Weekly, *March 23, 1861*).

The turmoil in north Texas had increased sharply to a point of near hysteria against the Indians of the Brazos reservations. Former Comanche agent John R. Baylor, a rabid white supremacist who had been forced to leave the Fort Gibson area after killing a man, led the foment. At one point he incited around 250 followers to invade one of the reservations and attack the Indians. One old Indian man was killed before U.S. troops arrived and drove the white mob away.[67]

This affair further convinced Agent Neighbors that the only answer to the Texas Indian problem was removal of the tribes to a reservation in Indian Territory. With the concurrence of the U.S. government, which arranged the lease of a large tract of land along the Upper Washita River from the proprietary Chickasaw and Choctaw Indians, Neighbors initiated removal of the Brazos reservation Indians. On August 1, 1859, under escort of U.S. troops, a caravan of over 1,400 Indians on foot and horseback set forth with their cattle, horses, and dogs, their wagons and two-wheeled Mexican carts loaded with paraphernalia.[68]

The Texas tribes were relocated on the Leased District, joining the Wichitas and other peaceful bands of prairie Indians under a newly created

Wichita Agency. The government soon established Fort Cobb three miles from the agency. The vast lands of Texas, once ruled by the Comanches and their allies, were now completely free of tribal claim. Removal of the Brazos reservation Indians, however, did little to halt the raiding by hostile elements of Indian Territory. Texas's Indian troubles were far from over.

Fort Laramie and the Road West

*It is not intended to take any of your lands away
from you, or to destroy your rights to hunt,
or fish, or pass over the country, as heretofore.*
—COMMISSIONER DAVID D. MITCHELL

The Treaty of Fort Laramie was one of the largest and most colorful Indian councils ever held in the West. Importantly, it established the first official designations of territory for the northern Plains tribes, creating areas of occupation that future treaties would be forced to recognize. It was significant also that in being reported in detail by an American newspaper, the *Missouri Republican*, the affair revealed the tribal cultures of the Plains Indians to the outside world.

By mid-century the western concerns of the young American nation had moved well beyond the waters of the Missouri River. The great demand for beaver pelts had subsided, and the westward movement began in full force. The government now looked to territorial expansion to the Pacific Coast and protecting the immigration that accompanied and supported it. During the 1840s the great avenues of western migration, the Oregon and Santa Fe trails, became flooded with caravans of home seekers and commercial transportation as the new nation enlarged its empire. Standing directly in the path of this territorial expansion were the native tribes of the Central Plains, whose early commitments to amity had been rubbed raw by the ever-increasing traffic across their lands that severely reduced the game and thereby their vital food supply.

Although the Plains tribes viewed the invasion of their lands with much consternation, they remained quiet during the early years of westward migration. Despite disputes arising from indiscretions committed by both whites and Indians, good relations generally prevailed.[1] Thus, it was less because of Indian troubles and more for the government's pursuit of a supposed Manifest Destiny that military expeditions were sent forth to pave the way for westward expansion. During 1845 a topographical party under Lt. James Abert probed the region of the mid-Plains, another under Capt. John C. Fremont marched to California, and Col. Stephen W. Kearny was sent up the Oregon Trail to the South Pass of southern Wyoming.

Guided by mountain man Thomas Fitzpatrick, Kearny arrived at Fort Laramie with five well-armed companies of U.S. Dragoons.[2] There, on June 16 he conducted a showy council with a large band of Sioux Indians who had never witnessed U.S. troops. Kearny told them that many white people would soon be coming across their land: "You must not disturb them in their persons or molest their property. Should you do so your Great Father would be very angry with you and cause you to be punished."[3]

To impress the Indians, he fired three booming shots from a howitzer and that night shot rockets into the sky. Although some offenses occurred in the months ahead, the tribes remained peaceful despite the flow of white caravans along the Oregon Trail. But the potential of trouble remained, and government officials sought new agreements with the tribes.[4]

To this purpose, a single grandiose council was arranged with many of the Plains tribes during the spring of 1851. Superintendent of Indian Affairs David D. Mitchell dispatched emissaries up the Missouri, Platte, and Arkansas rivers and as far west as Fort Bridger, inviting tribes to meet at Fort Laramie on September 1.[5] Most accepted the invitation, but the Comanches and Kiowas rejected the idea. When Thomas Fitzpatrick, appointed the first Indian agent for the newly created Upper Platte and Arkansas Rivers agency in 1846, met with those tribes on the Arkansas River, they said they had too many horses and mules to risk making a journey among such notorious horse thieves as the Sioux and Crows. The Pawnees, who had only recently suffered an attack by the Cheyennes, likewise refused to attend. The southern bands of Cheyennes and Arapahos, however, accepted Fitzpatrick's invitation.[6]

In coming west, Mitchell was joined at St. Louis by Col. George Knapp, a proprietor of the St. Louis *Missouri Republican*; Adam B. Chambers, editor of the paper; and correspondent B. Gratz Brown.[7] The men boarded a steamboat for Fort Leavenworth, where a military escort of the First Dragoons was provided for the long overland trip up the Platte Trail to Fort Laramie.[8]

Mitchell found the Sioux (Oglala, Yankton, Blackfoot, and Brulé bands), Cheyennes, and Arapahos waiting impatiently at the fort. He immediately called a meeting to explain the objects of the proposed treaty and to decide upon a better camping ground where there would be grass and water for the thousands of tribespeople and animals that would gather. The chiefs selected a site at the mouth of Horse Creek, which flowed into the Platte thirty-five miles east of Fort Laramie in present Nebraska. The move to that location was made early in September.[9]

One of the remarkable aspects of the Fort Laramie treaty council was the degree of friendliness displayed by tribes that had long warred with one another. There was, however, an exception. The Shoshones, or Snakes, under the tutelage of the famous Jim Bridger, arrived from the West, their men leading in battle array and their women, children, and baggage at the rear. As they approached over the California (or Salt Lake) road, a Cheyenne warrior charged a man and his son who were on the trail by themselves. Both were killed and scalped. When their bodies were discovered, the Shoshones commenced their death song, sent a number of their women and children back, and refused to proceed with the remaining eighty-three tribesmen until a military escort from Fort Laramie arrived.[10]

The Cheyennes resolved the matter, Plains Indian style, by giving a feast for the Shoshones. The hosts set up an arbor and provided their tribal guests, along with Brown and other whites, mats and skins to sit on. The preliminary smoke was conducted in silence before Cheyenne chief Porcupine Bear arrived and made a forceful speech to his young men. He instructed his tribesmen to treat the Shoshones as friends and to give them presents, then admonished them further to listen to the tribal elders and not go to war without permission of their chiefs.[11]

After this, a drum was beaten as the Cheyenne old men harangued the village, calling all forth to the arbor. The Shoshones, who would not eat dog as the Cheyennes and Sioux did, were feasted first from a large copper kettle filled with boiled corn that had been cracked and mashed. When the meal was over more speeches were made, and the Cheyennes presented gifts to the offended tribe. Among the goods were blankets, bolts of scarlet cloth, knives, and tobacco. A final offering was made of the two Shoshone scalps recently taken. They were presented to the dead man's brother, who received them with deep sorrow before embracing the warrior who had killed his brother and nephew. The issue had been resolved; the Cheyennes joined the Shoshones in nightlong dancing and revelry.

On that same evening the Assiniboines and Gros Ventres arrived from the Missouri River accompanied by Alexander Culbertson and Edward Chouteau, traders at Fort Union, and the noted Catholic priest, Father Pierre Jean De Smet.[12] Culbertson announced that the notorious Blackfoot tribe of Montana, whom U.S. officials greatly hoped would attend, had not come because of the lateness of the season. The campsite at Horse Creek now contained around 7,000 lodges, several thousand tribespeople, and an uncountable number of horses and mules. On Saturday, September 7, Mitchell announced that there would be no council on Sunday, "the white man's medicine day," and the tribes spent the day holding feasts and dances for one another. The drum beating and songs continued through the night.[13]

The initial grand council got under way on September 9. At nine o'clock that morning, artillery was fired and a flag was raised on a tall staff before Mitchell's tent to call the assemblage together. The boom of the cannon brought the prairie to sudden life as tribespeople surrounded the council grounds, some on horseback, some on foot: chiefs, warriors, women, youths, and children—Cheyennes, Arapahos, Sioux, Assiniboines, Shoshones, Arikaras, Gros Ventres, and Mandans. Brown was thoroughly impressed:

> Each nation approached with its own peculiar song or demonstration and such a combination of rude, wild and fantastic manners and dresses, never was witnessed. It is not probable that an opportunity will again be presented of seeing so many tribes assembled together, displaying all the peculiarities of features, dress, equipments, and horses. The manner of painting themselves and horses, and everything else, exhibited their wild notions of elegance and propriety.[14]

In this, Brown saw a strong similarity to prototypes in American cities. The dress of young men was often exquisite to a point of foppery, whereas the attire of young women, the tribal "belles," ranged in elegance reflective of the wealth and standing of their husbands or fathers. In observing the flirting interplay between the sexes, Brown realized that coquetry was not restricted to the white race.

Father De Smet further described the historic gathering of Plains tribes:

> During the eighteen days that the Great Council lasted, the union, harmony and amity that reigned among the Indians were truly admirable. Implacable hatreds, hereditary enmities, cruel and bloody encounters, with the whole past, in line, were forgotten. They paid mutual visits, smoked the calumet of peace together, exchanged presents, partook of numerous banquets, and all the lodges were open to strangers. A practice occurring but on the most amicable and fraternal occasions was seen—this is, the adopting of children and of brothers on each side.[15]

The council was arranged in a circle of skin shelters extending out from the branch-covered arbor of the commission party, with a portion of the ring left open facing east according to tribal custom. Commissioners Mitchell and Fitzpatrick held center stage along with Chambers, who served as secretary and also provided copy to his newspaper; other members of the commission retinue took seats beside and behind them. These included military officers headed by Col. Samuel Cooper, the journalists, Father De Smet, Fort Laramie founder Robert Campbell, a variety of interpreters and traders, and others. Among them were Bridger; John Simpson Smith, long associated with the Cheyennes; Edward Chouteau; and the wife of Lt. W. L. Elliott of the Mounted Rifles, the lone white woman present.[16]

When everyone had settled into position, Mitchell rose and addressed the chiefs, who waited patiently as his words were intermittently interpreted. He compared the Indian ritual of smoking the pipe of peace to the white man's swearing on the Bible and said he wanted no one to swear to anything with two hearts. He then instructed the Sioux interpreter to fill a three-foot red-stone pipe stem with kinnikinnick and light it. Mitchell and Fitzpatrick took the first puffs before passing it on to the Sioux and then to other tribes successively. Each chief took his puff and reverently pointed the calumet to the four points of the compass, then upward to the Great Spirit and down toward the bad spirits.

After the smoking was completed, Mitchell introduced Mrs. Elliott, indicating her presence as proof of the commission's belief in the Indians' good intentions. Immediately following his remarks, the meeting was suddenly interrupted. A Cheyenne woman, leading a horse that carried a ten- or- twelve-year-old boy, made her way to the front of the arbor and commenced a long chant. Her action stunned everyone for a moment or two before the Cheyenne chiefs came forward and led her off. Cheyenne interpreter Smith later explained what had taken place.

The woman's husband, father of the boy, had been killed years earlier by a Shoshone chief who was seated in the council circle. The Cheyenne widow had come to present the boy and the horse to him. By custom, the chief had no right to refuse the gift, and the boy thus adopted by the Shoshones would receive all rights and privileges of the tribe. The woman was forced to delay her presentation until another occasion.[17] After this, Mitchell outlined the government's plan, telling the chiefs:

> In order that justice may be done [to] each nation, it is proposed that your country shall be divided into geographical districts—that the country and its limits shall be designated by such rivers, mountains, and lines, as will show what country each nation claims and where they are located. In doing this it is not intended to take any of your lands away from you, or to destroy your rights to hunt, or fish, or pass over the country, as heretofore. But it will be expected that each nation will be held responsible for depredations committed within its territory, unless it can be clearly shown that the people of some other country committed them, and then that nation will be held responsible—Your Great Father only desires to punish the guilty and reward the good. When a horse is stolen, or a scalp taken, or a woman or child carried off, or any other wrong done, he wants to find out who did it, and punish the bad men or nation; and the nation will be held responsible for the acts of its people.
>
> Your condition is now changed from what it formerly was. In times past you had plenty of buffalo and game to subsist upon, and your Great Father well knows that war has always been your favorite amusement and pursuit. He then left the questions of war and peace to yourselves. Now, since the settling of the districts West of you by the white man, your condition has changed, and your Great Father desires you will consider and prepare for the changes that await you.
>
> He desires and it is now necessary that you should make and maintain peace between nations and bands as well as with the whites. Diseases, famine and the vices of bad white men are carrying your people off fast enough without the aid of war. Your Great Father desires to drive the bad white men out from amongst you, and I therefore expect you will freely give me the names of any bad men in your country.[18]

Leading chiefs answered in-kind and shook hands with the commissioner. Percival G. Lowe, who was present at the council as a U.S. Dragoon, described a technique government officials commonly employed in treating with the Indians that has been generally ignored: "Amidst the grunts of approval as the oratory went on, a chief was called in to headquarters and soon returned decked out in full major-general's uniform from head to foot."[19]

In addition, the chief was often presented with a glistening saber and silver peace medal to further adorn his presence, plus an official document with a large red seal and ribbon to testify to his stature in the eyes of the Great Father. These trappings were immensely influential for the chief among his tribesmen and increased his fidelity to the United States, as well as his propensity to sign a treaty document. This assuaging of chiefly egos traces back to and beyond the Choctaw leader Pushmataha, who aided Andrew Jackson at the Battle of New Orleans and commonly wore a U.S. general's uniform.

Correspondent Brown, Father De Smet, and Lowe recorded many of the interesting incidents and scenes of the huge intratribal encampment: the multitude of hieroglyphic-decorated lodges; the numerous dog feasts; the nightlong, drum-throbbing dances; the Indians' affection for oratory; and the adeptness of tribes with different languages to communicate effectively through signs and gestures. Both Brown and Father De Smet extensively described an ear-cutting ceremony a Cheyenne mother conducted on her young son. Brown described the mock charge of Cheyenne warriors on the commission camp and the display of a tribal war drill exercised with great precision before the white audience: "They would fire their guns, shoot their arrows, give a shout, make a charge, and then the horsemen would rush out around and through the footmen, indicating the manner of protecting their men when too closely pressed."[20]

Another grand council was called for September 10. But even as the affair was getting started, it was interrupted by word that the Crows were on their way.

"They came down the plain in a solid column singing their national songs," Brown wrote. "In front rode the two principal chiefs, each carrying a highly ornamented pipe[;] behind them the remainder of their party with their arms."[21]

Mitchell mounted a greeting party and rode out to welcome them. After a friendship smoke, he assigned them a campground and invited them to a place in the council. There, he asked the assembly for its response to his previous talk. He went to the Sioux, and a very old Brulé chief spoke first, saying: "Some things you propose are very well, but in some things we don't agree with you. We are a large band, and we claim half of all the country; but we don't care for that, for we can hunt anywhere."[22]

Big Yancton, another Sioux leader, insisted that he was willing to make peace with the whites who came through his country, but they destroyed the grass and timber and drove the game away. Painted Bear, who had met with whites twice before, said he did not understand their words. He knew they meant well, but he would have to let the half bloods who understood them do his speaking.

Other Sioux speakers stressed the fact that their people were all very poor and very hungry. Mitchell contended that since the government was buying all the Sioux land north of the Missouri River, it would be important for the Sioux to the south to unite, form one nation, and define their lands. "If you take one lodge pole," he said, "you can easily break it; but if you take all the poles together, it is very hard to break them."[23]

The Cheyennes were more amenable. The Bear's Feather, better known to whites as Old Bark, acknowledged that the buffalo were becoming scarcer. "As the sun looks down upon us—the Great Spirit sees me. I am willing, Grand Father, to do as you tell me to do. We regard this as a great medicine day, when our pipes and water shall be one, and we all shall be at peace. If all the nations here were as willing to do what you tell them, and do what they say as we are, then we could sleep in peace; we would not have to watch our horses or our lodges in the night."[24]

Arapaho chief Beka-chebetcha, or Cut Nose, expressed himself similarly and thanked the commissioners for coming. "It is a good earth," he said, "and I hope there will be no more [coming] on it—that the grass will grow and the water fall, and [there will be] plenty of buffalo."[25] Another chief, Authon-ish-eh, addressed his tribe, haranguing them not to be fools but to listen to the advice of the Great Father and hold no lies in their hearts.

Earlier, Mitchell had requested that the tribes select a single chief to represent them with the government. The Sioux had not done so, insisting on a chief for each band. They were asked to meet and try again to select a single chief. The Cheyennes gave the name of their own great medicine man, Wan-na-sah-tah (Who Walks With His Toes Turned Out) and the Arapahos chose Blah-at-sah-ah-kah-che (Little Owl).

When the Sioux returned to council the next morning, they had still not complied with Mitchell's request. Every band had vied to have one of its men become the principal chief. Mitchell explained again that he could not accept a chief for each band, that the chief must be the choice of the entire nation. He sent them back to hold a smoke and see if they could not come to an agreement.[26]

The Crows, a Rocky Mountain tribe that habitually traded with other tribes on the Missouri River and at Fort Union, had met in the meantime and joined the council circle as the Sioux departed. Their spokesman was a chief named Arra-tu-resash (Big Robber), a large, well–developed, elegantly dressed man with an intelligent face. The Crow said his delegation had been sent by the tribal elders to see what could be done for his people. Their big chief at home was only a child—indicating a hereditary line of headmen—but the boy would be a great chief one day. Big Robber admitted that the young men of the Crows sometimes went to war in defiance of the old men, but he believed they could be restrained in the future.[27]

He was followed by another Crow chief named Mountain Tail, who informed Mitchell that Big Robber had been selected to represent the Crows. The commissioners saluted Big Robber and gave him presents for his tribe. This done, each nation was asked to select five or more of their principal men to meet the next morning to determine their respective boundaries. The various traders, trappers, interpreters, and others—including Bridger and Father De Smet—were called in to join the commissioners in pouring over a map of the western region and designating on it the various tribal territories.

On the map, the Platte River separated the Sioux from the Cheyennes and Arapahos. This displeased the Sioux greatly, and when the council met on September 13, Oglala chief Black Hawk complained. He said the Sioux had fought the Crows and Kiowas for range south of the Platte and deserved a share of it. Mitchell was eventually able to persuade them that the line did not prohibit hunting there so long as they remained at peace.[28]

The debates continued for four more days until September 17, when the treaty document was signed by chiefs of the Sioux, Cheyennes, Arapahos, Crows, Assiniboines, Gros Ventres, Mandans, and Arikaras. The treaty document had been written out in longhand, with blank spaces left for signing. With guidance, each chief duly took the proffered pen and made his "x" where his name had been written in.[29]

The treaty called for friendship and a cessation of hostilities by the tribes, restitution for wrongs committed against American citizens, and permission for the United States to build roads, military posts, and trading posts within their respective territories. In return, the government promised to protect the Indians from depredations by U.S. citizens and to make like restitution for the wrongs they committed. A principal feature of the pact involved the designation and assigning of specific territories to the various tribes. Article Seven of the treaty stipulated that "for their maintenance and the improvement of their moral and social customs," the United States would pay $50,000 per annum to each tribe for fifty years.[30]

Considerable anxiety had existed throughout the camp over the arrival of the wagon train bringing the promised gifts of goods and food. After three weeks in camp, the hungry tribal members were anxious to return to the hunt. Finally, on the twentieth the train arrived, and goods to the expense of $60,000 were piled on the prairie: "Without delay, the occupants of the various camps flocked in—men, women and children— in great confusion, and in their gayest costume, daubed with paints of glaring hues and decorated with all the gewgaws they could boast. . . . The great chiefs were, for the first time in their lives, pantalloned; each was arrayed in a general's uniform, a gilt sword hanging at his side."[31]

The roll of chiefs was read, and each headman in turn parceled out the fare, which was then packed aboard horses and taken off to the camps. On the same day, even as the various tribes trailed off to their particular haunts, the commission party broke camp and returned back down the Platte River.[32]

Delegates selected from the various tribes to visit Washington accompanied Mitchell and Fitzpatrick up the Platte Road. The group was composed of White Antelope, Alights on the Cloud, and Little Chief for the Cheyennes; Eagle's Head, Storm, and Friday for the Arapahos; One Horn, Red Skin, Shellman, and Watchful Elk for the Sioux; Goose for the Assiniboines; Black Elk, his wife Eagle's Feather (or Plume), Black Bear, and his wife Singing Bird for the Otoes; and a Crow brave. Accompanying them were Chambers, Brown, Campbell, Father De Smet, and interpreters John S. Smith and Joseph Tesson Honore.[33]

When the group arrived at Fort Kearny, Nebraska Territory, on October 2, Mitchell arranged a council between the treaty delegation and a party of twenty Pawnee Loup Indians under Big Fatty. The historic enemies sat together and talked amiably. That night the Pawnees held a banquet for the travelers, with singing, dancing, and speech making.

"My heart bounds with delight," Big Fatty told his guests, "for it had never dreamed of meeting you face to face, and of touching your hand in friendship."[34]

Cheyenne Alights on the Cloud, however, abstained from smoking the peace pipe with the Pawnees. The reason, he said, was that his fellow Cheyenne warriors might even then be raiding a Pawnee village, and he would not betray his hosts by pretending to be at peace with them.

Upon arriving by steamboat at St. Louis, the Crow brave disappeared at Brunswick, Missouri, and his body was later found badly mutilated by hogs. It was speculated that he had committed suicide with a knife borrowed from Black Bear, distraught over the strange environment and the sickening motion of river travel compounded by the confusing noises of steam whistles, bells ringing, and the blowing off of steam by the "firehorse" (the steamboat).[35]

In Washington the delegation was housed at Maher's Hotel, where Mrs. Maher attended to the members' needs. They were soon taken to the office of Commissioner of Indian Affairs L. Lea, who lectured them on the government's desire for peace. From there, they went to the White House for a visit with President Millard Fillmore. The Indians had been concerned that the Great Father, of whom they had heard so much, would treat them harshly. The president, however, greeted them in a friendly and kindly manner, and they left with their fears greatly alleviated. That night they accepted Mrs. Lea's invitation to visit her home, and they appeared in full dress to the interested viewing of other guests.[36]

The Indians were duly impressed by a visit to the Washington Naval Yard and Arsenal, which included encounters with steam-powered lathes and other equipment, and other sights around the city. On January 6 they returned to the White House for a final interview with the president. On this occasion, Otoe chief Faithful Partisan, Arapaho chief Storm, Sioux chief Red Plume, and Cheyenne chief White Antelope gave short talks to the president. Fillmore responded in-kind, promising help for their impoverished people but threatening punishment if they did not behave. He presented the chiefs with "my likeness on a valuable medal" and an American flag for their tribe.[37]

Initial reports from Fort Laramie following the great council indicated a continuing amity among the treaty-signing tribes. But this goodwill was short-lived. By the time Fitzpatrick returned to Fort Laramie during October 1852 to deliver the first annuities under the new treaty, trouble had erupted. Even as the distribution of goods got under way on the post parade ground, a party of well-armed Sioux warriors arrived and began firing their guns in the air and demanding redress for an injury done to a tribal member when a soldier had slapped him. Fitzpatrick calmed the matter with a few pounds of sugar, but the chiefs complained further about the treaty they had signed. They professed that they did not understand or comprehend the nature of its provisions and obligations, that their chief had not clearly known what he was doing when he signed the treaty. Chief Fighting Bear said he had supposed the treaty parchment was something to live by but had now discovered it was something to die by.[38]

Other, more serious conflicts followed, causing the Treaty of Fort Laramie to fail in its central purpose of protecting white transportation along the Oregon Trail. There would be no halt to the intertribal warring that was standard fare on the Central Plains. During 1852, two Pawnee women had been killed and scalped in sight of Fort Kearny. The military commander there reported that the starving Pawnees dared not go afield to hunt. He feared that if the government did not provide the tribe some protection, many would perish.[39]

During the summer of 1853, a large Sioux, Cheyenne, and Arapaho war party suffered a severe defeat sixty miles south of Fort Kearny (Nebraska) when it attacked the Pawnees, who were supported by an alliance of Otoes, Iowas, Sacs, and Pottawatomies. This sizable battle, which reportedly involved warriors numbering in the thousands, resulted in ten Sioux and Cheyenne warriors left dead on the field and many others wounded. The Pawnees lost eighteen warriors in addition to several women and children, and their allies also suffered a number of casualties.[40]

During August 1853, Commissioner of Indian Affairs George W. Manypenny set forth from Washington to visit the various tribes of the region in an attempt to resolve Nebraska's Indian problems. He hoped to persuade the tribes to cede their treaty-recognized regions and remove to Indian Territory, thereby relinquishing their lands to white settlement.[41] Already, Congress had altered the stipulation of the 1851 treaty that awarded the tribes payment of $50,000 per annum for fifty years, reducing that time period to only ten years with an additional five years at the president's discretion.[42]

Of the tribes that had signed the pact in 1851, only three—the Cheyennes, Arapahos, and Sioux—accepted the amendments. The government, however, simply ignored the tribes that rejected the treaty alterations and continued to pay their annuities under the altered time span of only fifteen years.[43]

CHAPTER NINE

Protecting the Santa Fe Trade

*It has been my endeavor to reduce the amount [paid to the
southern tribes] as low as a sense of justice would authorize.*
—INDIAN AGENT THOMAS FITZPATRICK

With the mistaken notion that the Indian problem along the Platte Trail
had been resolved, U.S. officials turned their attention to the mid-Plains
where transportation along the Santa Fe Trail, particularly through western Kansas, suffered persistent attacks by tribal raiders. Of special concern were the Comanches, Kiowas, and Plains Apaches who controlled
the vast uncharted regions between the Arkansas and Red rivers.

The history of the Santa Fe Trail during the first half of the nineteenth century had been turbulent at best. Traders plying the long, difficult route between Westport, Missouri, and Santa Fe, New Mexico, did
so at great risk to both property and life. War parties were attracted to
the Santa Fe route for several reasons. Particularly enticing to tribal warriors were the horses and mules employed by travelers. Captured weapons and ammunition were special prizes of war. Santa Fe–bound wagon
trains carried more trade cargo than those on the migration-dominated
Oregon Trail, offering greater potential of securing sugar, coffee, and
other goods of the white man for the taking or as tolls for passage.
Beyond the rewards and love of battle, raids along the road constituted
a resistance to white intrusion for the Plains tribes, which had their own
notion of independence.

The first major incursion occurred on the route in 1816 when a band of 200 Pawnees attacked a party of around twenty traders led by Col. A. P. Chouteau near present Lakin, Kansas. The traders, returning east along the Arkansas River with their winter's take of furs, took refuge on an island of the river and defended themselves from behind their packs. In a fierce fight, they managed to hold off the Pawnees, with the loss of only one man and three wounded. Chouteau's Island became a place of note on the trail.[1]

During August 1825 the U.S. commission party surveying the road from Missouri to Santa Fe met with the Osages at Council Grove on the Neosho River in present Kansas and made a treaty allowing "for the passage of the road, and the unmolested use of the same to citizens of the United States and the republic of Mexico."[2] A similar agreement was made with the Kansa Indians.[3] After the route was surveyed, the number of wagons over the road increased sharply, as did forays by Indian raiders.

The United States provided its first military protection on the trail in 1829, sending Maj. Bennett Riley and four companies of infantry as escort for a Santa Fe–bound caravan under Charles Bent. With Texas still a Mexican province and its northern boundary in question, Riley was authorized to go as far as the upper crossing of the Arkansas River near Chouteau's Island. There, the trail broke off to the southwest instead of continuing on due west into present Colorado. On August 3, while waiting for the caravan to proceed to Santa Fe and return, Riley and his men were attacked by a sizable Indian force thought to be Comanches and Kiowas. Riley suffered the loss of five men, nineteen horses and mules, and a number of oxen.[4]

In following along the Arkansas River, the Santa Fe Trail coursed a dividing line between the country dominated by the Cheyennes and Arapahos to the northwest and the vast ranges of north Texas and Indian Territory to the south, controlled by the Comanches and Kiowas. By the Treaty of Fort Laramie, the territory of the Cheyennes and Arapahos had been defined essentially as lying between the Platte and Arkansas rivers from western Kansas to the main range of the Rocky Mountains in Colorado. During the early part of the century, the lure of hunting in Colorado's South Park and the advent of American traders along the Arkansas River had caused portions of the two tribes to drift south, splitting the tribes into northern and southern divisions.

But although the Southern Cheyennes camped their villages largely on the South Platte and Upper Arkansas, their war parties preyed upon the huge horse herds possessed by the tribes south of the Arkansas. The

A trade caravan meets a war party on the prairie (Gregg, Commerce of the Prairies*).*

abundance of these horses was noted by Thomas James, who traded with the Wichitas and Comanches on the Upper North Canadian in 1823 when wild herds still roamed the lower Plains. Wichita chief Alasares told James that his people owned no fewer than 16,000 horses.[5]

Following the massacre of a party of Cheyenne raiders by the Kiowas in 1838, a consolidated force of Cheyennes and Arapahos marched south and massacred a Kiowa/Comanche encampment on Wolf Creek in northwestern Indian Territory. The Wolf Creek attack led to a great Indian peace council by the four tribes (five, including the Plains Apaches) at Bent's Fort on the Arkansas River during the summer of 1841.[6]

Tohawson, the noted Kiowa peacemaker, initiated the peace by sending emissaries to arrange a great feast and exchange of presents. The tribes met near Bent's Fort, the Cheyennes and Arapahos camping on one side of the Arkansas River and the Kiowas and Comanches on the other. The host Cheyennes set up a special lodge for the feast, and the tribes mingled in friendship for a night of drumming, dancing, and singing. On the following morning, Tohawson invited all the Cheyenne and Arapaho people to his camp. There, the men were asked to seat themselves in a long row with their families behind them. Kiowa chief Satank walked along the line with a bundle of sticks, handing out one to each man. When they returned the sticks to his camp, he said, they would each be given a horse. Some of the Cheyennes and Arapahos received as many as six horses, with Satank giving up 250 of his own. The Cheyennes and Arapahos responded in-kind with calico, beads, brass kettles, blankets, and guns.[7]

From this peacemaking, the Cheyennes and Arapahos agreed not to raid the horse herds of the southern tribes in exchange for safe access to roam south of the Arkansas. This amnesty did not bring any amalgamation of tribal forces, but it did make the Santa Fe Trail even more vulnerable from raiders both north and south of the trail.[8]

Spurred by the Mexican War of 1846 and the 1849 California Gold Rush, traffic on the Santa Fe Trail increased dramatically. Gradually, the United States added dragoon escorts for wagon trains. Eventually, the small military post of Fort Mann was established west of present Dodge City, Kansas, during the spring of 1847, and, when that was closed, Fort Atkinson was established in 1850. These efforts, however, did little to halt the assaults. No treaty had been effected to award annuities to the Comanches, Kiowas, and Plains Apaches who frequented the Santa Fe Trail and preyed upon wagon trains that ventured along the route.

The attack on a Bent train returning from Independence, Missouri, in July 1862 was typical. Upon nearing Fort Atkinson, Bent found around 10,000 Kiowas and Comanches gathered there. The Indians attempted to stampede the wagon train and horse herd by galloping up close, whooping, and rattling their spears against their buffalo-hide shields. The wagon train was formed into a horseshoe and the Indians were held at bay until some dragoons from Fort Atkinson arrived in support. Bent eventually calmed the Indians by opening a barrel of sugar and doling out portions to the chiefs and headmen.[9] Such incidents pointed to the need for a new treaty with the Northern Comanches, Kiowas, and Plains Apaches to replace their limited pacts of 1835 and 1837. Thomas Fitzpatrick was assigned to the task.[10]

Fitzpatrick was generally liked and respected by the Indians. Known on the frontier as Broken Hand, Fitzpatrick had been one of the long-haired mountain men and explorers of the early West. He had guided traders and troops over the Santa Fe Trail and was with Jedediah Smith's party when unknown Indians killed the famous frontiersman on Cimarron Cutoff in 1831. After being appointed agent for the newly created Upper Platte and Arkansas agency in 1846, Fitzpatrick made annual pilgrimages up the Arkansas River, then north along the Rockies to Fort St. Vrain and thence to the Platte to counsel with his charges and deliver annuities called for by the Treaty of Fort Laramie. While at Washington in May 1853, Fitzpatrick was assigned to be the sole commissioner for conducting a new treaty with the Kiowas, Comanches, and Plains Apaches whose home ranges lay south of the Arkansas River.

Even as Fitzpatrick was making preparations for his return to the Indian country, these same tribes were among thirteen tribes that conducted their own grand council on the Upper North Canadian River. The meeting was sponsored by the Cherokee nation, which sent some of its "most intelligent men" to establish friendly relations between the Plains tribes and those recently removed to eastern Indian Territory. Jesse Chisholm, whose trading activities had made him well-known and well liked among the prairie tribes, was among the Cherokee representatives.[11]

Fitzpatrick's experience in conducting the Fort Atkinson treaty illustrates not only the difficulty of treaty making on the Plains but the political restraints in dealing fairly and equitably with Indian tribes. At the start, Fitzpatrick's order for supplies was delayed in shipment to St. Louis by low river water that hindered steamboat travel. These goods included those due the northern tribes under the Treaty of Fort Laramie, along with presents to encourage the southern tribes to agree to a new treaty. The delay in delivery meant the hungry tribes were kept waiting at the appointed meeting place, Fort Atkinson, through the torrid days of July, with growing doubts about Fitzpatrick's arrival and the promised rewards. The wait did little to improve tempers among the already belligerent warriors.

At Kansas City, Fitzpatrick encountered further impediment in the lack of wagon transportation to haul his sizable cargo once it had arrived. Seasonal fur traders such as Bent had already headed home from their market rendezvous. Once on the trail, the agent found it clogged with immense herds of cattle being driven west to feed the California mining camps.[12]

When Fitzpatrick arrived at Fort Atkinson in late July, once again accompanied by B. Gratz Brown who acted as secretary, the greater portion of the Kiowas, Comanches, and Plains Apaches were gathered along the Arkansas River, with other bands arriving daily. As a whole, they were "impatient, watchful, jealous, reserved, haughty," and angry because there was no game in the area.[13] And there was still another serious problem: a total lack of interpreters for communicating on treaty issues with the three tribes. Fitzpatrick had no way of talking directly with the Indians, and sign language proved inadequate. He had expected to find a trapper or trader among the tribes who could conduct interviews; instead, there was "no one who could speak a syllable of English."[14]

Eventually, a Mexican captive was brought forth, and a dialogue was conducted in Spanish. An Arapaho who had lived among the Comanches also proved helpful. Percival G. Lowe, stationed at Fort Atkinson, recalled the event:

> The big ox train came in, the wily Apaches (called Prairie Apaches to distinguish them from those ranging in southern New Mexico and Arizona), the Kiowas and Comanches having assembled in full force, the goods were unloaded, boxes and bales opened, the nabobs of the tribes decorated in brilliant uniforms, medals and certificates issued, goods parceled out, winding up with plenty to eat, feasting, sham battles, etc. The Apaches were off their home ground and anxious to return. Major Fitzpatrick seemed equally anxious to have the job over with and kept his little working force and a couple of clerks pushing things. The long drawn out dignity of the Horse Creek treaty was lacking.[15]

Despite the barriers to percipient communication, councils continued for several days. Tribal leaders made their feelings known. They stoutly opposed the establishment of military posts in their area, expressing great concern and hostility regarding the whites who moved through their country, destroying timber, driving off game, and interrupting the hunting grounds. And the chiefs adamantly rejected Fitzpatrick's proposal that they return their captive Mexican women and children, who by long-standing tribal custom were adopted into their clans and families.

The treaty instructions given to Fitzpatrick had called for the usual payment of annuity goods and provisions in exchange for certain rights and privileges conceded by the tribes. The latter included the right of the United States to lay off and mark roads, reserve land for depots, and establish military posts in territories inhabited by the tribes. The three tribes further agreed to cease their invasion of Mexico, return all captives, and halt all hostile activities against both white citizens and one another.[16]

In return, the United States agreed to pay the tribes jointly $18,000 in goods per annum for a period of ten years and for five years following at the pleasure of the president, who could then, if he so deemed, substitute agricultural implements or whatever fit the Indians' needs. All such rewards would be cancelled, however, if the Indians violated any of their treaty obligations. In the end, the chiefs and leading men of the tribe signed the document just as it had been prepared in Washington. Whether they simply did not understand that they were agreeing to much that they strongly opposed or whether they simply acquiesced is not clear.

Wulea-boo, or Shaved Head, led the signing for the Comanches. He was joined by four other chiefs, including Para-saw-a-man-no, or Ten Bears, who became a much-respected peace leader in the years ahead. Tohawson and Satank signed for the Kiowas.[17]

The tribal leaders had little comprehension of dollar value, current or otherwise. Fitzpatrick admitted that although the amount of country occupied by the three tribes was essentially equivalent, the $18,000 was only about a third of what had been guaranteed to the northern tribes by the Treaty of Fort Laramie. "It has been my endeavor," he reported to the Commissioner of Indian Affairs, "to reduce the amount as low as a sense of justice would authorize."[18]

From Fort Atkinson, Fitzpatrick continued on to the South Platte and old Fort St. Vrain, where he distributed the assigned annuity items. He also secured the signatures of Cheyenne leaders on the amendment to their 1851 Treaty of Fort Laramie that struck out the words "fifty years" in Article Seven and substituted "for the term of ten years, with the right to continue the same, at the discretion of the President of the United States, for a period not exceeding five years thereafter, in provisions, merchandise, domestic animals, and agricultural implements."[19]

Fitzpatrick then pushed his wagons north to Fort Laramie, where the Sioux had gathered in full to receive their annuity payment. He soon discovered that the hostility he had found there the year before had been exacerbated by still another conflict between Fort Laramie troops and the Sioux. According to officers at the post, some soldiers returning from the Fort Laramie farm across the Platte had taken the ferry away from some Minneconjous camped nearby. Someone from the village fired on the soldiers, whereupon a detachment was sent to arrest the man who fired the shot. The frightened villagers would not come out of their lodges. Firing began, and four Sioux were killed. Two were taken prisoner. The military at Fort Laramie was upset not only by the shooting infraction. The troops complained also that the Indians were persistently troublesome to the 23,000 persons, 150,000 cattle, and 6,000 wagons that had passed by the fort that season.[20]

Embittered over the deaths of their people, the Sioux leaders demanded that Fort Laramie, originally a trading post, be closed. They said that when it was put there, they had been told it was for their protection, "but now the soldiers of the great father are the first to make the ground bloody."[21] Although they at first refused to sign the amended treaty, the Sioux leaders were eventually persuaded to do so when Fitzpatrick threatened to withhold their annuities.[22]

The Treaty of Fort Atkinson attempted no definition or assignment of territory for the three tribes, as had the Treaty of Fort Laramie for other tribes. But the Senate saw fit to amend the 1853 pact by adding that the president could at any time cease the issuance of goods for annuity and instead establish farms so the tribes could raise corn and other crops in their country.[23]

Fitzpatrick died of pneumonia in Washington on February 7, 1854, and was replaced by J. W. Whitfield. When the tribes reassembled at Fort Atkinson to obtain annuities in July, Whitfield laid the treaty amendment before the chiefs for approval. He explained the Senate's alteration of the agreement in council, this time through an interpreter. Chief Tohawson rose to speak. He was pleased, he said, that the Great Father was taking pity on his people. But he also hoped that, since his people had none, the Great Father would send him land that would produce corn.[24]

"The Indians," Whitfield wrote, "will perish before the land thrives. Indeed, examples of all their race who have preceded them on the continent, would point to a condition of poverty, of humiliation, of extinction, as the natural result of the foster policy of our government."[25]

Whitfield reported that he had heard of no depredations being committed by either the Kiowas or the Comanches during the previous year. He believed the tribes had lived up to all their treaty obligations except one: that of making war on Mexico. But just as the Treaty of Fort Laramie had failed to resolve the basic conflict created by white intrusion onto Indian lands in the north, the Treaty of Fort Atkinson failed to do so with the tribes south of the Arkansas River.

The Kiowas and Comanches both insisted that they had never agreed not to make war on Mexico. If they did, they said, they would have no other place to get their horses and mules. Nor could they understand that New Mexico had become a part of the United States. From the Brazos reservations in Texas, Neighbors complained of depredations that occurred in his area.

"The evidence is full," he reported, "that they were northern Comanches, and my investigations show that they are the parties who have stolen most of the horses taken from our frontier citizens during the past year. . . . Those bands of Comanches and Kiowas, as they are now situated, commit serious depredations on the settlements of Texas, and continue their forays into Mexico."[26]

Neighbors called for the government to take action that would make the Indians not only restore stolen property and prisoners but also abandon their roving life. "I think the [U.S. Indian] policy at this day a bad one," he concluded, "and would respectfully suggest that the annuity be given only to those who settle down and cultivate the soil."[27]

For Colorado Gold

You are nearer Major Wynkoop than any one else, and you
can go to him [for protection] when you get ready to do that.
—COL. JOHN M. CHIVINGTON

The 1851 Treaty of Fort Laramie had assigned the Cheyennes and Arapahos the territory between the North Platte and Arkansas rivers from a line running north-south at the fork of the Platte in western Nebraska to the main range of the Rocky Mountains. By this, the boundaries for the two tribes were defined on the north by the Platte Trail and on the south in part by the Santa Fe Trail, although the treaty expressly permitted the two tribes to range beyond these limits.[1] Not unexpectedly, their warriors gravitated to those two routes.

Trouble erupted on the Platte Trail near Fort Kearny during August 1856 when young Cheyenne warriors pursued a U.S. mail wagon and wounded the driver. Although tribal elders punished the culprits for their actions, U.S. troops attacked the Cheyenne camp, killing and wounding a number of its occupants.[2] White immigration along the trail suffered from Cheyenne retaliation. This resulted in a major military campaign during the spring and summer of 1857 under Col. Edwin V. Sumner.

Sumner led an army up the Platte River to Fort Laramie, then turned south to the ruins of Fort St. Vrain on the South Platte. There, he joined with another arm of his command under Maj. John Sedgwick that had marched up the Arkansas Trail and moved north along the Rocky Mountains. Once consolidated, the force pushed eastward to the Solomon River of western Kansas, where it met a large force of Cheyenne warriors and drove them from the field.[3] When Agent Robert Millar arrived at Pawnee Fork with annuities the following summer, he found Cheyenne leaders compliant.

> They said they had learned a lesson last summer in their fight with the white man, who would soon with his villages occupy the whole prairie. They had eyes and were not blind. They no longer listened to their young men who continually clamored for war. They wanted peace, and [they needed a food supply], as the buffalo, their principal dependance for food and clothing, (which even now they were compelled to seek many miles from their home) would soon disappear entirely.[4]

When Millar broached the possibility of making a new treaty, the chiefs expressed their desire to be assigned the country on the headwaters of the South Platte, where they would be protected from the encroachment of their white brothers and could be taught to cultivate the soil. Fate, however, would intervene. Even as the chiefs spoke, an invasion of the South Platte region was imminent. Gold had been discovered, and during 1849 a great flood of Colorado gold seekers followed. With it came embryonic white settlements on land specifically assigned to the Cheyennes and Arapahos by the Fort Laramie agreement.

William Bent, who had replaced Millar as Cheyenne and Arapaho agent, reported that despite the onslaught of whites into their country, the Cheyennes and Arapahos had remained peaceful. He also noted the government's incapacity to restrain the ever-swelling concourse of white emigration and observed, "These numerous and warlike tribes, pressed upon all around by the Texans, by the settlers of the gold region, by the advancing people of Kansas, and from the Platte, are already compressed into a small circle of territory, destitute of food, and it bisected athwart by a constantly marching line of emigrants."[5]

Having been driven north by "the hostile front opposed to them in Texas,"[6] the Kiowas, Northern Comanches, and Plains Apaches continued to frequent the Santa Fe Trail and the Bent's Fort region in eastern Colorado Territory. In 1859 the U.S. Army established Fort Larned at the mouth of Pawnee Fork. With these developments came renewed friction. During the spring of 1860, Lt. J.E.B. Stuart and a company of First Cavalry pursued a band of Kiowas in the vicinity of the new fort Bent had built in 1853 near present Lamar, Colorado. Stuart's men captured Chief Satank's wife and family and turned them over to Bent. But when the Kiowas surrounded the fort and demanded their release, the trader was forced to comply.[7]

During this same time, Capt. Samuel D. Sturgis marched north from Fort Cobb into northwest Kansas. There, he engaged an estimated 600 Kiowa and Comanche warriors, but with little consequence.[8]

Upon receiving Bent's suggestion to remove the tribes from contact with whites, Commissioner of Indian Affairs A. B. Greenwood urged that new treaties be made with the Cheyennes and Arapahos. Congress responded by appropriating $35,000 for the purpose of holding a treaty council with the two tribes. In August 1860, Greenwood went to St. Louis and then to Kansas City, from where he sent word to Bent to request that the Cheyennes and Arapahos meet him at Bent's New Fort. Ignoring the military escort ordered for him by the secretary of war, Greenwood traveled the Santa Fe Trail with his son, a nephew, a brother-in-law, and a few private friends. Although accompanied by two Delaware scouts, the party had "nothing to guide them, except the river and the broad wagon road extending all the way."[9] Thirteen wagonloads of treaty goods and trinkets followed behind.

When Greenwood arrived at the fort on September 8, he found the Arapahos under Little Raven and Storm waiting for him. Only a few lodges of Cheyennes were present, however, their main body camped 250 miles away. Runners were sent to request that they repair to Bent's at once. While waiting, Greenwood was visited by three chiefs from a band of Comanches camped on the Arkansas River twenty-five miles above Bent's. When they asked for presents Greenwood refused, saying that the Great Father had heard they had not been good children because of their attacks along the trail.[10]

Greenwood did treat with the Arapahos, however, presenting their leaders with medals bearing the likeness of "Old Functionary," President James Buchanan. Frontier pranksters gave two Arapaho braves their own medals—political campaign buttons for Lincoln and Douglas.[11]

The construction of a new military post was taking place on the north bank of the Arkansas a few hundred yards above where Bent's New Fort stood perched on a rock bluff. A visiting journalist described Bent's post as a 125 by 200 foot stone structure with walls two feet thick and rooms opening onto a large unroofed plaza in the center, where abounded "Indians, Mexicans, half-breeds of all varieties, men from plains and mountains."[12]

Soldiers of the First Cavalry and the Tenth Infantry under Sedgwick quarried and hauled ledge stone from nearby bluffs to create barracks, officers' quarters, and corral that would become Fort Wise, named for the governor of Virginia.[13] When Cheyenne chiefs Black Kettle and White Antelope arrived with a small party, Greenwood hurriedly called a council. Greenwood commended them on keeping the peace. He displayed a map of the country assigned to them by the Fort Laramie treaty and found they understood it perfectly. Greenwood was greatly impressed by their "degree of intelligence."[14] He outlined propositions for settling the two tribes on a reserve that extended north from the Arkansas River to the head of Sand Creek and south to the New Mexico border between the Huerfano and Purgatoire rivers, the latter an area they had suggested to Bent in 1859.

"Notwithstanding they are fully aware of the rich mines discovered in their country," Greenwood chortled to the secretary of interior, "they are disposed to yield up their claims without any reluctance."[15]

The Cheyennes informed Greenwood that it would take at least twenty days for their bands to arrive. They refused to bind their people to a pact until the tribe had voted on the matter. Anxious to return home, the commissioner secured verbal agreements with the chiefs relative to a treaty. He then issued blankets, shirts, scissors, knives, kettles, flour, bacon, sugar, coffee, and tobacco—but distributed only a third of his goods with the promise that after the chiefs had signed the treaty, the rest would be provided. Placing the remaining goods under the care of special agent F. B. Culver, Greenwood and his party headed back to Washington.[16]

Bent, who had resigned as Cheyenne and Arapaho agent, was replaced by Albert G. Boone, grandson of Daniel Boone. In February 1861, Boone, who had established the settlement of Booneville several miles upriver, returned from Washington with the treaty document. He and Culver served as commissioners in holding a council with chiefs of the two tribes to explain the treaty terms. John Simpson Smith and Robert Bent served as interpreters, and Sedgwick and Stuart acted as witnesses.[17]

The Treaty of Fort Wise defined the new reservation area for the tribes as Greenwood had outlined to them. Additionally, it stated that the Cheyennes and Arapahos would be expected to give up their habitual mode of moving about and living by the hunt and settle down to an agrarian life, raising crops and livestock.

Each tribe would be paid $30,000 for a period of fifteen years. From this sum would be deducted costs of agricultural implements, machinery, livestock, fencing, and buildings. The United States would pay for a sawmill and a grain mill and other items not to exceed a cost of $5,000.

A postscript to the treaty awarded choice land along the Arkansas River to interpreters Bent and Smith, as well as to Smith's son Jack. The treaty also contained a clause whereby all U.S. commitments were subject to the discretion of the president, who could cancel them if the tribes failed to make satisfactory advancement.

Some chiefs of note represented the tribes. In addition to White Antelope, who had visited Washington in 1851, and Principal Chief Black Kettle, the Cheyenne signatories were Lean Bear, Little Wolf, Tall Bear, and Left Hand. Little Raven, Storm, Shave Head, and Big Mouth signed for the Arapahos. These men would play major roles in events on the Plains during and after the Civil War.

A clause in the original agreement permitted businessmen of Denver City to enter city and town lots on the reservation at $1.25 an acre. The U.S. Senate struck out this intrusive measure. During the fall of 1861, Boone brought the amended treaty to Fort Wise. There, the tribes, extremely destitute following a severe summer drought, had gathered to obtain their annuities. On October 29, the Cheyenne and Arapaho chiefs again signed the document, which was proclaimed by President Abraham Lincoln on December 5.[18]

Although generally unheralded in historical accounts, the Treaty of Fort Wise constituted one of the greatest landgrabs of the West. However judicious Greenwood and other officials considered the treaty arrangements to be, certain facts remain. Whereas he and others knew the value of the enormous land and mineral wealth the United States gained by the treaty, the Cheyenne and Arapaho chiefs had no inkling—even if they professed perfect acceptance, as Greenwood stated—of the poor bargain they were getting.

Not only were the chiefs without formal schooling, they also had no representation in a critical legal proceeding. In today's world, consummating such a weighty contract without legal counsel would be considered absurd. Having suffered a severe military defeat at the hands of Sumner and overwhelmed by the sheer magnitude of the gold rush invasion of their lands, the chiefs realized that their old way of life was direly threatened. Because of this and the diminishing supply of the buffalo, which left their people hungry, they bent to the persistent call for them to take up the white man's agricultural mode of existence.

In the end, tribal rewards so faithfully promised by the treaty were never realized. During the spring of 1861, the great national conflict between the states interceded, affecting Indian affairs on the Central Plains in a multitude of ways. The clouds of white militancy engulfed Colo-

When Black Kettle (seated center) led a delegation to Denver in 1864, it was like "coming through a fire" (Courtesy, Colorado Historical Society).

rado Territory, igniting an Indian war that nullified the promises of Fort Wise. The Treaty of Fort Wise had won Colorado politically; future events would win it militarily.

The government was greatly concerned about the interference the tribes presented to transportation across the Plains and to settlement of Colorado and other western territories. During the winter of 1862–1863, Samuel G. Colley, who had succeeded Bent as agent on the Upper Arkansas, worked to gather a delegation of the tribes for a peacemaking visit to Washington, D.C. He had been invited there for talks with President Abraham Lincoln and consummation of a new treaty. With the aid of John Simpson Smith, Colley recruited fourteen men and two women for the trip. The Kiowas were represented by chiefs Lone Wolf, Yellow Wolf, White Bull, Yellow Buffalo, and Little Heart, plus wives Coy and Etla; the Cheyennes by chiefs Lean Bear, War Bonnet, and Standing-in-the-Water; Spotted Wolf and Neva for the Arapahos; Ten Bears and Prickled Forehead for the Comanches; Poor Bear for the Plains Apaches; and Jacob for the Caddos. Smith accompanied the delegation as interpreter.[19]

The delegation arrived in Washington on March 26, 1863, and lodged in a hotel. On the following morning the Indians, dressed in full costume, were escorted into the East Room of the White House, where a large audience had gathered to witness the interview with the president. Taking his seat in an armchair, Lincoln shook hands with each chief in turn and, through Smith, invited them to speak. Chief Lean Bear rose to say that although he wished to keep peace with the white people, many white men on the Plains were not so disposed.

Lincoln responded by noting that the great number of people the delegates had seen on their trip were but a small portion of the pale-faced people. He called Professor Henry forward with a world globe to illustrate how the Indian tribes related to the rest of the world. Lincoln told them: "It is the object of this Government to be on terms of peace with all our red brethren. We constantly endeavor to be so. We make treaties with you, and will try to observe them; and if our children should sometimes behave badly, and violate these treaties, it is against our wish."[20]

The president leaned forward toward Lean Bear with a kindly smile and observed, "You know it is not always possible for any father to have his children do precisely as he wishes them to do."[21]

After daguerreotypes were made of the chiefs with notables such as Mrs. Lincoln, they were taken on tours of the city and the U.S. Capitol and to a play at Grover's Theatre. Newspaper accounts of their visit had caught the interest of showman P. T. Barnum, and the Cheyennes and Arapahos were invited to New York City, where they were put on display in Barnum's museum before gaping New Yorkers.[22]

The Comanches, Kiowas, and Plains Apaches remained in Washington. On April 6, chiefs of those three tribes signed a treaty in which, after the usual declarations for peace, they agreed not to "resort or encamp upon the *Overland Mail Route from Kansas City in Missouri to Santa Fé in New Mexico*" [original emphasis] and not to molest, annoy, or disturb the travel, emigration, or U.S. mail.[23] The tribes would recognize the right of the United States to establish mail stations along the route and to make use of on-site timber and coal. The agreements of the Treaty of Fort Atkinson in 1853 were reaffirmed, except for an increase from the original annuity payment of $18,000 to $25,000 per annum. Congress, however, rejected the 1863 pact.

Shortly after he had signed the agreement, senior Kiowa chief Yellow Buffalo, a noted peace leader, died. His friends prepared him for burial by painting his hands, feet, and face red and dressing his body in new clothes and blanket. The government provided a coffin and a site in

Washington's Congressional Cemetery, and Yellow Wolf was laid to rest. A number of other tribal leaders had died during visits to the nation's capital and were buried in the cemetery, among them Choctaw chief Pushmataha in 1825 and Cherokee John Rogers in 1846.[24]

Lincoln had touched on a fundamental truth regarding Indian-white conflict in his talk with Lean Bear. Events would soon prove that neither the White Father nor the tribal chiefs could control the actions of "their children" on the distant prairies. Reports of cattle thefts, some of them false, caused troops under District Commander John M. Chivington to attack several Cheyenne camps in northern Colorado Territory. At Fort Larned a great disturbance occurred when a Cheyenne attempting to enter the post was shot and killed by a guard.[25]

Gov. John Evans sent rancher Elbridge Gerry to meet with the Cheyennes at the headwaters of the Smoky Hill River. Gerry found them sick with whooping cough and diarrhea and still angry over the killing at Larned. The Cheyennes declared that the Treaty of Fort Wise was a swindle, insisting that the chiefs had not understood the treaty when they placed their mark on it.[26]

There were other incidents of friction between whites and the Cheyennes, but the most serious occurred in May 1864 on the Smoky Hill north of Fort Larned. A Cheyenne buffalo hunt under Chief Lean Bear was approached by a detachment of troops from Denver. When Lean Bear rode forward to show the peace medal given him at Washington and an official paper vouching that he was a peaceful Indian, the troops shot and killed him with no effort to parley.[27]

Infuriated by the killing of Lean Bear, the Cheyenne Dog Soldiers under Bull Bear, Lean Bear's brother, joined the Sioux, Comanches, and Kiowas in attacking frontier settlements and wagon trains along the Platte and Arkansas wagon roads. Hostilities continued until September, when an emissary arrived at Fort Lyon with a letter from Black Kettle offering to talk peace. This led Maj. Edward W. Wynkoop to take a garrison force to the head of the Republican River. There, he persuaded Black Kettle, White Antelope, Bull Bear, and four others to go with him to Denver and conduct talks with Evans and Chivington at Camp Weld.[28]

At Denver, Evans was brusque and accusative, making little or no effort toward a peace settlement. Chivington said very little until the end of the conference, when he told the chiefs, "You are nearer Major Wynkoop than any one else, and you can go to him when you get ready to do that."[29] Implicit in the instruction was that the Indians would be safe from military action if they went in to Fort Lyon.

But that was far from the case. When Black Kettle led his band to the fort, he was told by the new commander, Maj. Scott J. Anthony, to take his band to Sand Creek forty miles north of the fort. Black Kettle did so, and it was there, early on the morning of November 29, 1864, that Chivington, marching unannounced from Denver, launched a surprise attack. A number of chiefs—including White Antelope, Standing-in-the-Water, and War Bonnet—were killed, along with well over a hundred others, including women and children.

The Sand Creek Massacre was a signal event in relations with the Plains Indians, standing among the tribes as clear proof of the white man's perfidy. But in truth, even greater harm had been done the Cheyennes and Arapahos by the Colorado Gold Rush and the Treaty of Fort Wise. By these, their homeland had been lost.

Redefining Indian Territory

Our once powerful race is rapidly passing away as snow before the summer sun.
—CAMP NAPOLEON INVOCATION

With the outbreak of hostilities between the Union and the Confederacy during the spring of 1861, both North and South looked with concern toward Indian Territory. The territory's position as a buffer zone between Union Kansas and Confederate Texas could provide the enemy with an avenue of attack. Further, its Indian tribes offered potential military support. Most white men considered the Indian warrior, well noted for taking scalps of his victims, as too barbaric to serve as a civilized combatant. But all agreed, it would be far better to have the tribes on your side than to have them against you.

Indian participants in the Battle of Pea Ridge, Arkansas, did in fact take scalps of Union dead. Afterward, eleven captured tribesmen were sent north to be exhibited as "barbaric scalp-takers" in hopes of "firing the Northern heart."[1] En route, however, they were murdered by their Union guards, supposedly as they attempted to escape.

Early in the hostilities, the North realized that its military forts in Indian Territory—Fort Towson on the Red River and forts Arbuckle and Cobb—were untenable. Upon being ordered to withdraw all U.S. forces from the territory, Col. William Emory gathered the troops, their families, and their accouterments together in a wagon convoy and, guided by Delaware leader Black Beaver, led them to Fort Leavenworth, Kansas.[2] With the military withdrawal went the U.S. Indian Bureau vow of support to which the United States had committed itself through its treaties with the tribes.

This loss of food subsistence and other aid was devastating for the impoverished Plains tribes in western Indian Territory. Also it meant that they were once more under the oversight of the Texans, whose Confederate forces moved in behind the retreating federal troops and took over the posts and their associated Indian agencies. Because of their long-standing conflicts, the prairie tribes held strong suspicions of the aggressive Texans. In truth, with its manpower and resources siphoned off to Confederacy needs, Texas was neither capable of exercising effective control of the tribes nor able to provide them with adequate sustenance.

The immigrant tribes of eastern Indian Territory posed an entirely different situation. Although bound to the Union by treaties and thereby by subsistence, most of these large, partially acculturated tribes held strong affiliation to the South. Many of their wealthier members owned slaves. Further, tribes such as the Cherokees and Creeks were severely split over the issue of their forced removal, even to the point of internal assassination of their leaders. As a result, like the nation itself, the tribes became divided between pro-Union and pro-Confederacy elements that were bitterly hostile to one another.

The South quickly moved to establish treaty affiliations with the tribes of Indian Territory. Albert Pike, an Arkansas lawyer and poet, was selected to undertake the task of touring the region to talk with tribal leaders and initiate agreements. The flamboyant Pike had won frontier credentials in 1832 by accompanying a small party of trappers up the Red River to New Mexico and publishing his account of the journey.[3] Although he had once written a poem scorning the idea of secession, he accepted an appointment as a general in the Confederate Army and the treaty-making assignment.

During May 1861, Pike departed from Fort Smith, Arkansas, with two wagons and made his way up the Arkansas River to the Cherokee capital of Tahlequah. On the lead wagon he flew a specially designed flag containing eleven white stars set against a field of blue, each signifying a state of the Confederacy. Inside were four smaller stars representing the Choctaw, Chickasaw, Creek, and Seminole nations, with a place saved to add the Cherokees.[4]

Pike, however, failed to persuade Cherokee chief John Ross to take up the rebel cause. Although he had not given up on the Cherokees, Pike continued on to North Fork Town at the mouth of the North Canadian River, where he held council with the Creeks, Choctaws, and Chickasaws. He initiated treaties with each of these tribes, even though the Creek nation was severely divided between the pro-Confederacy faction under Chilly McIntosh, whose father had been assassinated prior to removal, and a pro-Union group under Opothle Yahola, formerly a national speaker for the Creeks. Moving westward, Pike met with the Seminoles at their agency north of the Canadian River, concluding a treaty with them on August 1.[5]

By these pacts, the Confederate States of America agreed to pay all annuities and payments due to the tribes under treaties with the United States; to guarantee ownership of their lands, with Confederacy rights to reserve tracts for roads, agencies, and military posts; and to establish district courts on tribal lands. The tribes would also be permitted to send delegates to the Confederate Congress, with the potential of jointly entering the Confederacy as a state. In return, the different Indian nations would furnish troops in support of the Rebel cause.[6]

While at the Seminole agency, Pike also met with a delegation of Comanches and other chiefs who had been brought there by Rebel Superintendent of Indian Affairs Elias Rector. The delegates agreed to meet with Pike at the Wichita agency. Escorted by a guard of Creek and Seminole warriors, Pike proceeded to that post, where he met with Comanche leaders—Buffalo Hump among them. Pike reported to Jefferson Davis, "On the 12th of August I concluded a convention [treaty] with the Chiefs and head men of these four bands, the Nokonis, Taneiwes, Yaparihcas, and Cochotihcas [Comanche bands], by which they agreed to come in and settle on Reserves in the Leased District, and I agreed that they should be fed and assisted like the Reserve Indians."[7]

On the same day, Pike signed an inclusive treaty with another group consisting of the Peneteka Comanches, Wichitas, Caddos, Wacos, Tahuacaros (Tawakaros), Anadarkos, Tonkawas, Ionis, Kichais, Shawnees, and Delawares.[8] By this extensive agreement, the tribes promised to maintain friendship and peace with the Confederacy, to return escaped slaves and stolen stock, to refrain from warfare, and to remain at peace with other tribes. Texas troops would be withdrawn to south of the Red River, and the treaty proclaimed optimistically that "[a]ll hostilities between Texas and Indians are ended and all will forgive and forget."[9]

In return, the Confederacy would be the friend and protector of the tribes against all enemies. It would further maintain an agency and supply rations such as beef, sugar, coffee, salt, soap, and vinegar, in addition to cows, hogs, a variety of agricultural implements, mills to grind corn, blacksmith shops, houses, water wells, plus a physician, blacksmith, gunsmith, wagon maker, and interpreter.

Noticeably missing from these agreements were the Kiowas, who continued to conduct raids into Texas and Mexico. Only recently, they had killed a white boy and some Texas soldiers near Fort Cobb. The Kiowas remained hostile even to overtures from Comanche chief Buffalo Hump, ordering him from their camp. Pike sent them a peace wampum and a bullet with a message telling them to take their choice. If they chose war, he threatened, he would send a thousand Creeks and Seminoles to wipe them out.[10] The Kiowas were not impressed. A year later, however, a single Kiowa chief appeared at the agency and signed a treaty accepting the stipulations put forth by Pike the year before.[11]

From the Wichita agency, Pike returned to Tahlequah. There, he found that the recent Rebel victory at Wilson's Creek, Missouri, in which some Cherokees had participated, had created intense pressure for Chief Ross to side with the Confederacy. Pike was now able to initiate a treaty aligning the Cherokee nation with the Confederacy. He arranged similar pacts with the Osages, Quapaws, Senecas, and Shawnees.

In the face of such strong sentiment for the South, the dissenting Opothle Yahola gathered a large band of loyal Creeks and Seminoles and their slaves during October 1861 and headed for Kansas. En route, during severe cold, Rebel-aligned Cherokee, Chickasaw, and Choctaw forces attacked the group. A number of the loyalists were killed and many more captured, whereas others suffered frozen fingers and toes before the remnant band finally reached safety in Kansas.[12]

The engagement of the immigrant tribes of eastern Indian Territory in the Civil War brought chaos to the region. Neighbor murdered neighbor, homes and barns were burned, fences were destroyed, stock was stolen, and once-productive fields were ravaged. During 1863 federal forces, supported by two loyal Indian regiments, drove south from Kansas and recaptured Fort Gibson. Several significant battles in the Indian Territory–Kansas-Missouri-Arkansas region were fought by Indian forces under Cherokee Rebel leader Stand Watie, who rose to the rank of general in the Confederate Army. Although the Indian Territory conflict had little effect on the final outcome of the Civil War, the disloyal tribes paid heavily in postwar treaties with the United States.

The Confederate treaties with the prairie Indians bore little fruit. For a time, Texas contractors who had supplied beef to the agency for the United States continued to do so for the Confederacy. But Pike had prom-

General Hancock and staff interview Kiowa chiefs at Fort Dodge in 1867 (Harper's Weekly, *May 25, 1867*).

ised the prairie tribes much that the hard-pressed Confederacy was totally incapable of fulfilling.[13]

Comanche and Kiowa war parties continued their usual activities of hunting and raiding, both along the Santa Fe Trail and south into Texas and Mexico. Following the withdrawal of Texas forces from the territory, the Wichita agency was left under the charge of former U.S. agent Matthew Leeper. When the Confederacy failed to meet its treaty obligations, hungry tribal members abandoned the reservation to seek food among the buffalo herds.

Buffalo Hump and his Comanche warriors became increasingly difficult to deal with. Leeper reported that they had destroyed most of the poultry belonging to trader John Shirley, shot arrows into his milk cows, and killed beeves belonging to the contractor. Warriors even invaded the bedroom of Shirley's wife. Buffalo Hump scornfully rejected all complaints.[14]

On August 3, 1862, Pike wrote to Jefferson Davis from Fort Washita to report that the Comanches and Kiowas, who were dissatisfied with Leeper, "have nearly all turned against us, and are preparing to enter and devastate the frontier of Texas, while the Reserve Indians are leaving the leased country, and the entire destruction of the reserve is looked for."[15]

Well-armed bands of Delaware and Shawnee Indians from Kansas had begun to appear on the reservation, inciting the remaining Indians of the agency to turn against Leeper and his men. Adding to this was many tribal members' festering dislike for the resident Tonkawas, who were not only friendly to the Texans but who reputedly practiced cannibalism. It was rumored that they had recently killed a Caddo boy and were preparing to feast on him.[16]

This rancor led to an after-dark attack against the agency on October 23, 1862, by a large force of Kickapoo, Delaware, and Shawnee warriors from Kansas. The attackers ravaged the agency, killing four white employees. Leeper, interpreter Horace Jones, and other agency employees managed to escape and flee to Texas. The Tonkawas, who were surrounded in a grove of trees where they had taken refuge, suffered the worse carnage. Over 390 Tonkawa men, women, and children were slaughtered, including the much-respected Chief Placido.[17]

The attack on the Wichita agency essentially destroyed any viability for Pike's treaties with the prairie tribes. Clearly, the Confederacy could neither feed nor protect the Indians clustered about the isolated agency. An exodus began of several hundred Wichitas, Caddos, Delawares, Tawakonis, Kichais, and Shawnees to southern Kansas, where they sought the protection and assistance of the Union.[18] Union officials sympathized, but they could or would do little for the destitute refugees. These small, splintered bands remained huddled around the mouth of the Little Arkansas River, starved and beset by cholera and other diseases, for the remainder of the war.

Still another tribe became caught up in the conflict between North and South. The Osage Indians, who resided in southeastern Kansas and northeastern Indian Territory, had long been major players on the Central Plains. On October 2, 1861, the Great Osage segment of the tribe accepted a lengthy treaty offered by Pike at Tahlequah. Heading the fifty-three signatories were Chief Ka-hi-ke-tung-ka of Chief Clermont's band, Chief Pawhuska of the White Hair band, Chief Chi-sho-hung-ka of the Big Hill band, and Chief Black Dog of the Black Dog band. Pike had hoped to include the Little Osages, who numbered about a thousand, but they resided in Kansas much closer to Union forces and had not attended the Rebel conference at Tahlequah.[19]

Among the many considerations of mutual friendship, support, and protection itemized for both the Confederacy and the Osages, the treaty declared: "The Great Osage Tribe of Indians hereby makes itself a party to the existing war between the Confederate States and the United States of America, as the ally and ward of the former."[20]

During the spring of 1863, however, an incident involving the Little Osage Big Hill band contradicted any cooperation with the Confederacy. On the morning of May 23, a war party from that band witnessed a group of twenty heavily armed, uniformed strangers with pack mules riding westward across their territory north of present Cherryvale, Kansas. Only recently, Union officials in Kansas had encouraged the Big Hill band to stop and arrest any unknown persons on their land and take them to the military post at Humboldt, Kansas.[21]

The strangers were a group of Confederate officers led by Charley Harrison, a former Denver saloon keeper widely noted on the frontier as a gunman, along with fiery Park McClure, onetime Denver postmaster. After being forced out of Colorado Territory by Union forces at the outbreak of the war, both men had joined with guerrilla leader William Quantrell on the Kansas-Missouri border. Now they were on their way back to Colorado to raid the lucrative gold mine routes on behalf of the Confederacy.

When the Osages stopped the party and one seized his reins, Harrison shot and killed the man. A running battle followed until the Osages cornered the Rebels in a bend of the Verdigris River and killed all except two who managed to escape down the river bottom. Uncertain as to whom they had just killed, the Osages hesitated in reporting the matter to Union officials. Eventually they did so, and Capt. Willoughby Doudna and a company of Union soldiers rode out to investigate. They found a bloody scene of scattered papers, dead horses, and decomposing human corpses that, by Osage warring custom, had been beheaded. The troops dug a trench and used long sticks to drag the bodies into it.

Three months later, on August 29, 1863, both the Great and Little Osages of Kansas signed a new treaty with the United States. Commissioner of Indian Affairs William P. Dole personally conducted the council held at Leroy, Kansas. By the agreement, the United States sought to secure not only Osage allegiance but Osage territory as well. With white settlement ever expanding westward, the government looked to a portion of the Osage lands as a place to relocate the Sac and Fox, New

York, and Kansa Indians. As its premise, the treaty presumed that the Osages had more land than they needed and, being impoverished by the lack of help from the government, wished to dispose of their surplus lands.[22]

As the Civil War came to an end in the spring of 1865, the immigrant tribes, which had actively fought with the Confederacy, and several Plains tribes, which had signed treaties with the South but remained largely ambivalent in their opposition, undertook an early effort at reconciliation. On May 26, following Lee's surrender, representatives of tribes still residing in Indian Territory met in a great council at a point dubbed Camp Napoleon near the Washita River. They included both the eastern tribes and those from the Plains, all seeking to form a league of Indian friendship for mutual protection.

At the meeting, the delegates invoked the memory of their forefathers and noted that their "once powerful race is rapidly passing away as snow before the summer sun."[23] In this brief moment of solidarity, the tribes pledged that "an Indian shall not spill an Indian's blood." After all was said, however, they remained as fractionalized as ever against the coming onslaught of postwar whites.

Jesse Chisholm attended the council as a friendly adviser, and Texas general James W. Throckmorton was there to secure protection for his state's northern frontier.[24] The meeting did nothing, however, to relieve Texas of Kiowa-Comanche raids or Kansas from the anger of Cheyenne Dog Soldiers seeking revenge for Sand Creek.

During the fall of 1865, the victorious Union set forth to arrange new treaties with various tribes of the Plains. Newly appointed commissioner of Indian affairs, Judge Dennis N. Cooley, looked to a radical change in the administration of Indian affairs. With the nation facing a debt of over $3 billion in connection with its Indian territories, he contended, it could not afford to let the mineral lands of the West go untitled. Further, the Indian wars had caused 30,000 troops to be stationed west of the Missouri River—many of them cavalry for whose horses corn had to be hauled long distances at great expense.[25]

The Indian Territory, populated by the rebellious immigrant tribes in the east and the troublesome Plains tribes in the west, presented one area of special concern. Cooley headed a commission to treat with the Indian Territory tribes at Fort Smith, Arkansas, during September 1865. He and other commission members Ely Parker, Elijah Sells, and Thomas Wistar gathered at Lawrence, Kansas. From there, they traveled overland to Fort Smith via Fort Scott and Fort Gibson with a train of thirteen six-mule wagons, six four-mule ambulances, private carriages, and an escort of a hundred Seventeenth Illinois troops.

The council convened at Fort Smith on September 8, attended by the immigrant tribes of eastern Indian Territory and several Plains tribes—namely, the Comanches, Wichitas, and Caddos. Cooley quickly laid forth U.S. demands. He sought a pledge of peace and amity from the tribes that had sided with the South, their assistance in controlling the unruly Plains tribes, the abolition of slavery among the tribes that indulged in that practice, and willingness of the Indian Territory tribes to consolidate under a single government. Importantly, the tribes would be required to surrender portions of their lands for the resettlement of Indians from Kansas and elsewhere.[26]

The Indian delegates, who had come thinking the council would merely restore harmony among the tribes, were taken aback by the demands. They did not have the authority, they said, to sign a treaty. They further argued that because the United States had withdrawn its protection from the territory, they had had little choice but to join the Confederacy. They strongly opposed the incorporation of former slaves into their nations, as well as the concept of a territorial government. The conference became further embroiled in the Cherokee issue of whether John Ross, their famous prewar leader, should continue as principal chief. After much oratory on both sides of the issue, the commission ruled against him.[27]

The delegates signed agreements of amity at Fort Smith, but formal treaties were deferred until a new council could be held at Washington, D.C., during the spring of 1866. The treaties signed there resulted in a significant change to the Plains Indian country of western Indian Territory. The Creeks were forced to cede 3.25 million acres of their treaty-assigned territory and the Seminoles 2.17 million acres. Having forced the cession, the federal government then purchased the ceded land, paying the Seminoles fifteen cents an acre and the Creeks thirty cents an acre. These were lands resided upon historically by the Wichitas, Comanches, Kiowas, and Plains Apaches but to which those tribes held no assignment under U.S. law other than occupation of the Leased District. The government was now free to use the district as it saw fit.[28]

At the same time the Fort Smith conference was in progress, U.S. peace commissions were meeting with other tribes and further shaping the destiny of the Central Plains.

CHAPTER TWELVE

The Cheyenne Resistance

Your young white soldiers I don't think listen to you. You bring
presents, and when I come to get them I am afraid they will
strike me before I get away. I take them up crying.
—CHEYENNE PRINCIPAL CHIEF BLACK KETTLE

During the fall of 1865, peace commission parties were in the field conducting talks with the Southern Plains tribes in southern Kansas and
with the Sioux at Fort Sully, Dakota Territory. In the face of continued
attacks against settlements and transportation routes, a bitter dispute
erupted in Kansas between Indian Bureau "olive-branchers" and the
military, stoutly supported by frontier whites, over how to deal with the
problem.

Calls by peace advocates for pacification of the Indian did not sit
well with Kansans who read daily newspaper accounts of mayhem along
the western trails. During September 1865 alone, a Lawrence paper printed
a number of reports of Indian atrocities. One came from a traveler on the
Platte route. The letter told of an attack wherein a war party ravaged a
Mormon family of eight, capturing four of the children: "The Captain
ordered his men in pursuit. But they had done their work of carnage and
gone around us, and at daylight next morning attacked a train of thirty
wagons, capturing and carrying off women and children, and burned the
train."[1]

Another account told of an attack by a Comanche war party on a
Mexican train on the Santa Fe Trail twelve miles below Cimarron Cross-

ing. Three men and two boys were killed. One story described the killing of troops at the Platte bridge in gruesome detail. Still another, taken from the *San Antonio Herald,* told of "fiendish depredations" committed by Indians in killing a German settler and his wife near Fredericksburg, Texas, and taking their only child captive.[2]

"The Indians never asked for peace," the paper charged. "As preliminary to any negotiations whatever, they demanded the Government to acknowledge itself whipped."[3]

Despite such frontier sentiment, officials set about to hold new treaty talks with the hostile tribes. To arrange this, Kiowa/Comanche agent Jesse Leavenworth sent Jesse Chisholm and Robert Bent separately into Indian Territory to gather the various bands.[4] The Treaty of the Little Arkansas, held in a cottonwood grove on the site of present Wichita, Kansas, featured an interesting assemblage of white and Indian personalities.

In support of its cause, the government had called forth some highly regarded men of the frontier: William Bent, Kit Carson, and interpreter John S. Smith—all of whom, like Chisholm, were married to and had families by Indian women. Army generals John R. Sanborn, William S. Harney, and James Steele, along with Indian superintendent Thomas Murphy and Agent Leavenworth, joined Bent and Carson as peace commissioners. Margaret Wilmarth, Thomas Fitzpatrick's Arapaho widow, and Smith served as interpreters.[5]

Notable among the Comanches were Buffalo Hump, Over the Buttes, Ten Bears, Horse Back, Iron Shirt, and Silver Broach. The Kiowas were headed by Tohawson, Satank, Satanta (White Bear), Lone Wolf, Kicking Bird, Big Bow, and Stinking Saddle Cloth. Little Raven, Storm, and Big Mouth represented the Arapahos. The Plains Apaches were headed by Poor Bear and Iron Shirt. George Bent brought in Black Kettle, along with Little Robe and a few other Cheyenne leaders. A large portion of that tribe, however, had been held back by dark threats from the Dog Soldiers.

Samuel A. Kingman, an Atchison, Kansas, lawyer working for Commissioner Murphy, wrote of the treaty council in his diary. His entries speak of the boredom of waiting in camp for the tribes to arrive—"eating, smoking, talking and sleeping make the whole day"; of how the men fished and hunted without much success at either; of the refugee Indians who lived nearby, impoverished except for their small crops of corn, pumpkins, beans, and watermelons; and of visits by brawny Osage warriors who "shave the head all but the scalp lock." He also told how concern had mounted among the commission when the train of treaty gifts was late arriving from Fort Leavenworth. Commission members had begun to fear that the $50,000 of goods may have become "the spoil of Kansas patriots."[6]

The commission treated with the Cheyennes and Arapahos first. Kingman characterized the talks as frank and friendly and Black Kettle's opening speech as eloquent: "[W]hen he spoke of the deserted wigwams, murdered braves, squaws & children on that occasion [Sand Creek], [he] sent a thrill throughout the whole of the Indians present & even in translations touched every heart there."[7] Black Kettle told the commissioners: "I am glad today to think that the Great Father has sent word to take pity on us. Your young white soldiers I don't think listen to you. You bring presents, and when I come to get them I am afraid they will strike me before I get away. I take them up crying. All my friends—the Indians that are holding back—they are afraid to come in; afraid they will be betrayed as I have been."[8]

Speaking as a commissioner, William Bent addressed the Cheyennes and Arapahos on October 13, noting: "I am well aware that we have both been deceived at prior times in the execution of our treaty by white men in authority, but we must not judge all white men alike. For instance, in the summer of 1864 I was sent to you by the Governor of Colorado [John Evans], and Colonel Chivington, to make a temporary treaty with you, which, I am sorry to say, was a deception on the part of the whites."[9]

"Our Great Father sent you here with his words to us," Black Kettle concluded, "and we take hold of them. Although the troops have struck us, we throw it all behind and are glad to meet you in peace and friendship."[10]

Arapaho chief Little Raven gave his view of the treaties that had been made previously: "When Major Fitzpatrick first came, he married this woman, (Mrs. Wilmarth) he laid off certain country on the North Platte. Major Fitzpatrick then came again, and they were called to another meeting on the Platte, then some tracts of land were talked of, and some of the Indians objected to signing the Treaty of 1851. After a long time there was another change of administration. [A. B.] Greenwood was sent to them. We did not understand him."[11]

By the treaty signed with the Cheyennes and Arapahos at the Little Arkansas on October 14, the two tribes were assigned a new reservation straddling the Kansas–Indian Territory border. The treaty further decreed: "*Provided, however* [treaty italics], That said Indians shall not be required to settle upon said reservation until such time as the United

States shall have extinguished all claims of title thereto on the part of other Indians." Until that time, the two tribes would be "expressly permitted to reside upon and range at pleasure throughout the unsettled portions of the country between the Platte and Arkansas Rivers."[12]

A portion of the new reservation involved lands assigned to the Cherokee nation by the Cherokee Treaty of 1828 as an "outlet" to the buffalo range, as well as a portion of the Osage reservation.[13] Two councils were held with the visiting Osages in an effort to persuade them to relinquish the part of their reservation necessary for the treaty. Having yet to receive compensation for lands sold to the United States on two occasions, the more experienced Osages replied skeptically "[h]eap talk, no money" and rode off.[14]

Until the Cherokee and Osage titles could be cleared, the Cheyennes and Arapahos would not be required to abandon their traditional range and confine themselves to the designated reservation. The tribes, however, were prohibited from camping within ten miles of roads, towns, or military posts without special permission. Further, the United States obtained the right to build roads and establish military posts through their country.[15]

The pact featured annuities for forty years, reparations for injuries done to the Indians at Sand Creek, and special grants of land to leading chiefs and various families related to the tribes. In return for these rewards and the pending reservation arrangement, the Cheyennes and Arapahos relinquished all claims or rights to all other areas in the United States and its territories—especially those defined for them by the Treaty of Fort Laramie.

Not only was the Cheyenne/Arapaho treaty predicated on uncertain future arrangements, it suffered still another fatal flaw. The absence of the belligerent Cheyenne Dog Soldiers in forming the agreement virtually guaranteed the continuance of war on the Kansas prairies.

On October 16 a council was conducted with the Kiowa, Comanche, and Apache bands. Commission president Sanborn addressed the Indians at length. He said that during the previous year, President Lincoln had directed him to punish the tribes for their depredations along the Santa Fe Road. But when word arrived that the tribes were ready to make peace, the president had held back his soldiers, who were "as numerous as the leaves of the forest or the grass on the prairie."[16]

Sanborn concluded by demanding that white captives held by the tribes be returned before a treaty could be made. The elderly Kiowa Tohawson answered him through Chisholm, the only man present who could translate the difficult Kiowa tongue: "The Kiowas own from Fort Laramie and the north fork of the Platte to Texas, and always have owned it. That all the branches, creeks, rivers and points that you see; all the deer and buffalo, wolves and turtles, all belong to him—were given to him by the Great Spirit. I want to tell you again and again to throw away your soldiers, and I will get all badness out of my heart, so that we can all travel kindly together."[17]

"I come in to-day to make a good wide road for my people," Noconi Comanche chief Eagle Drinking said. "Peace is what I want. I am not [involved] in the depredations on the Santa Fé road. I am away south. I ride around to find my people and try to keep them away from war."[18]

The chief pointed to the fact that the Texans still held Comanche prisoners captured in 1858 by Earl Van Dorn at the Wichita village. Although the captives were now being educated and did not wish to return to the tribe, the tribe very much wanted a chance to visit them. The council was then recessed so Kiowa chiefs Satank, Kicking Bird, and a few others could take a wagon out to bring in five white captives. They included Mrs. Caroline McDaniel, twenty-six, of Fredericksburg, Texas; her one-year-old daughter, Rebecca Jane; her niece, three-year-old Dorcas Taylor; and James Burrow, age seven, of Georgetown, Texas. Other captives were too far distant to retrieve just then, but the Kiowas promised to hand them over later.[19]

This done, the commissioners resumed council with the three tribes, and the parties consummated a treaty on October 24. By it, the Kiowas and Comanches were assigned a reservation that covered a large section of western Indian Territory, everything that is now the Texas Panhandle and the Oklahoma Panhandle, and a portion of west Texas. The Kiowa and Comanche chiefs agreed that their tribes would remain within that expanse of country and refrain from depredations against white transportation and settlements.[20]

Until title to the reservation area was settled, however, the Kiowas and Comanches would remain free to roam south of the Arkansas River as usual. Texas, which still held control of its public domain, stoutly resisted the establishment of any such reservation, and the treaty failed to create any substantial change in the status quo of the Kiowas and Comanches.[21]

The Plains Apaches, meanwhile, were given the choice of confederating themselves with the Cheyennes and Arapahos. They opted to do so upon Black Kettle's consent. Accordingly, they were made party to the Cheyenne/Arapaho treaty, even though they were only casually mentioned in the document.

Kingman, who felt the rewards promised the tribes by the commission were far too liberal, concluded of the commission members, "Their fate as com[missione]rs will be that they died of too large views."[22] Although Congress ratified both treaties in May 1866, their failure was not that, as Kingman put it, the agreements constituted "a large price to pay for peace."[23] Rather, in broad terms, it was the fault of the commission, and thereby of the U.S. government, to recognize the dire needs of the Plains tribes for survival in the face of white encroachment, constriction of their territories, and depletion of their food resources.

The refugee tribes residing near the confluence of the Arkansas and Little Arkansas rivers made it known to the commission that they wished to hold a council to address their condition and needs. These bands included the Wichitas, Caddos, Anadarkos, Wacos, Kichai, Tawakaros, Ionis, and Absentee Shawnees, all of which existed "in the most impoverished and destitute conditions."[24] They sadly illustrated the axiom on the Plains that the *most peaceful* tribes received the *least attention* from the United States.

After meeting with them the commission reported, "That they are poorly supplied is evident from their appearance, and the residence of the agent is distant from the Indian camps twenty-five miles, and this distance the Indians are compelled to go for what supplies they receive."[25] The commission recommended that they be sent back to their reservation near Fort Cobb and properly cared for. It would be two years, however, before the government finally returned the refugee tribes to Indian Territory. When finally they did, the tribes suffered the disaster of a cholera outbreak en route. Frontiersman Philip McCusker reported to Superintendent Murphy regarding the return march: "I travelled with them one day's march and really it was a pitiful sight to see the women and children, old men and old women trudging along on foot, most of them barefooted and nearly naked."[26]

The Absentee Shawnees lost fifty of their people and the Caddos forty-seven.[27] On his return to Kansas after freighting goods to Fort Arbuckle, Buffalo Bill Mathewson witnessed the corpses of victims lying dead "like rotten sheep" along what is now known as Skeleton Creek near present Enid, Oklahoma.[28]

During 1865 and 1866 the United States conducted new treaties with the immigrant tribes that had sided with the South. Constructed first at Fort Smith and then at Washington, these pacts dramatically affected titles to western Indian Territory lands that had long been the home range of the Plains tribes. In moving west originally, the Cherokees,

Creeks, Seminoles, Choctaws, and Chickasaws had been assigned lands extending westward to the 100th meridian, or the eastern boundary of the Texas Panhandle. By the reconstruction treaties of 1866, the government stripped the Five Civilized Tribes of their holdings in western Indian Territory, the unoccupied Cherokee Outlet along the Kansas border the important exception.[29]

To secure tribal approval of Senate amendments to the Little Arkansas treaty and to issue the promised annuities, Commissioner of Indian Affairs Lewis V. Bogy sent his brother, Capt. Charles Bogy, and W. R. Irwin as special agents to meet with the tribes at Fort Zarah, Kansas, in November 1866. They met there on the tenth with the Arapahos, headed by Little Raven, and the Cheyennes, represented only by Chief Little Bear and the famous warrior, Roman Nose. William Bent, Robert Bent, and John S. Smith were present. Bogy opened the council with a lengthy talk, reiterating that until they were assigned a reservation, the tribes were free to roam the country as before, with the exception that they must remain away from the white man's thoroughfares.

"If you will listen to your Great Father," Bogy said, "you will want for nothing. Should the Buffalo and other game at any time become scarce so that you will be unable to support yourselves with what assistance he now renders you, he will take care of you and supply your wants."[30]

In response, Arapaho chief Little Raven declared his tribe's desire for peace. Although he complained again about the steady increase of soldiers and military posts, he agreed to the treaty amendments. Roman Nose, the ultimate Cheyenne warrior, spoke far more bluntly, saying:

> I do not believe the whites. I do not love them. If I had plenty of warriors I would drive them out of this country, but we are weak [and] the whites are strong. We cannot count them. We must listen to what they say. At the treaty in the North the commissioners did not speak of making roads on the Smoky Hill. I did not come here to represent myself as a chief but as a soldier.[31]

On the twelfth, Bogy and Irwin met with the Comanches headed by bespectacled Yamparica chief Ten Bears, "a fine old man,"[32] and Cochetaka chief Shaking Hand. During the meeting, Agent Leavenworth demanded that a Texas boy, held captive by a Noconi chief, be returned. Six days later the youngster was delivered to the commissioners. He gave his name as John Charles Fremont Houston.[33] Another meeting with the Cheyennes was called when Black Kettle arrived from the Salt Plains of

Indian Territory where he had taken his band in fear of another attack by U.S. troops. He told the commissioners: "I have told our young men that you were here and what you have said to us. We will hold on to it and hope you will do the same. We are willing to sign your papers and wish you to give us a paper stating that our children [taken at Sand Creek] shall be given up to us."[34]

The grand promise Bogy had made in the name of the White Father, a tragically representative one, would not only be proven empty by the events at hand but would fail in the long course of history. A special agent had purchased the much-awaited treaty annuities from contractors at Fort Leavenworth. When the goods finally arrived on the twelfth, the Indians, who had grown wise to the white man's rewards from previous experiences, immediately questioned their quality. And well they did, as Irwin later reported. Half of the coffee grains were damaged. The sugar was dark and damp. The blankets were larger than ordinary but of inferior quality. Irwin wrote:

> The pants which the invoices claimed to have been purchased in Hartford, Conn., at a cost of $6.25 per pair, I saw an article in a sutler's store at Fort Ellsworth which I think was better, retailing at $5 per pair. Cotton shirts which were invoiced at $6.10 were also an inferior article, bearing U.S. Hospital brands and not worth perhaps 58 cents per price. In reference to the assortment of the original purchase of dry goods, there was no hardware except needles in the purchase for the Cheyennes and Arapahoes.[35]

William Bent agreed, saying the blankets issued the Indians were hardly fit to use as saddle blankets. Bogy himself was forced to admit that "[t]he goods generally were unsatisfactory to the Indians and they expressed their disappointment of the goods and remarked that they were hardly fit to take to camp let alone as a compensation for their lands."[36]

It was not the poor quality of the annuities, however, that posed the greatest barrier to peace. Black Kettle had taken his band south into Indian Territory, but the powerful Dog Soldiers held to the hard prairies of western Kansas and eastern Colorado between the Platte and Arkansas rivers. Work crews on the new Kansas Pacific Railroad were even then pushing their rails westward through the very heart of that country along the Smoky Hill River.

Dog Soldier leaders Tall Bull and Bull Bear met with the commissioners on November 20. Bogy told them: "The Great Chief holds you responsible for your conduct. We would like to hear from you and have you sign the papers. By so doing you will prove to your Great Father that you are working to comply with his requests."[37]

The two notable Cheyenne warriors smoked for a short time, then rose and left without signing the amendments or making a reply. Their silence was ominous. To them, the building of the Kansas Pacific Railroad and the stage line that preceded it along the Smoky Hill constituted a blatant betrayal of the treaty Black Kettle and others had signed.

War and Peace on the Platte

If we give you this [road] you will want another,
and if we give you that you will want a third."
—BRULÉ CHIEF SPOTTED TAIL

Hopes for peace along the Platte River quickly dissolved following the 1851 treaty at Fort Laramie. The troubles Thomas Fitzpatrick had found brewing between that post's garrison and the Indians in 1853 continued. During August 1854 a fracas ignited over the shooting by a Sioux of a stray cow from a Mormon caravan. The matter was exacerbated when Lt. John Grattan, who boasted greatly of killing Indians, invaded the Sioux village with twenty-nine men, an interpreter, and two artillery pieces. When Grattan attempted to make an arrest, the tribesmen resisted, and firing began. Grattan and all but one of his men were annihilated. The surviving soldier, whose tongue had been cut out, died later at Fort Laramie.[1]

Sporadic friction continued along the Platte Trail until U.S. officials concluded that the Indians must be punished. In the fall of 1855, Gen. William S. Harney marched from Fort Leavenworth with 600 men to Ash Hollow, west of present Ogallala, Nebraska. There, he found an encampment of Brulé Sioux Indians under Chief Little Thunder. Ignoring Little Thunder's declaration of friendship, Harney ordered his troops to attack the village from two sides. Eighty-six Indians were killed, and a like number of women and children were taken prisoner.[2]

Despite disturbances between white travelers and the Indians, a tentative peace had held over the Platte Trail in the years leading up to the Civil War in 1861. The U.S. military provided limited escort and oversight for the trail during that period. But once the Southern rebellion began, defections of soldiers from the South and the withdrawal of regular army troops for Civil War action left only volunteer soldiers to guard the trail. Still, even during the war, white influence advanced along the route. Settlers bound for Oregon, California, Colorado, Utah, and other western areas continued to migrate in caravans of from 10 to 100 wagons. Freighting convoys carrying supplies and goods to western settlements and mining camps were common as well.

Fortified ranch stops and military sutler stores sprung up along the way to provide respite and nourishment for travelers, some serving as relay stations for mail wagons, stage-line coaches, or the Pony Express. Settlers, trappers, hunters, bull whackers, soldiers, adventurers, and journalists—among them figures of note such as Artemus Ward, Brete Harte, Mark Twain, and Horace Greeley—passed along the trail that was now further defined by poles and lines of the Pacific Telegraph Company.[3]

Impoverished but compliant Pawnee, Ponca, and Omaha Indians resided in close proximity to the route.[4] From vantage points west of Fort Sedgwick, "the dangerous part of the line," however, roving parties of Sioux, Cheyenne, and Arapaho warriors watched the ever-increasing parade of white travel with angry distrust.[5] In essence, the Platte Trail was a long thread of Anglo-American culture stretching through what was still predominantly Indian country. Although a tenuous peace had held following Harney's strike, the 1862 Sioux uprising in Minnesota and the ensuing military strikes by generals Henry Sibley and Alfred Sully in the Dakotas exacerbated the unstable relationship of tribe and nation in Nebraska. This, in turn, brought an increase of depredations along the Platte Trail.[6]

During the spring of 1864, government officials sought to reach a peaceful resolution by holding a council with bands of the Brulé, Oglala, and Miniconjou Sioux that were active along the Platte. In hopes that the Cheyennes and Arapahos would behave once the Sioux were influenced to do so, those two tribes were not invited.[7] Capt. Eugene Ware expressed the military's view of the Indian problem on the Platte Road:

> It was cheaper to feed the Indians than to fight them, and the
> constant efforts of the commanding officers were to make treaties of
> peace, which resulted practically in our buying privileges and

immunities from them. The demands of the Civil War which was straining the nation's resources added much to the difficulties of the occasion. So we were in an attitude all the time of half war and half peace with the Indian tribes. We could not punish them adequately for what they did, nor could they drive us off from the Platte Valley.[8]

Importantly, by quieting the Indians along the Platte, the government hoped it could release troops on the frontier for use in Sherman's Atlanta campaign. Sioux bands had already begun appearing at Fort Cottonwood—also known as Cottonwood Springs and later as Fort McPherson—during April when Brig. Gen. Robert B. Mitchell, commanding the Military District of Nebraska, arrived to conduct the council. He and the officers of the post met with seventeen chiefs inside the roofless walls of an unfinished 25 × 25-foot sutler store. The Indians formed a semicircle on the dirt floor, and the officers sat on cracker boxes opposite them. Mitchell, postured in a large camp chair, towered above the assembly. After a few moments of silence, a Sioux produced a pipe from under his blanket.

> It had a stem about two and a half feet long. It was made of red pipestone, and had a good-sized bowl, but the orifice was scant for the tobacco. It was filled with great pomp and solemnity by the man who took it, and did it little by little, as if it was a great function. He felt the weight and importance of the ceremony. Then he passed the pipe down to the end of the line, and there an Indian with a flint-and-steel and a piece of punk started the pipe. Then it went mouth to mouth, the parties each taking three whiffs.[9]

After a pampering preamble in which he submitted his opinion that the Indians had actually prospered through contact with their white brothers, Mitchell got to his point: he wanted the Sioux to keep out of the Platte Valley. "If it takes more to feed you," he said, "if it takes more bacon or blankets and corn, we will give you more, but you must stay out of the Platte Valley."[10]

He also wanted the Sioux to keep away from the Smoky Hill in western Kansas where a new stage route had been opened. Big Mandan, the Brulé's principal orator, responded with charges that freighters had driven all the game away from the trail, that white whiskey dealers were corrupting his young men, and that his people were constantly cheated by their agents and traders.[11] The great Brulé warrior and chief Shan-tag-a-lisk, or Spotted Tail, forcibly repeated the complaints.

"We are not afraid of the white man," he told the general, "nor are we afraid to fight him. We will not give up the Platte valley to you until we have a regular treaty, and until we have all agreed to it, and have been paid for it."[12]

Then he very astutely observed: "If we give you this you will want another, and if we give you that you will want a third. Before we agree to anything you must stop the surveyors that are going west at this very time on the river Niobrara."[13]

Although Mitchell agreed to withdraw the surveyors, the council reached an impasse and was adjourned with an agreement to meet again after fifty moons. When that meeting was held in May, the same disputes prevailed. Mitchell called for a third council in another fifty days. On July 18 the Sioux bands had gathered en masse when he arrived at Fort Cottonwood to join them on a grassy meadow three miles east of the post. This time Mitchell brought with him a 50-man company of Seventh Iowa Cavalry to join the 100 men posted at Fort Cottonwood and a force of 80 Pawnee Indian scouts recruited and led by Capt. Frank J. North.[14]

Convinced that another council would fail to produce any satisfactory results, Mitchell had come prepared to make a strong military display that would intimidate the Sioux. He arranged his cavalry with drawn sabers flashing in the sun, positioned his artillery, and lined the Pawnee scouts on the opposite side of the Sioux. He then sent a trooper forward to mark a "talking place" by stabbing his saber into a large anthill. These things done, Mitchell rode to the place with his staff, saluted both the Sioux and the Pawnee, and began sounding bugle calls to bring his forces forward.

Mitchell addressed both the Sioux and the Pawnees through his interpreters, saying he had been sent by their Great Father in Washington. He insisted that the tribes pledge not to kill one another or steal the other's horses. But the principal demand remained: the Sioux were to stay out of the Platte Valley and not cross it to the south. The Pawnees expressed their willingness to comply with the Great Father's wishes to remain peaceful, but the Sioux were angry and obdurate. Their orators' speeches grew increasingly hostile to both Mitchell and the Pawnees. With the sun setting and no agreement in sight, Mitchell gave up. Sounding bugle calls to ready his cavalry and aiming his artillery directly at the Sioux, he sent orders for them to cross the Platte to the north and not stop for three days. Howling their defiance, they splashed across the river and rode away.[15] During August 1864, Mitchell had still another try at treating with the Sioux, this time at Fort Laramie. Only a small number of Sioux and none of their important leaders appeared, however, and the attempt failed.

The intensity of Sioux/Cheyenne resentment of white presence along the Platte Trail became apparent in July 1865 when a joint tribal council laid plans for conducting war against white transportation and military posts. The place chosen for an initial attack was the soldier stockade that guarded the bridge spanning the Platte River at the site of present Casper, Wyoming. A well-organized force of around 2,000 Oglala Sioux, Northern Cheyenne, and Northern Arapaho warriors took positions in the hills overlooking the bridge and prepared for the attack. A small decoy of men was sent down to show themselves and attempt to draw the soldiers out from the fort. The ploy failed because the troops were too wary to follow for any distance.

A short fight ensued, however, when the Indians met a party of soldiers seen approaching the fort. These soldiers were carrying word to the fort that a train of five supply wagons was on its way, oblivious to the current Indian threat. Lt. Caspar Collins, a young officer who had just arrived at the fort, volunteered to take a troop forth and provide escort for the train. When the Indians saw the soldiers ride out across the long bridge, it was precisely what they had wanted.[16]

One party of warriors was sent galloping down to cut the soldiers off from the fort while another blocked them at the front. Entrapped, Collins and his men had little chance against the massive force of warriors. Seeing their plight, they turned and attempted to fight their way back to the fort. Under support of cannon fire from the fort, some of them made it to safety. Eight men including Collins, however, were knocked from their saddles and killed. Collins was struck in the forehead by an arrow. His disembowled body was later found wrapped in telegraph wire, his hands and feet cut off and his heart and tongue cut out.[17]

A soldier who witnessed the affair from his post at the bridge wrote: "About 10 1/2 a.m., not less than one thousand Indians made an instantaneous rush toward where the soldiers would first be seen. . . . Two hours elapsed before the contest seemed to be over; then soon the wagons were on fire."[18]

The Collins massacre and other infractions along the Platte brought Gen. Patrick E. Connor marching north from Fort Laramie with a small army in a search for Indians to fight. On August 11 his Pawnee scouts found a small party of Cheyennes and killed twenty-four. Then on August

29, at the Tongue River, the scouts discovered an Arapaho village under Chief Black Bear. Connor attacked, driving the Indians upstream. After capturing the village, Connor burned the lodges and camp equipage, along with the bodies of dead villagers. Nearly a thousand horses and mules were taken. The Arapahos harassed the troops as they withdrew, recapturing some of the animals.[19]

In Washington, President Andrew Johnson appointed a six-man commission to conduct negotiations with the Sioux, Northern Cheyennes, and Northern Arapahos of the Upper Missouri and issued instructions to them through Secretary of Interior James Harlan. Newton Edmunds, governor and ex officio superintendent of Indian Affairs for Dakota Territory; Edward B. Taylor, head of the Northern Superintendency of Indian Affairs; Maj. Gen. Samuel R. Curtis; Brig. Gen. Henry H. Sibley; Indian commissioner Henry Reed; and Oran Guernsey were members of the commission.[20]

In acceptance of the concept of a Manifest Destiny for the nation, James Harian, Secretary of Interior, observed that "[o]ur hills and valleys are being occupied with an adventurous and rapidly increasing people, that must, in the progress of events, encroach upon the ancient abodes of the red man."[21] Harlan instructed the commissioners to be just and fair in removing them to "a district of the country as remote as practicable from any of the leading routes across the plains, or the usual thoroughfares of the people of the different Territories."[22]

"The nation cannot sanction the policy of exterminating them," the secretary observed. "Our self-respect, our Christian faith, and a common dependence on an all-wise Creator and benefactor, forbid it."[23]

Connors was still in the field when the new peace commission departed from St. Louis in September 1865, sailing up the Missouri River on the steamboat *Calypso*. The commissioners paused at the Yankton agency twenty miles below Fort Randall in Dakota Territory to hold a council with the Yankton, Yanktonais, Brulé, and Two Kettle bands. Yankton chief Pa-la-ne-ona-pe (the Man Who Was Struck by the Ree) told them he had seen none of the help promised by the Treaty of Fort Laramie: "My young men, squaws and children are starving—the black spots you see on the hills before you are the graves of many of my people."[24]

A correspondent with the party observed sympathetically: "All the Indians that I have seen complain bitterly of the treatment by the agents and traders, and I feel assured that they are justified in their hatred of the white man. Will this wholesale swindling of the Indians by their agents ever cease?[25]

The lack of grass for their horses and the scarcity of buffalo this late in the season, plus the great distance of their camps from Fort Sully, caused the Cheyennes, Arapahos, and many of the bands to hold back. The Miniconjou Sioux, considered the "most numerous, warlike, and mischievous"[26] division of the Sioux nation, were the first to arrive. Their chiefs were anxious to make peace, and the commission initiated a treaty with them on October 10. By the new pact, the tribe agreed to accept the exclusive jurisdiction of the United States, to cease all hostilities, to withdraw from all overland routes, and to use its influence in preventing other bands from molesting whites.[27]

In addition to the future assignment of a reservation and arrangements for the transformation of the tribe to agricultural pursuits, the treaty promised to provide annual annuities, schools, and other assistance. Similar agreements were subsequently made with other Sioux bands as they arrived: the Lower Brulés, Two Kettles, Blackfoot, Sans Arc, Hunkpapas, Yanktonais, and Oglalas.[28]

In its report to Harlan, the commission expressed its extreme dismay at the condition of the Dakota tribes and the way they had been treated. It noted "many instances of the utter disregard of the natural rights of the bands treated with, and of the injustices done them by residents and soldiers, as well as travelers through their country . . . and they reveal a condition of things alike disgraceful to the government."[29]

The agent for the tribes received condemnation as well. Despite the appropriation of large sums of money by Congress, the commission found that no appreciable improvements had been made for the tribes. The Miniconjous were in such a state of severe starvation that the commission ordered a special issue of provisions to the band. All this, the report noted, went against the fact that many of the Sioux had remained friendly to the government, rescued white women and children taken captive by others, and served as scouts and guides for the military against their own kindred.[30]

General Curtis affirmed these points in a separate report to Harlan. He charged that the former treaties with the tribes had been loosely defined and imperfectly carried out by the government. The annuity provided to them by the Treaty of Fort Laramie, he observed, was too small as distributed to each lodge to be worth going after: "The sum distributed among at least sixteen thousand [Indians] would only give to each about five dollars, and much of it is to be in agricultural implements, which are only loaned to the Indians. . . . There is a vast multitude of shivering, starving, anxious children of the prairies waiting the action of our Government, and hoping that a return of spring will bring with it the peace offerings contemplated by our treaties."[31]

The Fort Sully treaty council had addressed government concerns with the Missouri River Sioux, but it had been unable to reach the still-belligerent bands that resided along the Platte to the west. To do this, another commission was organized to work out new agreements with the Indians of the Fort Laramie region—namely, the Northern Cheyennes and the Brulé and Oglala Sioux. This commission was headed by Edward B. Taylor and included Robert N. McClaren, Thomas Wistar, and Col. Henry E. Maynadier, commanding officer at Fort Laramie.[32]

A council held at Fort Laramie on June 6, 1866, featured Brulé and Oglala Sioux leaders Red Cloud, Spotted Tail, Red Leaf, and Man-Afraid-of-His-Horses. The tone and spirit of these influential chiefs were reportedly conciliatory and peaceful, leading to hopes that a satisfactory treaty could be achieved.[33] People on the frontier, where Indian depredations were reported daily, were far more cynical. A Colorado newspaper suggested "that it is a pity the red devils didn't scalp the Commissioners sent out to make peace with them."[34]

A military officer present at Fort Laramie passed on an interesting, if questionable, treaty proposal the Sioux had reportedly made to the commission through a tribesman named Bad Hand:

> Red Cloud, Black Nable, One-afraid-of-his-horse, Bear Blanket, Thunderfire, Spotted Tail, Running Bear, Standing Elk; these Indians on here, give you Powder river road. You can make the wagon road on there for one hundred wagons loaded with Indian goods, 1,000 American horses, 1,000 rifles, 500 head of cattle, 500 head of cows, 2,000 head of sheep, 1,000 head of hogs, 500 roosters, 1,000 chickens, 200 colored men to raise corn.[35]

The treaty initiated at Fort Laramie on June 27 and eventually left unratified by the Senate called for the Brulé and Oglala bands to withdraw from the overland routes of the United States in return for an annual payment of $70,000 to each for twenty years. It was signed by Spotted Tail and seven other Brulé chiefs and Big Mouth plus five other Oglalas.[36] A similar treaty with the Northern Cheyennes arranged for that tribe to be paid $15,000 annually for twenty years. Chief Cut Nose and seven "Chief Soldiers" signed the document for the Cheyennes on June 28. Dull Knife and seven other chiefs reaffirmed the agreement on October 11.

Neither the Sioux nor the Cheyenne agreement made reference to any overland route in particular, stating that the tribes would "withdraw from the routes overland already established, or hereafter to be established through their country."[37] Nothing was said about the Bozeman Trail running from Wyoming to the Montana gold mines and cutting through the traditional range and prime hunting grounds of the northern tribes. This issue soon ignited bloody warfare that tragically involved an Eighteenth Infantry officer who had signed the 1866 treaty as a witness. His name was Capt. William Fetterman.[38]

By the 1866 treaty, the Sioux and Northern Cheyennes begrudgingly accepted the white man's road along the Platte River and on westward. But the Bozeman Trail was another matter. Just as Spotted Tail had wisely foreseen: when the Indians gave in to one trail, the whites wanted still another. Even before the Senate took the 1866 treaty under consideration, raids against wagon trains and their military escorts commenced along the Bozeman.

In their official report of the treaty council, Taylor and Maynadier had discredited "rumors of a discouraging character in daily circulation of the disinclination of the Indians to give Government the desired road to Montana by the way of the Powder River."[39] Such stories were spread, they insisted, by persons interested in keeping freight charges high. The two commissioners wrote, "Although the Indians, as might naturally be expected, were reluctant to allow the proposed road to pass through the best of their remaining hunting grounds, yet when informed of the wishes of the Government and of our disposition to give a liberal equivalent, they acquiesced in our request in a full council after a full expression of sentiment had taken place on both sides."[40]

Events soon revealed a stark disconnect between this reading of the Indians' attitude toward the Bozeman Trail and the reality of their fiercely determined opposition. Spotted Tail had led the treaty signing for the Brulés, Big Mouth for the Oglalas, and Cut Nose and Dull Knife for the Northern Cheyennes. But notably missing in giving approval to the Fort Laramie agreement was the Oglala war leader Red Cloud, who had held back from accepting presents from the commissioners. His fury soon wreaked havoc along the Bozeman.

Letters from two teamsters described incidents along the trail on July 24 when "twelve or fifteen men" were killed, among them army officer Lt. N. H. Daniels of Indiana, whose body was badly mutilated. One of the correspondents, whose train was attacked on the twenty-fourth, denounced the military for not providing better protection along the trail and concluded, "The [1866 Fort Laramie] treaty is not worth a damn."[41]

The other wrote: "The country is alive with game, such as bear, elk, deer, antelope, etc., but we can't enjoy it, as it is dangerous for one to go a great way from the train. We have about 150 miles of dangerous country to pass over, and if they [the Indians] let me pass over that, I will never bother their country again."[42]

It was only the beginning. The wagon trains continued to come, and Indian attacks increased daily. To provide protection for transportation to and from the Montana mines, the United States sent Brig. Gen. Henry B. Carrington to construct military posts along the trail. Marching north from Fort Laramie to Crazy Woman's Fork with 700 troops of the Eighteenth Infantry, Carrington upgraded Camp Connor and renamed it Fort Reno. This done, he led his forces farther up the eastern slopes of the Bighorn Mountains to Piney River. There, during August, he began construction of a new post that would become known as Fort Phil Kearny. A month later his men began work on another post, Fort C. F. Smith, on the Bighorn River in present Montana.[43]

It was at Fort Kearny that the U.S. Army suffered its largest defeat in the West to that date. A number of attacks against details sent to gather wood for the new post had drawn troops rushing out in pursuit. This also occurred on December 21, 1866, when Captain Fetterman led a force of seventy-eight officers and men from the post to rescue a wood train Sioux and Cheyenne attackers had surrounded. Despite orders not to do so, Fetterman pursued the Indians beyond Lodge Trail Ridge, where a mass of Sioux and Cheyenne warriors waited in ambush. Fetterman's entire force was wiped out.[44]

The Fetterman Massacre did not end U.S. efforts to secure its objectives in the North by way of councils and agreements on paper. Another treaty council would be held at Fort Laramie in 1868. But now began a decade of war, leading to an even larger military disaster—on the banks of the Little Bighorn of Montana.

A "Manifest Falsehood"

Now [the White Father] covers his face with the cloud of jealousy
and anger and tells us to be gone, as an offended master speaks to his dog.
Look at this medal I wear. By wearing this I have been made poor.
—KIOWA CHIEF SATANK

There was one last grand treaty gathering with the southern bands. Kansas had become a state in 1861, but much of its western region was still dominated by the Dog Soldiers. By a new treaty, the United States aimed to eliminate the remaining impediment to the lines of transportation and white settlements in Kansas, where Indian troubles persisted. Whereas Black Kettle and his amenable band held to the Indian Territory, the Cheyenne Dog Soldiers still dominated much of the country between the Platte and the Arkansas in 1867. During April of that year, Maj. Gen. Winfield Scott Hancock, commanding the Department of the Missouri with headquarters at Fort Leavenworth, launched an initiative to impress those bands with a show of force.

With a 1,500-man army composed of Seventh Cavalry under Lt. Col. George Armstrong Custer, four companies of infantry, and artillery units, Hancock marched from Fort Riley to Fort Larned and up the Pawnee Fork. In approaching a joint Cheyenne-Sioux encampment, the expedition was fronted by a commanding force of warriors under Roman Nose, Tall Bull, and others. A bloody clash loomed, averted only when Agent Edward Wynkoop rode forward to arrange a parley. The villagers, however, feared another Sand Creek attack, and that night they fled en masse.

Custer made an inept attempt to overtake them, but they constantly divided on the prairie until no discernible trail could be found. Not to worry—Custer, an avid sportsman, left his column to hunt buffalo, after which he led his troops on to Fort Hays, Kansas. Hancock, meanwhile, vacillated and eventually torched the deserted village. The act only added to the conviction among the tribes of the white man's duplicity.

Custer continued his search for Indians in June, leading the Seventh Cavalry on a long, difficult march through northwestern Kansas and on to the South Platte River. His only confrontation involved a brief encounter with an Oglala band under Pawnee Killer, who successfully eluded his cavalry. On his return march, Custer discovered the skeletal, arrow-spiked remains of a courier detachment under Lt. Lyman Kidder that had been massacred to the man. At the South Platte, Custer ordered the shooting of three regimental deserters. This and his own abandonment of the Fort Wallace post where he had been assigned led to his eventual court-martial and relief from active duty.

The military's inability to subdue the hostile Plains tribes added fuel to a rising humanitarian call for "a peaceable solution to the Indian troubles."[1] Following Chivington's attack on Black Kettle's camp at Sand Creek, Colorado, the spirit of benevolent sympathy for the native tribesman, so successfully exercised by the Quaker William Penn during Colonial times, reigned among certain religious groups and spread by way of the eastern press into the government bureaucracy. On the Kansas frontier, those of such bent were derisively called "olive branchers."[2]

Commissioner of Indian Affairs N. G. Taylor assumed tacit leadership of the peace movement when President Johnson appointed him to head a new treaty commission to deal with the western tribes. Joining him were four generals with Indian experience: William T. Sherman, J. B. Sanborn, William S. Harney, and Alfred H. Terry. Also serving were Senator John B. Henderson of Missouri, chairman of the Senate Committee on Indian Affairs, and Samuel F. Tappan, a liberal-minded former military officer in Colorado who had spoken out critically about the Sand Creek Massacre.

The peace commission's mandate included the northern tribes as well as those on the mid and lower Plains. After organizing at St. Louis, the commission traveled to Fort Leavenworth. There, interviews on the Indian problem were held with General Hancock, Kansas governor Samuel Crawford, and the missionary Father De Smet. From there, the commission traveled by boat up the Missouri River to Omaha, meeting with Maj. Gen. C. C. Augur and others. An attempt to reach Fort Rice failed because of low water in the Missouri, but the commissioners held councils with various tribes on the return downriver. Upon returning to St. Louis, Sherman, who had publicly denounced the peace commission as a "humbug," was recalled to Washington. He was subsequently replaced temporarily on the commission by Augur.[3]

In an effort to meet the September 13 date it had set with the Sioux and Northern Cheyennes at Fort Laramie, the commission headed up the Platte route by the new Union Pacific rail line. At the North Platte station it found a gathering of the two tribes there. The commission members learned from scouts that Red Cloud's band of Sioux would not be able to meet them on their schedule. Setting a new date for a meeting in October, they turned south to Fort Harker, Kansas.[4]

Central Indian Superintendent Thomas Murphy had arranged for a meeting with the southern tribes. Runners had contacted the various bands, and a council site was selected at the confluence of Medicine Lodge and Elm creeks seventy miles southeast of Fort Larned. An old Kiowa sun dance lodge stood nearby. By the time the commission reached Fort Harker at the small settlement of Ellsworth, the number of press "specials" (as correspondents were then called) had grown.

They included some highly regarded journalists of the day: S. F. Hall of the *Chicago Tribune*, John Howland of *Harper's Weekly*, George Brown of the *Cincinnati Commercial*, William Fayel of the *Missouri Republican*, James F. Taylor of *Frank Leslie's Illustrated Newspaper*, H. J. Budd of Cincinnati's *Semi-Weekly Gazette*, Milton Reynolds of the Lawrence *State Journal*, and Henry M. Stanley—the eventual finder of Livingstone in Africa—who worked for the *Missouri Democrat* but strung for other papers as well.[5]

These scribes added to the sizable army of commissioners and aides in ambulances, camp attendants, frontiersmen, half bloods hired as interpreters, teamsters commanding wagons loaded with treaty gifts and camping necessities, four companies of Seventh Cavalry under Maj. Joel Elliott to serve as escort, soldiers of the Thirty-eighth Infantry and their regimental band, artillerymen with their Gatling guns, and hundreds upon hundreds of horses and mules. All this merged into a huge caravan for the march to Fort Larned.[6]

Upon reaching that frontier post, the expedition rested briefly. While enjoying a libation session hosted by Agent Wynkoop at the sutler's store, officers and reporters were treated to a visit from the redoubtable Satanta. The Kiowa leader happily joined in the evening of drink and conversation, although he eventually announced that he wanted to get away from the fort because it "stink too much [of] white man here."[7]

Satanta made colorful copy for the reporters, catching their attention in an incident on the march to the treaty grounds. A huge herd of buffalo was encountered, exciting a number of officers and other members of the commission party to gallop forth from the line of the march to make their kill. After killing a large number of animals, the white hunters merely cut the tongues from the dead animals and left the remaining carcasses to rot on the prairie. An angry Satanta complained vigorously to General Harney about the matter, and the sport shooting was ordered to end.[8]

No Indian council had ever received the abundance of press coverage the one at Medicine Lodge did. Not only were more reporters present, but delays caused the affair to drag out for over two weeks. During this period of camping in tents on the hot, remote, wearisome, and sometimes dangerous prairie, the newsmen competed to write anything and everything about the Indians: their mode of tribal existence, their chiefly personalities, their depredations, camp life, verbatim speeches of commissioners and tribal orators, and the nuances involved in framing the new treaty. Stanley, the Englishman, proved to be among the most perceptive of these journalistic onlookers.

The often critical variance between federal and state views on Indian affairs arose during a precouncil meeting when Senator Henderson gave a discourse on treaty promises the United States had made to Indian tribes. He drew a relationship of that history to the effort at hand. Kansas governor Samuel Crawford, who had joined the commission party at Leavenworth, saw the matter much differently, arguing that the Indian forces presented a "powerful, well organized, and well equipped" army that was allied to wage war against whites.[9] Kansas editor Reynolds debunked Crawford's contention of an Indian alliance, writing: "The politics of this state [Kansas] are terribly muddled and mixed and a systematic attempt has been made by Governor Crawford and his partisans to drag the Indian question into the dirty pool. Political aspirants induce the government to proclaim the Manifest Falsehood that white settlers had a right to go onto the Indian lands in spite of treaty stipulations."[10]

Many of the various bands of Cheyennes, Arapahos, Comanches, Kiowas, and Prairie Apaches had arrived at the council site ahead of the commission party, their tepees and horse herds dotting the riverbank for miles. Of the Cheyennes, however, only the peacefully disposed band under Black Kettle was in camp at the site. The Dog Soldiers, who controlled the majority of the tribe, were noticeably absent, although they were known to be somewhere nearby. Earlier at the treaty site, the recalcitrant Roman Nose had threatened to kill Wynkoop, whom he mistakenly blamed for Hancock's burning of the Cheyenne/Sioux village. Wynkoop fled back to the safety of Fort Larned.[11]

Black Kettle met with the commissioners when they arrived on the morning of October 14. He warned them of the Dog Soldiers' continued hostility. He said, too, that the tribe was involved in its annual rite of renewing the Sacred Medicine Arrows, and it would be eight sleeps before they would be ready to hold council with the commission. That evening the commission camp stirred in alarm when a large party of heavily armed Cheyenne warriors under Tall Bull and Grey Head galloped unannounced into the commission camp. Grey Head, however, proffered a safe-conduct note Harney had issued to him nine years earlier on the Platte River. The two men—the warrior and the general—joyously slapped one another on the back in happy reunion.[12]

The following morning the commissioners conducted a preliminary conference with the Cheyenne leaders. The Indians came dressed in full regalia of feathered headdresses, robes, beaded moccasins, Mexican serapes, silver breastplates, peace medals, and other adornments. After both sides made speeches, it was agreed that a full council would be delayed until the Cheyennes' Sacred Arrows ceremonies were completed.[13]

That afternoon Harney conducted a critical inquiry into Hancock's campaign, taking testimony from Wynkoop and others on the matter. The agent related the torching of the Cheyenne/Sioux village and spoke at length of the fraud exercised with Indian annuities: blankets that were badly rotted and virtually worthless, barrels of sugar that were only half full, and other items such as ladies' gaiters and bonnets that were useless to the tribespeople.[14]

On October 20 the commission turned its attention to the Kiowas and Comanches. Satanta, who wore the coat of an army general above his bare legs with a bugle dangling at his side, spoke for the Kiowas; Ten Bears and Silver Broach (Toshowa) spoke for the Comanches. Although to the commission party his appearance was ludicrous, Satanta won high repute as an orator at the council. He spoke of his desire to roam the prairie and chase the buffalo freely, as had his fathers; he loved the open spaces of the wild country that were free of barns and hospitals. He hated houses, he said, because the Kiowas got sick in them. He closed with a stinging remark: "I have no little lies sticking about me. But I don't know how it is with the commissioners."[15]

Ten Bears agreed with Satanta, saying in effect: "I do not like one part of your talk about building houses. I was born on the prairie, and want to live and die there. I wish you would not insist on the Comanches going to a reserve."[16]

Silver Broach of the Peneteka Comanches said his people had been asked to settle down and were promised farming implements that never came. He had waited a long time for them, but if they did not arrive before next summer he would return to the prairie. He also had a word regarding white people who made treaties.

"It is a belief among the chiefs of the Comanches," he said, "that if they call upon the Great Spirit to witness, and make a false statement, they will be instantly destroyed. If the same belief existed among white men, I think a good many of their big chiefs would have died long ago."[17]

Other tribal speakers agreed with Satanta and Ten Bears, saying they had no use for the white man's houses, barns, or schoolhouses that the White Father so often promised them. When Senator Henderson persisted on the issue, Satanta replied sarcastically that the Indians would let him know when the buffalo were gone; then they could build houses.[18]

The fact was, however, that it did not matter what the chiefs said they wanted or did not want. The commission was fully determined to provide them with houses, schools, barns, blacksmith shops, and hospitals—the costs of which would be deducted from their $30,000 annual annuity. Further, Article 2 of the pact assigned the two tribes to a reservation south of the Washita in southwestern Indian Territory—on the fallacious assumption that the prairie nomads were prepared to settle down to an agricultural existence and drastically alter their traditional ways of life. These unwanted rewards stood as major elements of the treaty initiated the following day, October 21. Both Stanley and Major Elliott, who submitted an official report on the treaty signing, charged that the document was never read in full to the Kiowa and Comanche chiefs.

"The treaty with the Kiowas was something of a tremendous `goak,'" Stanley wrote, "a very farce, which had the people seen upon the stage, they would have laughed their very eyes out."[19]

Senator Henderson, he charged, selected only a few of the most pleasing portions of the long treaty articles—sixteen in number—to have interpreted for the Kiowas. Other correspondents concurred that the chiefs had little idea what the document said when they put their marks on it. Once the treaty was signed, the Kiowa and Comanche tribespeople came forward eagerly to collect their treaty goods, load them on travois, and take them off to their camp. The women excitedly garnered blankets, coats, shawls, calico, plumes, cords, beads, needles and pins, thread, yarn, and woolens. For the men, there were shirts, hats, and pants. Some of the handguns issued to them were faulty and exploded to bits when fired.[20]

The commissioners were still at their table when Satank rode up, accompanied by several of his warriors. Around his neck the elderly Kiowa warrior-chief wore a peace medal given to him by Fitzpatrick. Satank alighted from his pony and addressed the commissioners with a speech Stanley judged equal to those of the greatest Indian orators. Satank said in part:

> The white man once came to trade; he now comes as a soldier. He once put his trust in our friendship and wanted no shield but our fidelity. But now he builds forts and plants big guns on their walls. He once gave us arms, and powder and ball, and bade us hunt the game. We then loved him for his confidence; he now suspects our plighted faith and drives us to be his enemies; he now covers his face with the cloud of jealousy and anger and tells us to be gone, as an offended master speaks to his dog. Look at this medal I wear. By wearing this I have been made poor. Formerly I was rich in horses and lodges—today I am the poorest of all. When you put this silver medal on my neck you made me poor.[21]

All things considered, the commissioners were pleased with the session. They had at least one treaty to take back to Washington. But the Cheyennes and their Dog Soldiers posed a far more difficult problem. No one was sure when they would arrive or if they would come at all. There was, in fact, considerable trepidation among the commission party and newsmen alike about the potential danger the Dog Soldiers posed. Further, the fatigue and boredom of camp life were beginning to set in, and supplies were running low—especially the whiskey.

The Cheyenne situation grew even more threatening that night. An autumn storm with high winds had struck the camp when a party of rain-soaked Cheyenne chiefs, led by Black Kettle, appeared out of the dark. They asked to talk to the commission. Taylor arranged an interview in a commission tent by kerosene lamp, and John S. Smith was called forth to interpret.[22]

To the several reporters who were present, the Cheyennes appeared very imposing in the flickering lantern light. Black Kettle seemed ill at case as he told the commissioners that the Sacred Arrow ceremony would take four more days but that the Cheyennes wanted the Kiowas and Comanches to remain until they arrived. Tempers flared among the commissioners when Henderson said he was ready to leave Medicine Lodge Creek and declared he would wait no longer for the Cheyennes. Harney angrily threatened to place him under arrest if he tried to do so. After more heated debate, the delay was agreed to, and the Cheyennes rode off into the night.[23]

The sense of dread and outright fear increased on October 25 when Cheyenne half-blood Edward Guerrier, who had been sent to talk with the Dog Soldiers, returned to say he had found them to be belligerent and their camp heavily armed. The Cheyenne leaders said it would be three more days, the coming Monday, before they could meet with the commission. Word was sent back that the commission would wait that long but no longer.[24]

When the Cheyennes arrived, they did so unexpectedly and in a style that sent shock waves of fear throughout the commission camp. The commission party was basking in a quiet Sunday morning when the call sounded: the Cheyennes were coming! Stanley described their arrival:

> The Cheyennes, with tremendous display of numbers, with sound of gong, tinkling of bells, and a general salute of fire-arms, came into Medicine Lodge creek after having expressed their wish in a bombastic manner that no other Indians should be in the vicinity. The commissioners were dreadfully afraid, and nervously besought the aid of the military. As soon as the dreaded Cheyennes were announced, the cavalry and infantry were put under arms, and every citizen imbued with the same nervousness, loaded and otherwise prepared his weapons. When the Cheyennes, to the number of 1,500, were drawn up in lines before our camp, the commissioners, mustering up what courage they possessed, marched dignifiedly to the long line and affably shook hands with the most prominent men amongst them.[25]

Despite the tense situation, Taylor arranged a meeting for nine o'clock the following morning. At that time the Cheyenne and Arapaho chiefs gathered before the commissioners' tent in a semicircle, their warriors behind them. Brown of the *Cincinnati Commercial* described the Dog Soldiers as "armed to the teeth with revolvers and bows . . . proud, haughty, defiant."[26] For the commissioners, seated behind a table in the doorway of the tent, it was not a comforting view.

Henderson spoke first, laying out the government's position. After apologizing for Hancock having burned the village, he said that attacks on the Kansas Pacific Railroad and frontier settlements must stop. Hereafter, the tribes should do their hunting south of the Arkansas River. In return, the government would designate a reservation for them, build houses and a gristmill, provide annuity goods, and supply equipment and livestock so they could begin an agricultural existence.

Little Raven was the first Arapaho to reply. He stated that the Arapahos wanted a reservation near Fort Lyon and an honest trader. He spoke in part to the Cheyennes, saying the Arapahos were willing to join in making war on the Utes of western Colorado but would not war against the whites. There were none of the usual "Hows" of approval from the Cheyennes during his speech. Buffalo Chief, designated to speak for the Cheyennes, followed Raven. In a scolding tone, he told the commissioners that the Cheyennes owned the land north of the Arkansas River: "There the bones of our fathers lie buried. You think you are doing a great deal for us by giving these present[s] to us, but we prefer to live as formerly. If you gave us all the goods you could give, yet we would prefer our own life, to live as we have done. You give us presents and then take our land—that provokes war."[27]

Clearly, the Dog Soldiers spoke for the Cheyennes, and just as clearly they were not willing to give up their hunting grounds in western Kansas. The white man wanted peace, they said, and they were willing to comply—but on their own terms. They were adamant and held a threatening position at the council. This did not square at all with the prepared treaty document awaiting the Indians' signatures. The commissioners were perplexed. They were sorely fatigued with life in the wilds, filled with dread of the Dog Soldiers, and more than anxious to get signatures on the treaty and be gone.

When a break was called in the speech making, Henderson stepped forward. Politicians knew how to settle such an impasse. Calling some of the Dog Soldier leaders aside, along with John Smith and George Bent, he talked to them at length, saying that so long as they stayed away from white settlements and so long as the buffalo remained, they could continue to range north of the Arkansas River. The Cheyennes interpreted this to mean they would continue to control the country along the Smoky Hill and Republican rivers of western Kansas and eastern Colorado.[28]

The Dog Soldiers, thus led to believe something opposite what the official treaty stipulated, were satisfied and returned to the document table. As they waited for the Arapahos to begin the signing, however, someone in camp made the tactical mistake of opening the treaty presents prematurely. When the Cheyennes' turn came, not a chief was

Kiowa chief Satanta voices his love for the land at the Treaty of Medicine Lodge (Harper's Weekly, *November 16, 1867*).

present. John Smith was sent flying to find them and bring them back to the table. Even then, Tall Bull refused to sign until Henderson employed the art of flattery, saying the Great Father in Washington would not recognize the treaty if the "great Cheyenne brave" had not signed it.[29]

Tall Bull made his "x" on the document along with thirteen other Cheyenne leaders, including Bull Bear, head leader of the Dog Soldiers, who signed the treaty first ahead of Principal Chief Black Kettle. Absent were Roman Nose and Medicine Arrow, reflecting the suspicion and distrust they still held.[30] And with good reason. Stanley bitterly noted that, as with the Kiowas and Comanches, the Cheyennes and Arapahos had only a hearsay concept of the legal contract they were making in placing their mark on the prepared document:

> The Chiefs have signed it merely as a matter of form. Not one word of the treaty was read to them. How, therefore, can the treaty have been a success. Bull Bear and Buffalo Chief, even while they signed, said: "We hold that country between the Arkansas and the Platte together. We will not give it up yet, as long as the buffalo and elk are roaming the country." Do the above words seem anything like giving up all claims to that country? And yet, if a white man, acting under the knowledge that all that country belongs to the whites, will go and make a home for himself, it will soon be a burning

brand—a signal for war. If war is once thus commenced who are to blame? The commissioners.[31]

Indeed, the Treaty of Medicine Lodge committed the tribes to certain stipulations that, by all evidence, the Cheyennes were far from ready to accept: deliverance of tribal depredators to U.S. officials; a new reservation between the Arkansas and Cimarron rivers in northern Indian Territory; the presence of surveyors on their lands; farming as a means of existence; federal oversight of tribal governance; compulsory education for tribal children; substitution of articles of white man's clothing in lieu of money and annuities; relinquishment of rights to all lands outside the reservation area; and forbearance of wagon trains, stagecoach lines, cattle drives, railroads, military posts, and transportation routes on both their reservation and lands elsewhere.[32]

"What the treaties did," concluded historian William T. Hagan, "was not to provide the peace on the Plains Congress had hoped for but to give the stamp of legitimacy to United States efforts to concentrate the Indians and open the region to white exploitation."[33]

Having thus produced documents the Senate could accept as valid treaties, the peace commission turned its attention back to Indian problems on the Platte and headed once again for Fort Laramie. It left behind in Kansas a situation as troubled as before. Stanley's predictions of more trouble were validated within a year's time. The falsity of the Medicine Lodge treaties was not the only cause for war, however. The commission had not resolved the issues it had set out to resolve. The press of settlements, the intrusion of white transportation, and Dog Soldier militancy continued to create friction on the Kansas frontier. But a new departmental commander, Gen. Phil Sheridan, arrived to replace Hancock. He would give new impetus to the prevailing view on the frontier that the United States government should employ its military might to overwhelm the tribes and remove them to Indian Territory.

Red Cloud's Demand

Father, your young men have gone on the path, and have killed my game and my buffalo. They did not kill them to eat; they left them to rot where they fell. Father, were I to go to your country and kill your cattle, what would you say?
—CROW CHIEF THE BEAR'S TOOTH

The obstinacy of the Cheyenne Dog Soldiers and the trying circumstances of treaty making on the Kansas plains had produced a pretense of agreement with the southern tribes. A similar set of circumstances led to like results with the Sioux and Northern Cheyennes north of the Platte River and yielded still another fraudulent treaty. There, the Oglala Sioux under Red Cloud fiercely resisted white intrusion on the Powder River country, "the only hunting ground left to his nation."[1] Red Cloud insisted that the military garrisons would have to be withdrawn from his region before he would cease to make war and sign a new treaty.

"Red Cloud refused [to agree to the treaty terms]," Lt. George H. Palmer wrote from Fort Phil Kearny in December 1867. "The road which is now untraveled and utterly useless, was established, and the graves of butchered soldiers along the road from Fort Laramie to Fort C. F. Smith, bear witness to the fact that Red Cloud has kept his word."[2]

The N. G. Taylor–led peace commission, with some of its reportorial accompaniment and rejoined by General Sherman, returned to Fort Laramie in November 1867 with the intent of consummating treaties with the Sioux and Northern Cheyennes. Sherman's reinstatement reflected a resurgence of military influence in Indian affairs. When the commissioners reached the Platte River fort, they found that the tribes had not appeared as requested. A party of Crow Indians arrived, however, and the commission met with them on the twelfth. The commissioners and chiefs exchanged speeches, each stating their cause. Chief Bear's Tooth made his position clear:

> Father, listen well. Call your young men back from the Big Horn. It would please me well. Your young men have gone on the path, and have destroyed the fine timber and green grass, and have burnt up the country. Father, your young men have gone on the road, and have killed my game and my buffalo. They did not kill them to eat; they left them to rot where they fell. Father, were I to go to your country and kill your cattle, what would you say?[3]

The peace commission waited at Fort Laramie for the absent Sioux and Northern Cheyennes, but they did not come. The commissioners offered the excuse to Washington that the winter season was too far developed in Wyoming and Montana for the tribesmen to travel such distances with their families. Although this was true, as the commission should have known in advance, the principal reason was Red Cloud's steadfast determination not to treat with the commissioners until every white man had left the Powder River country.[4]

The commission party headed homeward back down the Platte Trail, leaving behind Special Agent H. M. Mathews to hold discussions with the Indians preliminary to the commission's return in the spring. Lieutenant Palmer attended a meeting Mathews held with the Sioux, Cheyennes, and Crows at Fort Phil Kearny on January 2, 1868. In his account, Palmer criticized Mathews for not telling the Indians that the government had offered to withdraw from the Bozeman Trail. He was bitter also that Mathews issued gunpowder and shot to the Indians.

"How many lives the giving of this powder to the Indians will cost," Palmer observed, "we do not know. These repeated failures of making peace with hostile Indians are additional proofs of the folly of both the Interior and War Departments attempting to carry on jointly our Indian Affairs."[5]

The peace commissioner had arrived back at the settlement of North Platte, Nebraska, on November 24. There, Spotted Tail and his Brulé band hosted a dog feast honoring generals Sherman and Harney. The event provided colorful copy for correspondent Stanley, who soon after accepted a challenging new assignment from the *New York Herald* and began his adventures in Africa.[6]

Despite its failure twice to conduct a council with the Sioux and Northern Cheyennes at Fort Laramie, the peace commission regrouped for another effort during the spring of 1868. Once again, runners were sent out to remote corners of present Wyoming and Montana to invite the tribes to meet with the commissioners in April. During that month the commission, accompanied by Father De Smet, entrained at Omaha for Fort Laramie, taking with it a wealth of treaty goods and a treaty document crafted to U.S. demands. Henderson was held in Washington by the impeachment trial of President Andrew Johnson. Sherman, too, was detained temporarily to give testimony, but he eventually joined the others at Fort Laramie.[7]

Dark clouds of conflict loomed ahead of the commission in Wyoming. Only recently, reports of mayhem had been sounded, one telling of an attack by 50 Indians against a ranch on the road between Cheyenne and Fort Fetterman. A boy had been killed and the rancher's wife carried away. Another account told how a party of 100 warriors attacked a ranch but was held off by the two owners' rifles. Two of the attackers were killed along with four horses, but the Indians burned the ranch buildings and stables. The two ranchers escaped to another ranch, where other whites joined them in their flight. An attack and firefight occurred as the party fled, resulting in one white man and five Indians being killed. All the settlers between forts Laramie and Fetterman, it was reported, had taken refuge at those posts.[8]

At North Platte the commission again met with Spotted Tail, who consented to attend the Fort Laramie council only after his band had been issued a copious amount of arms, ammunition, and other goods.[9] Continuing by rail to Cheyenne, Wyoming, and thence overland to Fort Laramie, the commissioners arrived on April 10 and once again found that the tribes had still not assembled as requested. Nor had any shown by the twenty-third.[10] When Spotted Tail and his Brulés finally reached Fort Laramie, the commissioners, desperate to make some headway, met and initiated a treaty with them on April 29.

Sanborn, acting as president pro tem of the commission, wired Sherman, who was on his way west at Omaha: "Everything looks most favorable for peace, with the exception of the small war parties."[11] Hopes for a peaceful resolution increased when the Northern Cheyennes and Northern Arapahos arrived and jointly signed a new treaty on May 10.

By this pact, the two tribes relinquished claim to all territory outside either the new reservation assigned to the Southern Cheyennes and Southern Arapahos in Indian Territory or the reservation most recently assigned to the Brulés. Significantly, however, they were given the triple option of attaching themselves within one year to the Indian Territory reservation, to an agency soon to be established on the Missouri River near Fort Randall, or to the Crow agency near the conflux of Otter Creek and the Yellowstone River. This unresolved issue would resurface as a major cause of conflict in the years ahead when the tribes were removed to Indian Territory and a year later when they made their famous retreat back north. Notable among the Northern Cheyenne signatories were Black Bear, Medicine Man, Little Wolf, White Crow, Little Shield, and Dull Knife. [12]

But the one principal player in the Fort Laramie treaty effort—Red Cloud—still remained resolutely aloof. When runners were again ordered afield with promises of enticing rewards for bands that came in, Red Cloud sent back a message. He and his warriors were waiting in the mountains for the military posts in his country to be evacuated, he said. Only when they were completely abandoned would he meet with the commissioners.[13]

The discouraged commission decided it could wait no longer. Leaving Sanborn, Harncy, and Secretary A. S. White to sign up newcomers, on May 14 the remainder headed off to other assignments: Sherman and Tappan to treat with the Navajos in New Mexico; Augur to meet the Snakes and Shoshones at Fort Bridger, Wyoming; and Terry to forts Randall and Sully, Dakota Territory, to receive the Sioux bands being transferred there.[14]

Word that arms and ammunition were being passed out at Fort Laramie was hard for the tribes to resist. Eventually, other small bands of Sioux and some Northern Arapahos began appearing to place their marks on the treaty and be rewarded with arms, rations, blankets, kettles, axes, knives, and other goods. Gradually, the treaty became more inclusive, and in its final form it bore the title "Treaty with the Sioux—Brulé, Oglala, Miniconjou, Yanktonai, Hunkpapa, Blackfoot, Cuthead, Two Kettle, Sans Arc, and Santee—and Arapaho, 1868." But Red Cloud and other important Sioux leaders did not appear.[15]

In addition to assigning the Sioux to a reservation in Dakota Territory, the lengthy treaty made the usual pledges of peace, punishment of offenders on either side, education of tribal children, farming assistance, annuities, and other rewards from the United States. Of critical importance, the government agreed that the country north of the Platte River and east of the Bighorn Mountains *would remain unceded territory totally excluded to white people.*

Another significant promise was the government's commitment that within ninety days after the conclusion of peace with all the bands of the Sioux nation, the military posts along the Bozeman Trail would be abandoned and the road closed. In truth, the forts had been able to do little more than defend themselves. This bending of the United States to Red Cloud's demands had been done reluctantly by General of the Army Ulysses S. Grant in the interest of railroad construction and national advancement in the West.[16]

On May 25, Sanborn and Harney secured the signatures of a large contingent of Oglala Sioux on the treaty document, including Man-Afraid-of-His-Horses. This done, the two commissioners departed, leaving the pact in the hands of the Fort Laramie commandant, Bvt. Brig. Gen. A. J. Slemmer. It was hoped, with the help of trader Seth Ward and interpreter Charles E. Geren, that Slemmer would achieve this last and most important task. Sanborn and Harney headed back to Omaha, where they boarded the steamboat *Ben Johnson* for Fort Rice on the Missouri River in southern Dakota Territory. During the period July 2–4 they joined Terry in holding another grand council with the Sioux of the Upper Missouri River, including some who came with the commissioners from Fort Laramie.[17]

The Jesuit missionary Father De Smet was sent to the mouth of the Powder River to bring in leaders of the hostile bands. He was escorted by eighty Sioux warriors and several Sioux leaders, including Two Bears, chief of the Yanktonai Sioux, whom De Smet described as "a very remarkable man, from his great zeal for peace, his valor and his eloquence."[18]

De Smet found the hostiles camped at the juncture of the Yellowstone and Powder rivers. Sitting Bull, "generalissimo of the warriors," presided over the camp. Although he received "Black Robe" (De Smet) graciously, he was blunt in his denunciation of the United States, whose very flag the hostiles hated. A major reason for their bitterness, Sitting Bull stated, was "the cruel, unheard of and wholly unprovoked massacre at Fort Lyon [Chivington's Sand Creek attack on the Cheyennes]."[19]

Despite this rancor, De Smet persuaded Sitting Bull, Gall (Co-kam-i-ya-ya, or the Man That Goes in the Middle), and other hostile leaders to accompany him back to Fort Rice, arriving there on June 30, 1868. The peace council convened on July 2. "Fifty thousand Indians were there represented," De Smet observed. "It was the greatest council that had been held on the Missouri in fifty years."[20]

In *Rekindling Camp Fires,* frontiersman Ben Arnold (Connor) described the occasion:

Sioux chief Red Cloud talks with President Ulysses S. Grant at the White House (Harper's Weekly, June 18, 1870).

Indians were already gathering in cavalcades from all directions and making camp as fancy or caprice dictated. Warriors and young men came on horseback; the old men, women, and children came by travois, wagon, and on foot, bringing with them their tents, bedding, dogs, dance costumes, medicine bags, and all other household plunder. Tepees arose as if by magic, while the ponies scattered out to graze and the dogs and children enjoyed themselves underfoot.[21]

A bevy of foodstuff and other presents were unloaded from the commission's steamboat. The hungry tribespeople scrambled forward to take food from the barrels of hardtack, sugar, coffee, beans, sorghum, and pickled pork and the tubs of butter, cases of dried fish, and caddies of tobacco set out on the dock. The dividing of presents consumed much of the day before the council got under way. Harney led the speech making for the commission, doing so in the name of the Great Father. He once again promised to close the Bozeman Trail forts north of the Platte River.

"You are today living in a country owned by the `Great Father,'" Harney told the gathering. "You are his children. He wants you to live on the piece of land reserved for you and live at peace. Today we are to lay before you the plans of the `Great Father.'"[22]

Gall, who had been seriously wounded when the U.S. military attempted to capture him at Fort Berthold, was unimpressed with Harney's rhetoric. He replied with contempt:

> Many of these men before me were at the treaty of Fort Laramie [in 1866]. The promises the "Great Father" made to us there were utterly false. He told us one thing and did another. He told us that the land set aside for us would not be invaded by white people, that we would be unmolested. Did he keep his compact? Before the treaty was a year old the white people built roads and bridges across our best hunting land, without our consent and in [the] face of our protests.[23]

Despite his bitterness, Gall placed his mark on the treaty document along with seventeen other Hunkpapa leaders. Also signing at Fort Rice were ten chiefs for the Blackfoot Sioux, five for the Cutheads, three for the Two Kettles, four for the Sans Arc band, and seven for the Santees.[24] This success greatly pleased the commissioners. Sitting Bull, however, remained adamantly belligerent and refused to sign. This would prove to be a serious failure of the Fort Laramie/Fort Rice treaty.

As the commission returned to Omaha, it received a report from Fort Laramie revealing another disturbing fact: Red Cloud, as well, had not come in to sign the treaty. Accordingly, the commissioners dispatched De Smet, the missionary Rev. Samuel D. Hindman, and interpreter Franc La Framboise—all of whom had been of great assistance at Fort Rice— to Fort Laramie to help commanding officer Maj. William McE. Dye in the critical task of persuading Red Cloud to accept the treaty.

The army's dismantling of the Bozeman Trail forts had already begun. In conveying Grant's edict, General Sherman listed forts Reno and Phil Kearny in Wyoming and Fort C. F. Smith in Montana but excluded

Fort Fetterman, which sat on the south bank of the Platte. The garrison at Fort C. F. Smith fell into formation on July 29 and marched away, leaving the palisaded fort on the Bighorn River vacant. The following morning the Sioux under Red Cloud swooped down and burned the post to the ground. A day later Fort Phil Kearny suffered a similar fate, being torched by the Northern Cheyennes under Little Wolf. Fort Reno, abandoned on August 18, was also destroyed by the Indians.[25]

Red Cloud took his time going to Fort Laramie, continuing to hold out during October and causing peacemakers and the army alike to agitate over his intentions. When the peace commission held its final meeting in Chicago on October 9, the generals, led by Sherman, held the upper hand. With Henderson not present, Taylor and Tappan found themselves a weak minority bucking a military alliance consisting of Sherman, Harney, Terry, Sanborn, and Grant—who was in Chicago and sat in with the commission.[26]

Taylor and Tappan joined in voting for Sanborn's resolution to feed, clothe, and protect the western tribes that accepted their respective agricultural reservations. They also approved the significant resolution submitted by Terry: to recommend to Congress that the government should cease to recognize the Indian tribes as domestic dependent nations and hereafter that all Indians should be individually subject to the laws of the United States except as required by existing treaties.[27]

Likewise, full agreement was given to Terry's resolution that, because of recent outrages in Kansas, the right granted by the Treaty of Medicine Lodge for the Indians to roam and hunt outside their reservation be abrogated. It was agreed further that the military should be used to compel the Indians to go to their reservation.

Dissension arose when Terry submitted a resolution that the Bureau of Indian Affairs be transferred from the U.S. Interior Department to the War Department. Tappan countered with a substitute motion that the Bureau of Indian Affairs be made into either a department of the government or an independent bureau. Tappan's motion was defeated by a five-to-two vote, Tappan and Taylor voting in the affirmative. Terry's resolution carried.

Tappan then sparked heated debate by offering a motion declaring that although the Cheyennes and Arapahos deserved punishment, their action "does not justify the declaration of war against all the Cheyennes or Arapahos, Apaches, Kiowas and Comanches, who seem to be in flight, having no other alternative than that of acting on the defense."[28] It would be recommended to Congress, therefore, not to abrogate any of their treaties and to guarantee all peaceful Indians protection and subsistence.

Sherman in particular took strong exception to this exculpation of recent Cheyenne depredations in Kansas and won even Taylor's vote in defeating the motion six to one. Further, the old soldier pushed through a resolution dissolving the peace commission. Sherman emerged from the meeting as a dominant force in national Indian affairs, particularly when Congress specified that he would be in charge of distributing the funds designated by treaties.[29]

Finally, in early November, Red Cloud arrived at Fort Laramie, accompanied by an impressive entourage of 125 chiefs and headmen. With the peace commission having been dissolved, the treaty process was left basically in the hands of Major Dye and his aides. When the conference got under way, Red Cloud made it clear that he was far more interested in getting powder and lead with which to fight the Crows than in taking part in a treaty. Further, he was not pleased to find he would be dealing with low-ranking officers and not the commissioners.

Aided by the diplomatic efforts of De Smet, Hindman, and La Framboise, Dye made the case that many other Sioux leaders had already signed the treaty. He told Red Cloud that only General Harney had the authority to issue powder and lead to the Sioux, and then only to those who were not at war. That night Dye "gladdened" Red Cloud's delegation with a feast. The next morning the chief, "with a show of reluctance and tremulousness[,] washed his hands with the dust of the floor"[30] and made his mark on the treaty document. He disdained to study the details of the pact, however, and clearly did not fully understand its implications for him and his people, particularly the issue of being removed from their Powder River haunts to a reservation on the Missouri River.[31]

Thus, the 1868 Treaty of Fort Laramie and Fort Rice with the Sioux was finally completed. Once again the peace commission, in the name of the president and the Congress and thus the nation, had consummated a treaty based on an untruth. Although the Bozeman Trail had been closed, the chances of keeping white men out of the country north of the Platte were as unimaginable as keeping them out of western Kansas.

The 1868 Sioux treaty embraced still another significant treaty injustice. The reservation area ceded to the Sioux had encompassed 96,000 acres north of the Niobrara River that had been assigned to the Ponca Indians by their treaty of 1865. In doing so, officials conducted no consultation whatever with the Poncas. When humanitarians railed against this outright theft of Ponca land, the government chose not to right its wrong but instead removed the tribe to Indian Territory in one of the nation's notorious Indian death marches.[32]

Through the presence of General Sherman, aided by the hostility of tribal warring elements, a resurgence of the army's influence on Indian affairs had emerged. South of the Platte, treaty councils gave way to military campaigns under Sheridan and Custer. There, the tenuous peace had, in fact, already begun unraveling. Soon it would do so north of the Platte as well.

CHAPTER SIXTEEN

By a Sweep of the Sword

This amounts to war. If the President does not approve, notify me.
 —GENERAL W. T. SHERMAN

The Treaty of Medicine Lodge in 1867 and the 1868 Treaty of Fort Laramie were the last formal treaties conducted with the Plains tribes. Jealous of the Senate's prerogative to finance and to approve or disapprove such treaties, the U.S. House of Representatives soon enacted legislation, as had been recommended by the 1868 Chicago conference, ending the acceptance of Indian tribes as independent nations.

The rising influence of the military on Indian matters strongly affected this evolution of U.S. policy. A number of northern military men who had risen to political power following the Civil War began to exert their will on national Indian affairs. Significant among these men were Grant, Sherman, and Sheridan. In 1868, with the impeachment of President Andrew Johnson under way and prior to President-elect Ulysses S. Grant taking office, it was Sherman—soon to become general of the army—who directed the course of Indian policy on the Central Plains toward stricter military controls rather than pacification by treaty. "Little Phil" Sheridan, who is said to have fathered the frontier platitude that "the only good Indian is a dead Indian,"[1] became the enforcer through generals such as Nelson Miles, George Armstrong Custer, Ranald Mackenzie, George Crook, and others. He, too, would exert considerable influence on Indian policy behind Sherman.

The Treaty of Medicine Lodge served as a point of demarcation in U.S. relations with tribes south of the Platte River. Before that time, with its military potential wanting, the government had sought to resolve disruptions and disputes by arranging compacts with the tribes. Physical conflicts with bands and tribes had been mostly isolated events, and even though military men were often sent afield to secure predetermined agreements, U.S. Indian policy on the Plains had been constructed principally by civilian government officials.

Even as the Fort Laramie/Fort Rice treaty effort was in progress during mid-August 1868, a large war party consisting of Southern Cheyennes—including some from Black Kettle's band, which had come north into Kansas—along with Arapahos and Sioux, had headed off from western Kansas on a raid against the Pawnees. On the way, however, they found some whiskey and ended up attacking white settlements along the Saline and Solomon rivers. They killed a number of settlers and carried off several women and children as captives.[2] Sherman, commanding the Division of the Missouri at Chicago, considered this a wanton violation of the Treaty of Medicine Lodge. On that basis, he preemptively ordered Sheridan, as commander of the Department of the Missouri at Fort Leavenworth, to drive the tribes in Kansas into Indian Territory and to kill those who resisted.

"This amounts to war," Sherman wired the secretary of war. "If the President [Johnson] does not approve, notify me promptly."[3]

Sheridan devised a plan of operations that would deprive the Indians of a sanctuary by striking both north and south of the Arkansas River simultaneously. By agreement with the Indian Bureau, Fort Cobb in Indian Territory, abandoned by the North during the Civil War, was reactivated to serve as an Indian agency and refuge for bands wishing to remain friendly. Excepted, however, were the Cheyennes and Arapahos. Sherman and Sheridan refused to allow those two tribes, including Black Kettle's band, the benefit of sanctuary.[4]

Sheridan sought and gained authority to enlist a company of frontier scouts under Maj. George A. Forsyth to lead a foray into the Dog Soldier domain of northwestern Kansas and eastern Colorado. A belief persisted that a small number of well-armed white frontiersmen could outfight a superior force of Indians. Not only was the notion dubious— many military men considered the Cheyennes the best fighters on the Plains—but many of the fifty-three men Forsyth had recruited as scouts were green and untested, with no Indian-fighting experience.

On the morning of September 17, 1868, the scouts were at breakfast on Arikaree Fork of the Republican River when they were attacked by a large force of Cheyenne warriors under Roman Nose. The highly lauded war chief was killed during one of several charges on the sandbar island of the creek where the scouts had taken refuge. But the scouts lost several men as well, including Lt. Frederick Beecher and physician Dr. John G. Mooers.[5] The scouts, who remained pinned down on the sandbar for eight days, were driven to eating the rotted flesh of their horses before a force finally arrived to rescue them. Sheridan and the military reported the event as a heroic military victory, but the fiery hero of Shenandoah saw that this was no way to fight Indians.

At the same time Forsyth was in the field, a much larger and better outfitted expedition under Brig. Gen. Alfred Sully, commanding at Fort Larned, invaded northwestern Indian Territory to search for unfriendly Indians to fight. This venture proved inept and ineffective as well. Sully's force consisted of nine companies of Seventh Cavalry and one of Third Infantry. Frontiersmen John S. Smith, Amos Chapman, and Ben Clark served as guides as the long wagon train lumbered south from the Arkansas River to the point where Beaver and Wolf creeks form the North Canadian.

Indian snipers harassed the expedition as it went, but when the cavalry pursued, it found that the army mounts were incapable of catching the agile Indian ponies in the sandhills adjoining the river. Warriors stood on the backs of their animals at a distance and thumbed their behinds at the troops. Finally, his supplies running low, Sully gave up and trudged back to Fort Larned. He had seen twenty or thirty Indians fall from their ponies, he said, and claimed many were killed—even though he admitted, "It is too much the custom to report a very large number of the enemy killed."[6]

Having twice failed to punish the hostiles, Sheridan decided on a three-pronged winter campaign that would catch the Indians in their home camps. The main force led by Sully and Custer, who had been recalled from exile, would drive south from Kansas. Other army units would march from Fort Lyon in Colorado and Fort Bascom, New Mexico. Once Camp Supply was established at the mouth of Wolf Creek in northwestern Indian Territory, Sheridan ordered Custer and the Seventh Cavalry into the field to search for Indians. An early snowstorm had struck and blanketed the countryside as Custer marched southwestward up Wolf Creek and turned south to the Antelope Hills.

There, a scouting party under Maj. Joel Elliott located the trail of a war party heading south. Custer followed it on a forced march to the

Artist's rendering of Crook's battle with the Northern Cheyennes at the Rosebud (Dodge, Our Wild Indians).

Washita River, where his Osage scouts discovered an Indian camp of around fifty lodges. Custer surrounded it during the night and waited until dawn to attack. By prearranged signal, Custer's troops charged the village on the morning of November 27, 1868, driving its occupants from their lodges and killing many. The hapless camp proved to be that of Black Kettle's Cheyennes, which Chivington had struck almost exactly four years earlier at Sand Creek, Colorado. This time Black Kettle and his wife were among the victims.[7]

When the firing had subsided, Custer ordered the village and its accouterments burned. He also destroyed the captured horse herds. Then, as warriors appeared from the Cheyenne, Kiowa, Arapaho, and Comanche camps immediately downstream, Custer feinted a movement forward. As dark began to fall, however, he retreated hurriedly back to Camp Supply with the fifty-three women and children he had captured. He did so without making a determined effort to learn what had become of Major Elliott and a detachment of seventeen men who had charged off from the battlefield in pursuit of Indians.

Although Black Kettle's band represented the peace element of the Cheyennes, Custer, Sheridan, and the military in general hailed the surprise attack as a great military victory. Sheridan built on it by leading the Seventh Cavalry, now accompanied by the Nineteenth Kansas Volunteer Regiment, to old Fort Cobb on the Washita. In revisiting the battlefield, troops found the bodies of Mrs. Clara Blinn and her young son, who had been held captive and killed during the Custer attack. The mutilated bodies of Elliott and his men were found a short distance from the village site.

During the ensuing march to Cobb, a confrontation occurred with a large body of Kiowa warriors under chiefs Satanta and Lone Wolf. Custer took the two Kiowa leaders prisoner and placed them in irons. Sheridan threatened to hang them unless their tribe capitulated. After a short stay at Cobb, the military expedition moved south to the Wichita Mountains and established a new post that eventually became known as Fort Sill. After spending the winter there, Custer led the Seventh Cavalry and Nineteenth Kansas on a foray into the Texas Panhandle, where he rescued two Kansas women who had been captured by the Cheyennes.

Custer's attack on the Cheyennes at the Washita and the killing of Black Kettle rekindled the great debate concerning U.S. Indian policy. Sheridan contended that evidence found in the camp proved that Black Kettle's band had "massacred the settlers on the Saline and Solomon, and perpetrated cruelties too fiendish for recital."[8] Commissioner of Indian Affairs George W. Manypenny countered that neither Custer nor reporter DeB. Randolph Keim, who had been Sheridan's constant companion during the campaign and written extensively on the battle, had mentioned any such evidence.[9]

Another prong of Sheridan's winter campaign under Col. A. W. Evans pushed east from Fort Bascom across the Texas Panhandle to the Wichita Mountains. There, on Christmas Day 1868, scouts discovered a Comanche/ Kiowa tepee village, attacked it, drove the occupants away, and destroyed the camp.[10] Sheridan's invasion and military occupation broke the resistance of the bands in western Indian Territory and forced them to reservations. The Kiowas and Comanches were assigned to an agency at Fort Sill. The Southern Cheyennes and Arapahos were strongly dissatisfied with the area assigned to them by the Treaty of Medicine Lodge. By edict in 1869, President Grant assigned them a new reservation between the North Canadian and Washita rivers. Their new agency on the North Canadian became known as the Darlington agency after its first agent, the Quaker Brinton Darlington.

Sheridan's strike effectively reduced the Indian threat against southern Kansas and the Santa Fe Trail. Cheyenne Dog Soldier leader Tall

Bull, however, refused to give in to the restrictions of a reservation and the military-supported oversight of an agent. During the spring of 1869, he led his eighty-four lodges northward to join the Northern Cheyennes. He was intercepted on June 11 in northeastern Colorado by Maj. A. E. Carr, who earlier had led the third prong of Sheridan's campaign into the Texas Panhandle, without success. Carr's command of Fifth Cavalry and Pawnee scouts attacked Tall Bull's camp by surprise, killing fifty-two of the Cheyennes—including Tall Bull—and capturing around 400 horses and mules. A white captive, Maria Weichell, was rescued by Carr's men, but Susanna Alerdice was found murdered.[11]

As Custer had effectively stifled tribal control over western Indian Territory, so had Carr's victory over Tall Bull effectively ended Cheyenne Dog Soldier dominance over western Kansas and eastern Colorado. Sherman's Indian policy and Sheridan's military enforcement of that policy did much to secure the Santa Fe Trail and western Kansas. But northern and western Texas still remained prey to Indian Territory raiders, particularly those from the Kiowa and Comanche bands.

The Sheridan-Custer campaign, plus widespread corruption among the Indian agents and traders, had ignited a firestorm of criticism from peace advocates and the eastern press. In December 1868 a move to place the Bureau of Indian Affairs under the U.S. Army was defeated in Congress.[12] Upon taking office the following spring, President Grant initiated a significant change in Indian policy, turning administration of Indian affairs over to church groups. He appointed the peace-minded Society of Friends, the Quakers, as custodians over the tribes of the Central Superintendency. Soon the new agents, most of whom had never dealt with Indian people, were making their way to the distant agencies in Nebraska, Kansas, and Oklahoma.[13]

But not even the most determined benevolence could overcome the habits of raiding and war making that had long played a significant role in Plains Indian society. Particularly active were Kiowa and Comanche war parties that continued to raid in Texas and beyond into Mexico. The massacre of a wagon train by a Kiowa party under Satanta between forts Richardson and Griffin in north Texas during May 1871 proved critical. It so happened that at the time, General of the Army Sherman was making a tour of frontier military posts and had gone over the trail only a few hours earlier. Sherman continued on to Fort Sill, where he confronted Satanta and others of the war party. Satanta, Satank, and Big Tree were arrested and placed in irons. As they were being taken off by wagon to face trial at Jacksboro, Texas, Satank rebelled. He was shot and killed by guards. Satanta and Big Tree were sent to prison at Huntsville, Texas.[14]

In September 1872 a delegation consisting of Kiowa, Comanche, Plains Apache, Caddo, Arapaho, and Delaware leaders departed from the Wichita agency on a peace mission to Washington, D.C. In compliance with Kiowa wishes, the government brought Satanta up from Huntsville to St. Louis, where a joyous reunion was held. Satanta was sent back to prison, and the delegation continued on to Washington, where it met with President Ulysses S. Grant and Commissioner of Indian Affairs Francis A. Walker. Kiowa chief Lone Wolf promised that if Satanta and Big Tree were released, his people would remain peaceful. For some time, however, Satanta's release was held up by the governor of Texas, Edmund J. Davis.[15]

Matters continued to deteriorate in western Indian Territory, north Texas, and the Texas Panhandle under the relaxed oversight of the Quakers. The mounting confidence among tribal hostiles came to a head in 1874 with a series of depredations: the murder of a party of surveyors, an attack on a buffalo hunters' camp at Adobe Walls in the Texas Panhandle by a joint war party, and the massacre of Pat Hennessey and three teamsters by a Cheyenne war party. These and other infractions caused Sheridan to organize still another invasion of the region.

In a five-pronged campaign that became known as the Red River War, Gen. Nelson Miles marched southwest from Camp Supply; Col. William Price east from Fort Union, New Mexico; Lt. Col. John W. Davidson west from Fort Sill; Lt. Col. George P. Buell north from Fort Griffin, Texas; and Col. Ranald Mackenzie north from Fort Concho, Texas. Of the several engagements that occurred during late 1874 and early 1875, most involved skirmishes that drove Indians from their villages. Although the Indian deaths were minimal, the tribes suffered severe loss of shelters, living equipment, robes, food, and horses.[16]

A major defeat for the tribes occurred when Mackenzie located a large joint encampment on the floor of Palo Duro Canyon in the Texas Panhandle. On the morning of September 27, his Fourth Cavalry troops descended the steep cliffs of the canyon and launched a surprise attack. After capturing and burning the village and its winter's supply of meat and corn, Mackenzie destroyed most of the 1,414 captured horses and mules that were so vital to tribal existence on the Plains.

Following this, on November 8, Lt. Frank D. Baldwin—a two-time Congressional Medal of Honor winner—attacked a Cheyenne camp on McClellan Creek in the Texas Panhandle, destroyed the village, and rescued two of the four Germain girls who had been taken captive when their family was massacred in Kansas.

By the following spring, virtually all of the hostile bands, starved and defeated, had surrendered at either Fort Sill or Darlington agency. At this point, Sherman introduced a new innovation to U.S. Indian policy. Enlarging upon the occasional practice of incarcerating hostile Indian leaders, he ordered the imprisonment of hostile chiefs and warriors. Seventy-two tribal members were placed in irons and sent to Fort Marion at St. Augustine, Florida, where the Seminole leader Oceola had once been held.[17]

Lt. Richard H. Pratt, who had recently served in the Indian Territory cavalry and had experience with the tribes, was placed in charge of the prisoners at Fort Marion. Pratt eventually founded the Carlisle Indian School in Carlisle, Pennsylvania, dedicated to the acculturation of tribal children to the livelihood and ways of white society.[18]

The Red River War, abetted by the Modoc killing of Gen. Edward Canby and the Reverend Eleasar Thomas during peace talks in California in 1873, reestablished the dominance of U.S. military influence in national Indian affairs. Military officers began replacing the Quakers as Indian agents, and the United States no longer looked to treaty making and policies of pacification to achieve its aims with the now-acquiescent and totally dependent Southern Plains tribes.[19]

The government joined the agency schools under various religious denominations in the goal of assimilating Indian children. There would be no more making formal treaties because the U.S. House of Representatives had nullified the treaty system with an obscure clause in the Indian Appropriation Bill of March 3, 1871: *"Provided.* That hereafter no Indian nation or tribe within the territory of the United States shall be acknowledged or recognized as an independent nation, tribe, or power with whom the United States may contract by treaty."[20]

There would still be disputes and settlements that needed to be worked out and more land that whites wanted—particularly for railroad rights—but these were conducted as "agreements." Ultimately, the Indians of the territory and elsewhere were driven to assume private ownership of lands, drastically altering their traditional tribal systems and modes of life.[21] Many of the agreements forced on them by the Dawes and Jerome commissions still entailed the same manipulations and faults of the old pacts and at times were even worse.

CHAPTER SEVENTEEN

And the Stroke of a Pen

The men the President sends have no heart. What has been done to my country? When we first had this land we were strong, now we are melting like snow on the hillside while you are growing like spring grass.
—OGLALA CHIEF RED CLOUD

When he finally signed the 1868 treaty at Fort Laramie, Red Cloud did so fully intending to remain in the proximity of the Platte River. There, he and his people could continue to trade at Fort Laramie as they had done in years gone by. Even as he made his mark on the treaty, the Sioux leader declared his strong opposition to moving to the new reservation site on the Missouri River.[1] Sherman, on the other hand, fiercely rejected the notion of the Sioux remaining, believing they were a threat to the Platte or to the Wyoming/Montana region, and insisted that they be placed under General Harney at Fort Sully, Dakota Territory.

"Sheridan has knocked the Cheyennes, Arapahoes and Kiowas all to pieces," he said in a letter to General Augur in December 1868, "and they are running for [the] reservation. I think the same process will have to be applied to those Powder River Sioux and by early spring we will have the troops available."[2]

Once again, a significant disconnect occurred between treaty participants. Before signing the document, Red Cloud had stated that he wanted his people, like the whites, to be able to go where they pleased. Further, he had made it clear that he would oppose moving to the Missouri River reservation. The United States, however, stood on its right to relocate the Northern Sioux as provided by the treaty.[3]

Although Sherman remained committed to the use of force to settle the disagreement, Grant and Secretary of Interior Jacob D. Cox looked to another often-used technique for persuading Indian leaders. They suggested that Red Cloud and a few of his chiefs be brought to the nation's capital, where they could be dealt with under more advantageous conditions. Accordingly, in June 1870, Red Cloud's party of sixteen chiefs and four of their wives arrived in Washington. They were surprised to find a delegation under Spotted Tail already there.[4]

By long-standing procedure, Red Cloud and his people were shown the sights of the city, including visits to the Arsenal and the Naval Yard, all designed to impress them with the magnitude of U.S. military power. In a series of meetings with Secretary Cox, Commissioner Ely S. Parker, and eventually Grant himself, Red Cloud eloquently stated the case for his people.

"The men the President sends," he told Cox, "have no heart. What has been done to my country, I do not want [and] do not ask for it. The white children have surrounded me and have left me nothing but an island. When we first had this land we were strong, now we are melting like snow on the hillside while you are growing like spring grass."[5]

The existence of Fort Fetterman still disturbed Red Cloud. As he felt had been promised at Fort Laramie, he demanded that this last "war house" of the white man be removed from his country. In his interview with the president, Grant rejected the idea on the grounds that the post served the interests of both whites and Indians. Disappointed by this much-heralded meeting with the Great Father, the frustrated Red Cloud angrily denounced the recent Fort Laramie treaty as "all lies."[6]

Faced with the total failure of the visit, Cox and Parker managed to pacify Red Cloud with a compromise: instead of going to the Missouri River reservation to receive their goods, the Sioux would be permitted to reside northeast of Fort Fetterman on the headwaters of the Big Cheyenne River. Upon hearing this, Red Cloud recanted and begrudgingly voiced his acceptance of the treaty despite "all the false things in it."[7]

This did not mean, however, that he and other Sioux leaders accepted the treaty stipulation that they forsake their country and move east. This most critical issue remained to irritate and inflame U.S.-Sioux relations. Red Cloud's visit to Washington and later to New York had established him as an Indian icon to many whites, but it was not the same among his own people. A Seventh Cavalry officer reported from

Fort Shaw, Montana, that many of Red Cloud's followers had left him to join Sitting Bull. Another officer suggested one reason: "Red Cloud saw too much [in Washington]. The Indians say that these things cannot be; that the white people must have put bad Medicine over Red Cloud's eyes to make him see everything and anything they please."[8]

In further talks at Fort Laramie, Indian commissioner Felix Brunot refused to supply Red Cloud with the hunting ammunition he requested. The Sioux leader also lost his arguments with the government on both the continuing existence of Fort Fetterman and the wagon road that intruded for a ways along the north bank of the Platte. When he complained of these things and of soldiers cutting hay on his land, Brunot questioned whether he really wanted peace. Red Cloud stated the matter bluntly: "If the Great Father looks after my interest, and keeps white men out of the country, peace will last forever, but if they disturb us there will be no peace."[9]

Red Cloud was also denied his choice of an agent for his people. He did succeed in getting an agency, which bore his name, located on the Platte just west of the Wyoming-Nebraska line. But in 1873, after operating the Red Cloud agency there for only two years, the government moved it north to Nebraska's White River near where Camp Robinson would soon be established.[10]

Red Cloud and Spotted Tail had ended their militant opposition to the government, although both adamantly refused to go to their assigned reservations. Both tribal leaders proved more than capable negotiators, perplexing government officials with their considerable political skills.[11] Many Sioux still held to the north country where Red Cloud's nephew, Crazy Horse, Sitting Bull, Gall, and others had emerged as the new leaders of hostile elements who had either not signed or now rejected the 1868 treaty.[12] Their anger with the United States stemmed from multifold reasons, but in general it emanated from white disregard for Article 16 of the 1868 treaty: "The United States hereby agrees and stipulates that the country north of the North Platte River and east of the summits of the Big Horn Mountains shall be held and considered to be unceded Indian territory, and also stipulates and agrees that no white person or persons shall be permitted to settle upon or occupy any portion of the same without the consent of the Indians[,] first had and obtained, to pass through the same."[13]

The Sioux interpreted this clause to mean they could still freely hunt and range over their homeland north of the Platte and that white men would be kept out. The government and white citizens, however, not only saw certain geographical limitations to the ill-defined territory but found ample reasons for intrusion. Thus, as with the Treaty of Medicine Lodge, the pact established a situation of confusion and misunderstanding that agitated Indian-white relations and led to certain conflict. White ranchers, miners, teamsters, would-be settlers, travelers, soldiers, and other whites who ventured into northern Wyoming and Montana suffered the wrath of Sioux war parties.

A major intrusion in the north of the territory obliquely defined by the treaty was, in fact, already under way. By 1871 surveyors for the Northern Pacific Railroad had arrived at the new town of Bismarck, Dakota Territory, on the Missouri River preparatory to laying out a rail route through the Montana domain of the Sioux. In the face of fierce resistance by the enraged Sioux, army expeditions under Col. David S. Stanley and Lt. Col. George A. Custer served as military escorts for the surveyors. Custer and the Sioux twice fought battles along the Yellowstone River before the debilitating financial Panic of 1873 temporarily shut down the railroad operations.[14]

No sooner had this issue subsided than a new crisis developed to evoke an even more passionate disturbance among the Sioux and Northern Cheyennes. The Black Hills of present South Dakota, long held sacred by the two tribes, had been included within the reservation area assigned to the Sioux by the treaty of 1868. The title was unequivocal; but for all their pine-studded beauty, the Black Hills suffered a severe detriment: to the white man, they smelled of precious ore.[15]

Public clamor for a government investigation into the mineral wealth of the region found support from Phil Sheridan and led to Custer's Black Hills Expedition of 1874. With ten troops of cavalry and two of infantry, Custer explored and mapped the region. Miners with him searched for minerals and found traces of gold in some of the streams. Public reports of the expedition, spiced by memories of bonanzas in California, Colorado, and Montana, excited a similar stampede of white prospectors to the Black Hills. The army made a token but unsuccessful effort to halt the intruders, who soon occupied the lands that legally belonged to the Sioux.[16]

Unable and unwilling to resist popular demand that the Black Hills be opened legally to ownership by U.S. citizens, officials sought desperately to obtain title to the region. In August 1875, Congress employed its most potent weapon: it cut off all subsistence to the Sioux until they agreed to relinquish their treaty claims to the unceded territory and the portion of their reservation west of the 103rd meridian, which included the Black Hills.[17]

In September a commission under Senator W. B. Allison arrived at Fort Robinson with a mandate to purchase not only the Black Hills but the Powder River and Bighorn country as well. But the commissioners found they had walked into a wasp's nest of 20,000 angry Sioux whose discontent was exacerbated by the commission's failure to bring the customary treaty presents. The ensuing councils were both difficult and dangerous. At one point Sioux warrior Little Big Man charged the commission camp, threatening to kill the white men who were attempting to take his land. Chief Young Man Afraid of His Horse (actually, "Young Man Who Is So Brave That His Enemies Fear Even His Horse"), however, arrived with his band of Oglala soldiers and threatened to kill anyone who harmed the commissioners.[18]

The commission soon realized that the Sioux valued the Black Hills far beyond the government's capacity to pay. Further, the Indians strongly suspected that opening the Black Hills to whites would ultimately lead to the same for their entire reservation.[19] Although the 1868 treaty required a favorable vote of a three-fourths majority of the tribe's adult males for amendment,[20] the commissioners concluded that no purchase agreement could possibly be reached with the entire tribe present. Even when the chiefs were met alone in council, they refused either to sell the Black Hills for $6 million or to lease mining rights at $400,000 annually. The Allison group gave up in exasperation, although they were much relieved to be returning home.

In the face of Sioux obstinacy, the government threw off all ethical pretense and laid plans for taking the land by military force. Because of Sioux strikes against the railroad and other intruders into their territory, Sherman recommended that Congress abrogate the 1868 treaty altogether.[21]

"The true policy, in my judgment," a government inspector asserted, "is to send troops against them [the Sioux] in the winter, the sooner the better, and whip them into subjection."[22]

The military found support for such a move even from Commissioner of Indian Affairs Edward P. Smith. On November 3, 1875, a White House meeting involving President Grant, Secretary of War William Belknap, Secretary of Interior Zachariah Chandler, General Sheridan, Gen. George Crook, and Smith was convened to address the Sioux problem. A two-part plan evolved. Troops would be withdrawn from the Black Hills, permitting increased penetration of the region by white gold seekers.[23]

As a result, Smith issued an edict directing that all Indians should abandon the unceded territory and settle on their assigned reservations

Secretary Carl Schurz addresses a Sioux assembly on the Spotted Tail Reservation (Frank Leslie's Illustrated Newspaper, *October 4, 1879).*

within two months. At the same time, a punitive campaign would drive the Sioux and Northern Cheyenne hostiles out of the north country and force them to the reservation. The end purpose of these actions would be to release the United States from commitments it had made by the treaty of 1868, thereby freeing both the unceded territory of Wyoming and Montana as well as the Black Hills to white citizens.[24]

As a first move, in December 1875 the Indian Bureau sent runners afield with orders commanding all tribal members to go to their reservations by January 31, 1876. When the Indians displayed no willingness to comply immediately, Chandler and the Indian Bureau abandoned responsibility for them, giving Sheridan full authority to act.[25]

Hearkening to the success of his winter campaigns in 1868 and 1874 against the southern tribes, Sheridan was determined to hit the Sioux quickly before spring, when the Indians would be even more difficult to catch. Once again he laid plans for a multipronged thrust into Indian-held country. Gen. Alfred H. Terry would strike west up the Yellowstone from Fort Abraham Lincoln on the Upper Missouri, Crook would lead an expedition northward from Fort Fetterman in Wyoming, and Gen. John Gibbon at Fort Ellis, Montana, would drive eastward down the Yellowstone.

The ensuing military campaign brought the defeat of Crook on the Rosebud by Northern Cheyennes and the calamitous massacre of Custer (under Terry) and much of his Seventh Cavalry on the Little Bighorn by Sioux and Northern Cheyennes. Eventually, however, U.S. forces under Crook, striking from the south, and Gen. Nelson A. Miles, who operated from the newly established Fort Keogh on the Yellowstone, were able to strike the Indians in their camps and drive most of the two tribes to the reservation. Sitting Bull and his band took refuge in Canada until starvation finally drove them to return to the United States and surrender.

During 1876 a new commission was sent forth, including former Indian commissioner George W. Manypenny, former Dakota Territory governor Newton Edmunds, and Bishop Henry B. Whipple, long a leading defender of Indian rights. But even this august group found it expedient to breach the treaty of 1868. Meeting with Sioux chiefs at the Red Cloud agency on September 18, the Manypenny commission, in direct violation of the 1868 treaty, satisfied itself with securing their marks alone for the land cession.

Having done their official and moral duty as they saw it, the group reported to the commissioner of Indian affairs: "We finished our labors in the Indian country with our hearts full of gratitude to God, who had guarded us and protected us, and directed our labors to a successful issue."[26] With minds swollen with piousness, the Board of Indian Commissioners praised their work while condemning previous treaty efforts. Oblivious to the blatant betrayal of both Articles 12 and 16 of the 1868 treaty, the board members apparently did not realize that by looking into the historical window of past U.S. Indian treaties they had seen their own reflection when they declared, "We would, if possible, have the public conscience aroused to a full comprehension of the utter want of good faith, the oft-repeated violations of the most sacred promises and agreements, which have characterized the intercourse of this nation with its helpless wards."[27]

Almost as if to validate the charge, in February 1877 Congress passed a bill abrogating Sioux title to the Black Hills, ignoring the treaty pledge that the region "set apart for the absolute and undisturbed use and occupation of the Indians herein named" would be left to the Sioux forever.[28]

The U.S.-Sioux treaty of 1868 was the last with that tribe to be ratified by Congress.[29] There would, however, be a number of agreements whereby the United States sought railroad rights-of-way and, as always, more and more land through diminution of treaty-assigned reservation areas.

By 1870 the peace policy instituted by the Grant administration had been deemed a dismal failure. As the falseness of the treaty system and the corruption of the Indian Bureau became more and more apparent, church reformers' challenges to national Indian policy increased. Also, the idea of placing the War Department in charge of Indian affairs re-emerged, although unsuccessfully.[30]

Even beyond the connivance of the commissioners who conducted the treaties and the officials who instructed them, the carrying out of solemn promises by the government, its agents, and private contractors produced practices that invalidated the government's part of the agreements. Added to this, tribal treaties were commonly broken by invasions of Indian lands by U.S. citizens, and eventually the pacts were ripped asunder by military action. Clearly, at times the penchant of the Indians' young men and war societies to raid and make war instigated conflicts, but in many, perhaps most, cases the root cause of troubles between Indians and whites stemmed from infractions by American citizens acting in violation of treaties initiated and legally confirmed by the federal government.

Government records are filled with testimony to annuities that reeked with weevil-infested flour, hard corn that was virtually unpalatable, corrupted sugar, sick and emaciated beef cows, charred coffee beans, and other spoiled edibles that were the refuse of white society. Promised health care was often extremely limited or nonexistent. The list of U.S. violations to treaty agreements is virtually endless. In its 1872 report, the Board of Indian Commissioners recited a litany of misdeeds occurring under the existing system:

> partnerships between agent and trader, or the agent and contractors;
> receipting for supplies never delivered; overestimating the weight
> of cattle for the contractor; taking vouchers in blank to be filled
> with fraudulent sums; carrying false names on the rolls; paying
> employees for whom there was no employment; reporting employ-
> ees at higher or lower salary than provided by law, and using the
> difference for other purposes; farming out the appointments
> controlled by the agents; using the annuity-goods for the agents or
> employees trading with the Indians, selling them for their own

goods; selling annuity-goods to whites; contriving with others to swindle Indians out of annuities after distribution; having Indian concubines and allowing similar license to employees; and other abuses.[31]

The specifications delineated by solemn treaty were further subject to the whims of an often-parsimonious Congress that could manipulate Indian annuities through its annual appropriation bills. One stark instance of this occurred in bringing an end to the Indian treaty system. The U.S. House of Representatives had long been annoyed that it did not enjoy the same power of treaty ratification as the Senate. Finally, in a move to obtain that stature, the House refused to pass an Indian appropriation bill for fiscal year 1870.[32] The action temporarily denied all Indian tribes the rewards legally due them under the terms of their treaties. This, of course, translated into food being withheld from impoverished families that, confined by troops to reservations, desperately depended on their annuities to avoid starvation.

In enacting its appropriation bill for the following year, the House inserted a clause stating: "That hereafter no Indian nation or tribe within the territory of the United States shall be acknowledged or recognized as an independent nation, tribe, or power with whom the United States may contract a treaty."[33]

Nullification of the system of treaties with native tribes, however, did not, could not, end the need for making legal arrangements. A new terminology was adopted whereby the mechanisms through which legal matters to be worked out were termed "agreements" rather than "treaties."[34] But the stature of the tribes as "dependent nations" had been severely reduced. And although councils with tribal chiefs continued, they became less and less "grand," losing the primitive beauty and glamour of early America.[35]

In the end, the United States won title to the Central Plains by military force, having often failed to do so legitimately on paper. Today, some of the inequities created by Indian treaties have been resolved in courts of law. Some neither time nor money will ever amend. As with slavery, the United States of America cannot erase the stain of its Indian treaty misdeeds on its historical past.

CHAPTER EIGHTEEN

Conclusion: A Racial Parallel

As stated earlier, the concept of making treaties with the many Indian tribes residing on ground now comprising the United States of America may well have been the best available system for resolving the great conflict of vital interests between native and nonnative peoples. Like democracy or even life itself, it was far from perfect and often severely unfair. Yet who among us can suggest anything better? No one can rightly imagine, despite how much the native resident may have wished it, that the European invader would simply go back to where he came from. Equally as impossible would be the hope that the intruders would not multiply and aggressively seek lands that were Indian domain.

Time and again, the U.S. government initiated pacts with tribal groups, assigning them specific land areas, only to return later and abort solemn contracts entered into previously. New demands were made that reduced the Indian homeland or removed the tribes to other localities or to reservations. The demise of Indian lands during the nineteenth century is a stark feature of U.S. history, nothing less than a racial parallel to the practice of slave ownership.

The only apparent alternative to the treaty system, however, would have been an overt military conquest in which the European immigrant, it appears—coming as he did from a far more advanced world of armament and weaponry—would have ultimately succeeded. This, it could be argued, is what did occur in essence, although achieved under the guise of a constructed legal instrument—the formal treaty.

The conquest of Indian tribes in Latin America and the Caribbean islands differed from that in North America. There, the European invader principally sought gold and riches rather than territory to colonize, and his intrusions were even more harsh and brutal than in North America.

The great faults of Indian treaty making were (1) the political deception and dishonesty often employed in the pursuit of territorial agreements; (2) the failure of both government officials and the general public to honorably fulfill solemn treaty commitments faithfully, as promised by the executive branch and fully consented to by Congress; and (3) the woeful effects of treaty-designated displacements and removals on Indian people.

Despite its many faults, however, the Indian treaty did offer more than outright oppression. Most important, it avoided the potential of outright genocide and other grievous defects of pure brute force. It is significant as well that formal treaties bound the United States legally to certain obligations that, even though originally evaded, have stood in place to provide belated remedy in the longer course of history.

Even today, many native descendants feel they were cheated and robbed of their land. It is difficult indeed to read history honestly and deny the existence of much truth in this charge. Nor is it necessary to rely upon the Indians' oral accounts of the past as evidence. The white man's own records—the words and actions of non-Indian participants documented in archives and libraries—bear unequivocal testimony to endless fallacies and indiscretions in the making and conduct of Indian treaties.

But this is not to cast unredeeming indictment against all of those involved. The range of reproach for treaty malfeasance spans the spectrum from damnable guilt to innocent miscalculation, with many persons in between who believed—sometimes rightly and many times wrongly—they were acting for the Indians' good within the moral boundaries of the Christian faith they professed.

Nor is this to say that the Indian was completely void of fault. His, we must surely admit, was the right to defend his homeland and his people. But the inclination of young tribal members to war indiscriminately created fear and animosity among non-Indians and exacerbated the conflict and bloodshed on both sides. Any charge that can be made against the Indian warrior for illegal or inhumane acts, however, can be countered with similar instances of white atrocities.

A great structural flaw in the Indian treaty process lay in the issue of oversight and responsibility. As Lincoln commented to Cheyenne chief Lean Bear in 1863 at Washington, it was not always possible for any father to control his children—that is, his soldiers and citizens on the Plains. Not only distance but also the slowness of communication of that day created a troublesome disconnect between policy decisions at the highest level and actions of soldiers and civilians in the field. Thus, conflicts on the distant frontier were often initiated by individuals who were subject to little or no restraint in regards to stipulations set forth in a treaty.

The tribes themselves suffered from a loose system of tribal governance. White people generally thought tribal chiefs had the authority to autocratically represent and control their tribal body. In the main, both assumptions were false. Treaty-making decisions were subject to the approval of other chiefs or, at times, the full tribe. Chiefs normally possessed an essentially persuasive power, measured largely by the stature they held within the tribe.

Although the chief was generally a man who had been a great warrior at one time, as a tribal leader he was largely responsible for the peace and security of the tribe. Seldom did he have a police entity to enforce his wishes, although some tribes maintained light-horsemen. Thus, although a Plains Indian chief could represent his people in a treaty council, he had little power to enforce the commitments an agreement he made placed upon his tribe. Although he could influence and persuade other chiefs, he seldom had restraining control over warrior clans, which were reared body and soul to hunt and make war—both vital activities for tribal survival.

Such was the case of Cheyenne principal chief Black Kettle, who was actually a member of the Suhtai band that had joined the Cheyennes in the early nineteenth century. Although he was a noted warrior as a younger man, he lost face following the Sand Creek disaster and was unable to restrain the powerful Dog Soldier war society. He could still sign treaties at the Little Arkansas in 1865 and at Medicine Lodge in 1867, but he exercised direct influence over his one band only—and even then not over his young men.

Sioux chief Red Cloud maintained a strong tribal following so long as he forcibly resisted white encroachment onto Sioux lands. When at long last Red Cloud won concessions from the government and signed the Fort Laramie treaty of 1868, Crazy Horse and Sitting Bull emerged as principal leaders. Among the Kiowas, Satanta, Lone Wolf, and Maman-ti continued to head the warrior element of the tribe even as Kicking Bird and Stumbling Bear, both noted warriors, sought to make peace.

Still, the most severe breakdown of Indian treaties, as indicated earlier, lay in the posttreaty intrusion onto Indian-designated areas by military expeditions such as Custer's Black Hills venture, gold seekers, land speculators, white home seekers, railroads, and others in violation of treaty agreements. At times, these occurred in spite of government efforts to restrain them. On occasion, they took place with the full recognition and approval of government officials. In many instances, the public was badly misled concerning government title to or control of certain lands.

The historical time frame of the Plains Indian treaty period—essentially from 1815 to 1871—bears heavily on its character. During this expansion period of U.S. history, the nation at large permitted and fully believed in the enslavement of African-descended people. Likewise, even white women were held to a societal substandard that prohibited voting and severely limited their participation in economic affairs.

These social injustices stemmed directly from the majority-accepted attitude of white-male superiority. Thus, it is little wonder that Native Americans were broadly considered an inferior race that was far less deserving of basic rights and land ownership than its white counterparts. Churchmen and military officers who served as peace commissioners tried at times to overcome this innate fallacy in conducting treaties. Still, the fundamental belief of racial inequality invariably meshed with the desire to serve the government's end in manipulating the provisions of a given treaty.

It is to the credit of the United States that over the years it has been able to overcome some of its gross imperfections of governance and public attitude. Its consideration of the now-citizen native has improved, and some long-standing treaties have been readdressed in courts of law. Today, many Native Americans have emerged to win recognition as writers, artists, lawyers, doctors, teachers, soldiers, and government figures, as well as in other roles of American life.

Even yet, however, much of the U.S. Indian population exists apart from the main body of American society, cast onto isolated reservations by treaties devised behind the force of arms. Although many Native Americans may prefer their separation from outside society, there still lingers the Jeffersonian hope that one day the Indian and non-Indian can live together in mutual respect.

Plains Indian Treaties With the United States, the Republic of Texas, and the Confederate States of America to 1871

K = Kappler, comp., *Indian Treaties*
D&D = Deloria and DeMallie, *Documents of American Indian Diplomacy,* 2 vols.
CSA = Confederate States of America
MS/OHS = Manuscript Division, Oklahoma Historical Society

ANADARKO INDIANS

August 12, 1861, at Wichita agency, near present Anadarko, Oklahoma—CSA—
D&D 1: 630–635

APACHE INDIANS—SEE KIOWA APACHE, LIPAN APACHE

ARAPAHO INDIANS (AS UNIFIED TRIBE)—SEE ALSO
NORTHERN ARAPAHO, SOUTHERN ARAPAHO

September 17, 1851, at Horse Creek east of Fort Laramie, Nebraska—Treaty of
Fort Laramie—*K: 594–596*
September 18, 1859, at Upper Platte agency, Deer Creek, Neb. Terr.—Rejected
by Congress—*Sen. Ex. Doc. 35, 36/1, 9-11; D&D 2: 858–886*

ARIKARA INDIANS

July 18, 1825, at Arikara village on Upper Missouri River—*K: 237–238* September 17, 1851, at Horse Creek east of Fort Laramie, Nebraska—Treaty of Fort
Laramie—*K: 594–596*

July 27, 1866, at Fort Berthold, Dak. Terr.—Unratified—*K: 1052–1056; D&D 2: 1379–1383*

ASSINIBOINE INDIANS

September 29, 1826, at Mandan village on Upper Missouri River, North Dakota—Unratified— *D&D 2: 1247–1248*

September 17, 1851, at Horse Creek east of Fort Laramie, Nebraska—Treaty of Fort Laramie—*K: 594–596*

July 18, 1866, at Fort Union, Mont. Terr.—Unratified—*K: 702–705; D&D 2: 1376–1379*

CADDO INDIANS

July 1, 1835, at Caddo agency, near present Shreveport, Louisiana—*K: 432–434*

May 28, 1843, at Tehuacana Creek, near present Waco, Texas—Republic of Texas—*D&D 1: 576–578*

September 29, 1843, at Bird's Fort, near present Fort Worth, Texas—Republic of Texas—*D&D 1: 579–582*

October 9, 1844, at Tehuacana Creek, near present Waco, Texas—Republic of Texas—*D&D 1: 582–585*

May 15, 1846, at Council Springs, near present Waco, Texas—Treaty of Comanche Peak—*K: 554–557*

December 10, 1850, at Spring Creek, tributary of San Saba River, Texas—Unratified—*D&D 2: 1270–1275*

October 28, 1851, on San Saba River, Texas—Unratified—*D&D 2: 1293–1296*

CHEYENNE INDIANS (AS UNIFIED TRIBE)—SEE ALSO NORTHERN CHEYENNE, SOUTHERN CHEYENNE

July 6, 1825, at mouth of Teton River (Bad River), Dak. Terr. at present Pierre, South Dakota—*K: 232–234*

September 17, 1851, at Horse Creek east of Fort Laramie, Nebraska—Treaty of Fort Laramie—*K: 594–596*

COMANCHE INDIANS

August 24, 1835, at Camp Holmes, I.T., Oklahoma—*K: 435–439*

May 29, 1838, at Houston, Texas—Republic of Texas—*D&D 1: 572–574*

August 9, 1843, on Red River—Republic of Texas—*D&D 1: 578–579*

October 9, 1844, at Tehuacana Creek, near present Waco, Texas—Republic of Texas—*D&D 1: 582–585*

May 15, 1846, Treaty of Comanche Peak at Council Springs, near present Waco, Texas—*K: 554–557*

May 9, 1847, at Fredericksburg, Texas (with German Emigration Company)—
D&D 2: 1493–1494

December 10, 1850, at San Saba, Texas—Unratified—*D&D 2: 1270–1275*

October 28, 1851, at Spring Creek, tributary of San Saba River, Texas—Unratified
—*D&D 2: 1293–1296*

July 27, 1853, at Fort Atkinson on Arkansas River west of present Dodge City,
Kansas—*K: 600–602*

August 12, 1861, at Wichita agency, I.T., near present Anadarko, Oklahoma—
CSA—*D&D 1: 630–635*

October 18, 1865, at mouth of Little Arkansas River, present Wichita, Kansas—
K: 892–895

October 21, 1867, at Medicine Lodge Creek, near Medicine Lodge, Kansas—*K:
977–984*

GROS VENTRE (HIDATSA) INDIANS

July 30, 1825, at Lower Mandan village on Upper Missouri River, North Dakota—*K: 125*

September 17, 1851, Treaty of Fort Laramie at Horse Creek east of Fort Laramie,
Nebraska—*K: 594–596*

July 27, 1866, at Fort Berthold, Dak. Terr.—Unratified—*K: 1052–1056; D&D 2:
1379–1383*

July 13, 1868, at Fort Hawley, Mont. Terr.—Rejected by Congress—*K: 705–708;
D&D 2: 937–940*

HAINAI INDIANS—SEE IONI INDIANS

IONI (HAINAI) INDIANS

February 23, 1836, at Colonel Bowles village on Neches River, northeast Texas—
Republic of Texas—*D&D 1: 566–568*

March 28, 1843, at Tehuacana Creek, near Waco, Texas—Republic of Texas—
D&D 1: 576–578

September 29, 1843, at Bird's Fort, near present Fort Worth, Texas—Republic of
Texas—*D&D 1: 579–582*

October 9, 1844, at Council Springs, near present Waco, Texas— Treaty of
Comanche Peak—Republic of Texas—*K: 554- 557*

October 28, 1851, on San Saba River, Texas—Unratified—*D&D 2: 1293–1296*

KANSA (KAW) INDIANS

October 28, 1815, at Portage des Sioux, near St. Louis, Missouri—*K: 123–124*

June 3, 1825, at St. Louis, Missouri—*K: 222–225*

August 16, 1825, at Sora Kansas Creek, near Fort Osage, Missouri—*K: 248–250*
January 14, 1846, at Methodist Mission, Kan. Terr.—*K: 552–554*
October 5, 1859, at Kansas agency, Kan. Terr.—*K: 800–803*
March 13, 1862, at Kansas agency, Kansas—*K: 829–830*
June 11, 1864, at Washington, D.C.—Rejected by Congress—*D&D 2: 875–879*
February 13, 1867, at Washington, D.C.—Rejected by Congress—*D&D 2: 893–895*
March 13, 1869, at Kansas (Kaw) agency, Kansas—Rejected by Congress—*D&D 2: 971–974*

KIOWA INDIANS

May 26, 1837, at Fort Gibson, I.T., Oklahoma—*K: 489–491*
July 27, 1853, at Fort Atkinson on Arkansas River of present Dodge City, Kansas—*K: 600–602*
April 6, 1863, at Washington, D.C.—Rejected by Congress—*D&D 2: 867–869*
October 18, 1865, at mouth of Little Arkansas River at present Wichita, Kansas—*K: 892–895*
October 21, 1867, at Medicine Lodge Creek, near Medicine Lodge, Kansas—*K: 977–984*

KIOWA APACHE (ALSO KNOWN AS PLAINS APACHE, PRAIRIE APACHE) INDIANS

May 26, 1837, at Fort Gibson, I.T., Oklahoma—*K: 489–491*
July 27, 1853, Fort Atkinson on Arkansas River west of present Dodge City, Kansas—*K: 600–602*
April 6, 1863, at Washington, D.C.—Rejected by Congress—*D&D 2: 867–869*
October 17, 1865, at mouth of Little Arkansas River at present Wichita, Kansas (signed Cheyenne and Arapaho treaty)—*K: 892–895*
October 21, 1867, at Medicine Lodge Creek, near Medicine Lodge, Kansas—*K: 977–984*

KICHAI (KITSAI, KEECHI) INDIANS

September 2, 1838, at mouth of Washita River, I.T., Oklahoma—Republic of Texas—*D&D 1: 574–575*
May 15, 1846, at Council Springs, near present Waco, Texas—Treaty of Comanche Peak—*K: 554–557*
August 12, 1861, at Wichita agency, near present Anadarko, Oklahoma—CSA—*D&D 1: 630–635*

LIPAN APACHE INDIANS

January 8, 1838, at Live Oak Point, Live Oak Co., Texas—Republic of Texas—*D&D 1: 569–571*

October 9, 1844, at Tehuacana Creek, near present Waco, Texas—Republic of Texas—*D&D 1: 582–585*

May 15, 1846, Treaty of Comanche Peak at Council Springs, near present Waco, Texas—*K: 554–557*

December 10, 1850, at Spring Creek, tributary of San Saba River, Texas—Unratified—*D&D 2: 1270–1275*

October 28, 1851, on San Saba River, Texas—Unratified—*D&D 2: 1293–1296*

MANDAN INDIANS

July 30, 1825, at Mandan village, Upper Missouri River, North Dakota—*K: 242–244*

September 17, 1851, at Horse Creek east of Fort Laramie, Nebraska—Treaty of Fort Laramie—*K: 594–596*

July 27, 1866, at Fort Berthold agency, Dak. Terr.—Unratified—*K: 1052–1056; D&D 2: 1379–1383*

NORTHERN ARAPAHO INDIANS

May 10, 1868, at Fort Laramie, Wyoming—*K: 1012–1015*

NORTHERN CHEYENNE INDIANS

September 18, 1859, at Upper Platte agency, Deer Creek, Neb. Terr.—Rejected by Congress—*D&D 2: 858–860*

June 28, October 11, 1866, at Fort Laramie, Wyoming—Unratified—*D&D 2: 1370–1373*

May 10, 1868, at Fort Laramie, Wyoming—*K: 1012–1015*

OMAHA INDIANS

July 20, 1815, near St. Louis, Missouri—*K: 115–116*

October 6, 1825, at Fort Atkinson, Council Bluffs, Mich. Terr.—*K: 260–262*

July 15, 1830, at Prairie du Chien, Wisconsin—*K: 305–310*

October 15, 1836, at Bellevue, Upper Missouri River, Nebraska—*K: 479–481*

January 27, 1854, at Council Bluffs agency, Nebr. Terr.—*D&D 2: 1301–1304*

March 16, 1854, at Washington, D.C.—*K: 611–614*

March 6, 1865, at Washington, D.C.—*K: 872–873*

OSAGE (GREAT AND LITTLE) INDIANS

November 10, 1808, at Fort Clark (Osage, Missouri)—*K: 95–99*

September 12, 1815, at Portage des Sioux, Mo. Terr.—*K: 119–120*

September 25, 1818, at St. Louis, Missouri—*K: 167–168*

August 31, 1821, at Marais de Cynges, Missouri—*K: 201–202*
June 2, 1825, at St. Louis, Missouri—*K: 217–221*
August 10, 1825, at Council Grove, Missouri—*K: 246–248*
January 5, 1835, at Fort Gibson, I.T., Oklahoma—Unratified—*D&D 2: 1258–1263*
August 24, 1835, at Camp Holmes, I.T., near Norman, Oklahoma—*K: 435–439*
January 11, 1839, at Fort Gibson, I.T., Oklahoma—*K: 525–527*
August 29, 1863, at Leroy, Kansas—rejected by Osages—*D&D 2: 1031–1036*
September 13, 1865, at Fort Smith, Arkansas—Unratified—*D&D 2: 1344–1358*
September 29, 1865, at Canville Trading Post, Kansas—*K: 878–883*
May 27, 1868, at Drum Creek, Kansas—Rejected by Congress—*D&D 2: 918–926*

PAWNEE INDIANS

June 18, 1818, at St. Louis, Missouri—*K: 156–157*
September 30, 1825, at Fort Atkins, Council Bluffs, Mich. Terr.—*K: 258–260*
October 9, 1833, at Grand Pawnee village on Platte River, Nebraska—*K: 416–418*
August 6, 1848, at Fort Childs, Nebr. Terr.—*K: 571–572*
September 24, 1857, at Table Creek, Nebr. Terr.—*K: 764–767*

PONCA INDIANS

June 25, 1817, at St. Louis, Missouri—*K: 140*
June 9, 1825, at mouth of White Paint Creek (now Bazile Creek) in northeastern
    Nebraska—*K: 225–227*
March 12, 1858, at Washington, D.C.—*K: 772–775*
March 10, 1865, at Washington, D.C.—*K: 875–876*

SIOUX INDIANS

September 23, 1805, at mouth of St. Peters River, Indiana Terr.—*K: 1031*
July 18, 1815, at Portage des Sioux, near St. Louis, Missouri (Teton band)—*K:
    112–113*
July 19, 1815, at Portage des Sioux, near St. Louis, Missouri (Sioux of the Lakes)—
    K: 113
July 19, 1815, at Portage des Sioux, near St. Louis, Missouri (Sioux of St. Peter's
    River)—*K: 114*
July 19, 1815, at Portage des Sioux, near St. Louis, Missouri (Yankton Sioux)—
    K: 115
June 1, 1816, at St. Louis, Missouri (Eastern band)—*K: 128*
August 9, 1820, at St. Peters, Mich. Terr.—Unratified—*D&D 2: 1246–1247*
June 22, 1825, at Fort Lookout, Missouri (Teton, Yanton, Yanktonai bands)—*K:
    227–230*
July 5, 1825, at mouth of Teton River (Bad River), Dak. Terr., at present Pierre,
    South Dakota (Oglala band)—*K: 230–232*

July 16, 1825, Hunkpapa band at Arikara village on Missouri River, North Dakota—*K: 235–236*

August 19, 1825, at Prairie du Chien, Mich. Terr., Wisconsin—*K: 250–255*

July 15, 1830, at Prairie du Chien, Mich. Terr., Wisconsin (Mdewakanton, Santee, Sisseton, Yankton bands)—*K: 305–310*

September 10, 1836, at unnamed site—*K: 466–467*

October 15, 1836, Yankton band at Bellevue, Upper Missouri River, Nebraska—*K: 479–481*

November 30, 1836, Mdewakanton, Santee, Wahpekute bands at Bellevue, Upper Missouri River, Nebraska—*K: 481–482*

September 29, 1837, at Washington, D.C. (Sioux of the Mississippi River)—*K: 493–494*

October 21, 1837, at Washington, D.C. (Yankton band)—*K: 496–497*

July 31, 1841, at Oeyoowarha, Iowa (Eastern mixed-bloods, Sisseton, Wahpekute bands)—Unratified—*D&D 2: 787–790*

August 11, 1841, at Mendota, Minn. Terr. (Mdewakanton band)—Rejected by Congress—*D&D 2: 790–791*

October 9, 1849, at Mendota, Minn. Terr. (Eastern mixed-bloods)—Rejected by Congress—*D&D 2: 791–798*

July 23, 1851, at Traverse des Sioux, Minn. Terr. (Sisseton, Wahpekute bands)—*K: 588–590*

August 5, 1851, at Mendota, Minn. Terr. (Mdewakanton band)—*K: 591–593*

September 17, 1851, at Horse Creek east of Fort Laramie, Nebraska—Treaty of Fort Laramie—*K: 594–596*

March 1–5, 1856, Blackfeet band at Fort Pierre, Northwest Terr., South Dakota—*House Ex. Doc. 130, 34/1, 6–8*

April 19, 1858, at Washington, D.C. (Yankton band)—*K: 776–781*

June 19, 1858, at Washington, D.C. (Medawakanton and Wahpahoota bands)—*K: 781–785*

September 18, 1859, at Upper Platte agency, Deer Creek, Nebr. Terr. (Brule, Oglala, and Wasagaha bands)—Unratified—*D&D 2: 858–860*

October 10, 1865, Minniconjou band at Fort Sully, Dak. Terr.—*K: 883–884*

October 19, 1865, Blackfeet band at Fort Sully, Dak. Terr.—*K: 898–899*

October 19, 1865, Two Kettle band at Fort Sully, Dak. Terr.—*K: 896–897*

October 20, 1865, Sans Arc band at Fort Sully, Dak. Terr.—*K: 899–901*

October 20, 1865, Hunkpapa band at Fort Sully, Dak. Terr.—*K: 901–903*

October 20, 1865, Yanktonai band at Fort Sully, Dak. Terr.—*K: 903–904*

October 28, 1865, Upper Yanktonai band at Fort Sully, Dak. Terr.—*K: 905–906*

October 28, 1865, Oglala band at Fort Sully, Dak. Terr.—*K: 906–908*

June 27, 1866, Brule, Oglala bands at Fort Laramie, Wyoming—Unratified—*D&D 2: 1368–1370*

February 19, 1867, Sisseton, Wahpeton bands at Washington, D.C.—*K: 956*

April 29, 1868, Brule, Oglala, Minniconjou, Yanktonai, Hunkpapa, Cuthead, Two Kettle, Sans Arc, and Santee bands at Fort Laramie, Dak. Terr.—*K: 998*

SOUTHERN ARAPAHO INDIANS

February 18, 1861, at Fort Wise (Fort Lyon), Kan. Terr. (Colorado)—*K: 807–811*

October 14, 1865, at mouth of Little Arkansas River, Wichita, Kansas —*K: 887–891*

October 28, 1867, at Medicine Lodge Creek, near Medicine Lodge, Kansas—*K: 984–989*

SOUTHERN CHEYENNE INDIANS

February 18, 1861, at Fort Wise (Fort Lyon), Kan. Terr. (Colorado)—*K: 807–811*

October 14, 1865, at mouth of Little Arkansas River at site of present Wichita, Kansas—*K: 887–892*

October 28, 1867, at Medicine Lodge Creek, near Medicine Lodge, Kansas—*K: 984–989*

TAWAKONI (TAWACANO, TOWACANAI, TOWOCARRO) INDIANS

May 26, 1837, at Fort Gibson, I.T., Oklahoma—*K: 489–491*

September 2, 1838, at mouth of Washita River, I.T., Oklahoma—Republic of Texas—*D&D 1: 574–575*

March 28, 1843, at Tehuacana Creek, near Waco, Texas—Republic of Texas—*D&D 1: 576–578*

September 29, 1843, at Bird's Fort, near Fort Worth, Texas—Republic of Texas—*D&D 1: 579–582*

October 9, 1844, at Tehuacana Creek, near Waco, Texas—Republic of Texas—*D&D 1: 582–585*

November 16, 1845, at Torrey's Trading Post No. 2 on Brazos River—Republic of Texas—*D&D 1: 585–586*

May 15, 1846, at Council Springs, near present Waco, Texas—Treaty of Comanche Peak—*K: 554–557*

December 10, 1850, at Spring Creek, tributary of San Saba River, Texas—Unratified—*D&D 2: 1270–1275*

October 28, 1851, on San Saba River, Texas—*D&D 2: 1293–1296*

August 12, 1861, at Wichita agency, near present Anadarko, Oklahoma—CSA—*D&D 1: 630–635*

TONKAWA INDIANS

November 22, 1837, at Bexar, Texas—Republic of Texas—*D&D 1: 571–572*

April 10, 1838, at Houston, Texas—Republic of Texas—*D&D 1: 571–572*

May 15, 1846, at Council Springs, Texas—Treaty of Comanche Peak—*K: 554–557*

WACO INDIANS

September 2, 1838, near mouth of Washita River, I.T., Oklahoma—Republic of Texas—*D&D 1: 574–575*

March 28, 1843, at Tehuacana Creek, near Waco, Texas—Republic of Texas—*D&D 1: 576–578*

September 29, 1843, at Bird's Fort, near present Fort Worth, Texas—Republic of Texas—*D&D 1: 579–582*

October 9, 1844, at Tehuacana Creek, near Waco, Texas—Republic of Texas—*D&D 1: 582–585*

November 16, 1845, at Torrey's Trading Post No. 2 on Brazos River—Republic of Texas—*D&D 1: 585–586*

May 15, 1846, at Council Springs, near present Waco, Texas—Treaty of Comanche Peak—*K: 554–557*

December 10, 1850, at Spring Creek, tributary of San Saba River, Texas—Unratified—*D&D 2: 1270–1275*

October 28, 1851, (party to) on San Saba River, Texas—*D&D 2: 1293–1296*

August 12, 1861, at Wichita agency near present Anadarko, Oklahoma—CSA—*D&D 1: 630–635*

WICHITA INDIANS

August 24, 1835, at Camp Holmes, I.T., near Norman, Oklahoma—*K: 435–439*

September 2, 1838, near mouth of Washita River, I.T., Oklahoma—Republic of Texas—*D&D 1: 574–575*

March 28, 1843, at Tehuacana Creek, near Waco, Texas—Republic of Texas—*D&D 1: 576–578*

November 16, 1845, at Torrey's Trading Post No. 2 on Brazos River—Republic of Texas—*D&D 1: 585–586*

May 15, 1846, at Council Springs, near present Waco, Texas—Treaty of Comanche Peak—*K: 554–557*

October 28, 1851, (party to) on San Saba River, Texas—*D&D 2: 1293–1296*

August 12, 1861, at Wichita agency, near present Anadarko, Oklahoma—CSA—*D&D 1: 630–635*

Notes

CofIA = Commissioner of Indian Affairs
HR = House of Representatives
KHS = Kansas Historical Society
LR = Letters received
NA = National Archives
OHS = Oklahoma Historical Society
OIA = Office of Indian Affairs
RG = Record Group
WHC/OU = Western History Collection, University of Oklahoma

PREFACE

1. Prucha, *The Great Father* 1: xxviii.
2. Ibid., 194, citing Israel, *State of the Union Messages* 1: 308–310.
3. Royce, *Cherokee Nation*, 81–82; *U.S. Statutes at Large* 7: 148–149.
4. Cohen, *Handbook of Federal Indian Law*, 46–47.
5. Horsman, *Race and Manifest Destiny*, 2.
6. White Americans seldom realized that they themselves were but a few generations removed from tribal clans in Europe and elsewhere. The invention of the Cherokee Syllabary by Seqouyah during the 1820s persuaded some

Americans to respect native intellect, but they respected only a few and mostly in an abstract sense.

CHAPTER I

1. Prucha, *The Great Father* 1: 169–177.
2. Walker, "The Indian Question," 8–9.
3. Whipple, "The Indian System," 450–451.
4. Slattery, *Felix Reville Brunot*, 156.
5. Deloria and DeMallie, *Documents* 1: 177.
6. *Peace treaty* was a long-standing term relating to agreements worked out for the purpose of ending hostilities between organized states with governmental bodies. With such, peace was usually the essential goal. In treaties initiated by the United States with Indian tribes, an end to Indian warfare was always desired; but in the main the government inevitably sought to obtain certain nationalistic benefits. It never promised to curtail its own use of military force.
7. Prucha, *Indian Policy in the United States*, 99–100.
8. Ibid., 103.
9. In *Documents*, 1: 9, Deloria and DeMallie cite the use of a bright silver covenant chain used by colonial officials to symbolize the need to brighten relationships that had become dirty or tarnished through acts of bad faith.
10. "A Treaty Between Virginia and the Catawbas and Cherokees, 1756," 238–239.
11. Williams, *Henry Timberlake's Memoirs*, 59.
12. *New American State Papers, Indian Affairs* 1: 41.
13. *American Magazine*, October 1760, 118–119.
14. Williams, "Tatham's Characters," 177–178.
15. *CofIA Report, 1872*, 98–99.
16. *Friends' Review* 27 (June 17, 1874): 716.
17. Deloria and DeMallie, *Documents* 1: 177.
18. Ibid., 179.
19. Ibid., 180.
20. Schmeckebier, *Office of Indian Affairs*, 60–61.
21. Jackson had once personally gained a tract of Creek Indian land as a treaty negotiator.
22. Satz, *American Indian Policy in the Jacksonian Era*, 99–100.
23. Dodge Report, *Sen. Ex. Doc. 1*, 23/2: 87.
24. Schmeckebier, *Office of Indian Affairs*, 59.
25. Schoolcraft, *Personal Memoirs*, 383.
26. Miles to CofIA, January 17, 1881, *Sen. Ex. Doc. 34*, 46/3: 2.
27. Hoig, *Battle of the Washita*, 36–38, citing Henry M. Stanley, *New York Tribune*, November 8, 1867.
28. Schmeckebier, *Office of Indian Affairs*, 61.
29. For a detailed account, see Hagan, *Taking Indian Lands*.

CHAPTER 2

1. Even as Lewis and Clark made their way back down the Upper Missouri in 1806, an interesting intertribal peace council was being conducted in the region. Such attempts to settle differences among themselves were vital to the tribes of the Plains, which warred perpetually with one another, and their peace councils were conducted with great deliberation and style. Canadian trader Alexander Henry provided a graphic account of the peacemaking effort. See Coues, ed., *New Light on the Early History of the Greater Northwest*, 354–355.

2. "Extracts From the Diary of Major Sibley," 205–206.

3. Ibid.

4. Nichols, *General Henry Atkinson*, 47–48.

5. Kappler, ed., *Indian Treaties*, 110–124; *Niles' Register*, January 6, 1816: 328–329; January 13, 1816: 344–345.

6. Kappler, ed., *Indian Treaties*, 126–130. Although not listed among current records, *Niles' Register* of November 29, 1816, reported that another pact had been signed at St. Louis in October 1816 with the Kansa nation.

7. During October 1819, Indian agent Benjamin O'Fallon held a council with the Otoes, Missouris, and Pawnees at Council Bluffs, where Engineer Cantonment had been established, but no treaties were signed. Barry, *Beginning*, 86–87.

8. Kappler, ed., *Indian Treaties*, 156–159.

9. James, *Account of an Expedition*, 258–261.

10. Reid and Gannon, eds., "Journal of the Atkinson-O'Fallon Expedition," 6–7.

11. Ibid., 91–95.

12. Ibid., 8, 10, n. 4.

13. Ibid., 8–9.

14. Ibid., 14.

15. Ibid.

16. *New American State Papers, Indian Affairs* 2: 605–608. The Oglalas were reportedly camped six miles up the Teton River, the Saones thirty miles, and the Cheyennes eighty miles. Reid and Gannon, eds., "Journal of the Atkinson-O'Fallon Expedition," 26.

17. Reid and Gannon, eds., "Journal of the Atkinson-O'Fallon Expedition," 22–23.

18. Ibid., 26.

19. Ibid., 27–28.

20. Ibid., 28.

21. Ibid., 29–30.

22. Ibid., 31.

23. The site is now known as the Larson Mandan Site. Ibid., 34, n. 50.

24. Nichols, *General Henry Atkinson*, 101.

25. Ibid., 102.

26. Ibid., 103–104. In *Adventures of Captain Bonneville,* Washington Irving states that while the brigade officers were at the council meeting, some of the Crow warriors spiked their artillery pieces with dirt and, knowing this, had become insolent. In 1867 at Fort Laramie, Crow chief Bear's Tooth recalled the hitting incident. Gen. William S. Harney concurred, saying, "The white chief was crazy. I was there and saw it done." Stanley, *My Early Travels,* 269.

27. Now known as the Poplar River, it was considered to be 2,000 miles distant from the Mississippi River.

28. Deloria and DeMallie, *Documents* 1: 189; Kappler, ed, *Indian Treaties,* 250, 256, 258, 260.

29. Atkinson and O'Fallon to Barbour, November 7, 1825, in *New American State Papers, Indian Affairs* 2: 607–608.

30. Kappler, ed., *Indian Treaties,* 250–251.

31. *Niles' Register,* October 9, 1825: 84.

32. Ibid., November 19, 1825: 187.

33. Ibid.

34. Ibid.

35. Ibid.

CHAPTER 3

1. The instances of this are many, but two notable cases were the massacre of the Kiowa village in 1833 and that of a group of Confederate soldiers on the Verdigris River in Kansas in 1863. See Hoig, *Tribal Wars,* 102–104, 212–214.

2. Lewis to Sec. of War, July 14, 1808, in Carter, ed., *Territorial Papers* 14: 190.

3. Ibid., 109.

4. Clark to Sec. of War, August 18, 1808, in ibid., 209.

5. Jefferson to Lewis, August 21, 1808, in ibid., 220.

6. Clark to Sec. of War, September 25, 1808, in ibid., 225.

7. Clark to Eustis, February 20, 1810, in *New American State Papers, Indian Affairs* 2: 765.

8. Gregg, "History of Fort Osage," 443. The Clark treaty was never ratified by the U.S. Congress.

9. Clark to Eustis, February 20, 1810, in *New American State Papers, Indian Affairs* 2: 765.

10. Foley and Rice, *The First Chouteaus,* 135.

11. Carter, ed., *Territorial Papers* 4: 230. See also *New American State Papers, Indian Affairs* 2: 766.12. Sibley's account is presented in James, *Account of an Expedition* 2: 246. The final Fort Osage treaty sustained a gift of land the Osages made to Chouteau in 1792. Deloria and DeMalie, *Documents* 2: 1212–1213. Foley and Rice, *The First Chouteaus,* 135, comment that "Sibley's resentment toward Chouteau emanated more from his belief that Chouteau had attempted to use the treaty for personal gain than from objections to the agent's negotiating tactics."

13. Lewis to Jefferson, December 15, 1808, in *New American State Papers, Indian Affairs* 2: 766.

14. Clark to Sec. of War, December 2, 1808, in Carter, ed., *Territorial Papers* 14: 243.

15. Kappler, ed., *Indian Treaties*, 167–168.

16. Ibid., 201–202.

17. *Daily National Intelligencer*, July 11, 1825.

18. *House Ex. Doc. No. 1*, 19/1: 89–92.

19. The treaty defined the tract of land as "beginning at a point due East of White Hair's village [located on the Verdigris River near the town of Shaw in Neosho County, Kansas], and twenty-five miles West of the Western line of the State of Missouri, fronting on a North and South line, so as to leave ten miles North, and forty miles South, of the point of said beginning, and extending west, with the width of fifty miles, to the Western boundary of the lands hereby ceded and relinquished." The western boundary was defined as "a line to be drawn from the head of the Kansas [River], Southwardly through the Rock Saline." Kappler, ed., *Indian Treaties*, 217–221.

20. Ibid.

21. *Daily National Intelligencer*, July 11, 1825; *Niles' Register*, September 10, 1825.

22. Unrau, *Kansa Indians*, 107–108; Kappler, ed., *Indian Treaties*, 222–225; *Kansas Daily Tribune*, November 20, 1888. The land area also includes a small portion of present Nebraska. Article 8 of the pact called for the tribe to pay $500 it owed for credit in trade to Francis G. Chouteau, who with his wife, Berenice, had come among them in 1822 and were the first whites to reside on the site of present Kansas City, Missouri.

23. Unrau, *Kansa Indians*, 149–154.

24. Ibid., 154.

25. Kappler, ed., *Indian Treaties*, 552–554.

CHAPTER 4

1. Foreman, *Pioneer Days*, 104–105; Young, "Ranger Battalion," 468–469; Foreman, ed., "Colonel James B. Many," 125.

2. Grinnell, *Bent's Old Fort and Its Builders*, 2.

3. *Daily National Intelligencer*, November 28, December 8, 1828; January 27, February 26, 1829.

4. Ibid., May 11, August 28, December 1, 1829; February 8, 1830. See also Young, *First Military Escort, 1829*.

5. Ghent, *The Early Far West*, 250.

6. *Niles' Register*, March 23, 1833; *Daily National Intelligencer*, November 25, 1833.

7. Foreman, *Pioneer Days*, 116–119.

8. Hildreth, *Dragoon Campaigns*, 125.

9. Perrine, ed., "Journal of Hugh Evans," 180–181.

10. *Daily National Intelligencer*, September 30, 1831; Dodge Report, *Sen. Doc. 1*, 23/2: 10–11.

11. Catlin, *North American Indians* 2: 37.

12. Foreman, *Pioneer Days*, 117–119.

13. Perrine, ed., "Journal of Hugh Evans," 182; Wheelock Report, *Sen. Exec. Doc. 1*, 23/1: 74.

14. Wheelock Report, *Sen. Exec. Doc. 1*, 23/1: 75–76.

15. Catlin, *Letters and Notes*, 50–51; Catlin, *North American Indians* 2: 51; *Daily National Intelligencer*, July 28, 1835.

16. Wheelock Report, *Sen. Exec. Doc. 1*, 23/1: 77, 91.

17. Hildreth, *Dragoon Campaigns*, 154.

18. Perrine, ed., "Journal of Hugh Evans," 189.

19. *Arkansas Advocate*, October 3, 1834; Wheelock Report, *Sen. Exec. Doc. 1*, 23/1: 80.

20. Wheelock Report, *Sen. Exec. Doc. 1*, 23/1: 79, 83.

21. Ibid., 81–82.

22. Ibid., 84–85.

23. Ibid., 85.

24. Ibid., 87.

25. Ibid.

26. Ibid., 90.

27. *Daily National Intelligencer*, October 23, 1834.

28. It was estimated that around 150 of the 500 men involved in the expedition died. Foreman, ed., "Journal of Proceedings," 394.

29. "Proceedings of a Council Held at Fort Gibson, Sept. 1834," RG75, NA.

30. Ibid., 47.

31. Ibid., 48.

32. Ibid., 52.

33. Ibid., 56.

34. Ibid., 67.

35. Ibid.

36. Ibid., 58.

37. Ibid., 59.

38. Ibid., 65.

39. Ibid., 69.

40. Ibid., 56.

41. Berthrong, *Southern Cheyennes*, 76.

42. "Expedition of Colonel Dodge," *Senate Report No. 654*, 131.

43. Kappler, ed., *Indian Treaties*, 416–418. See also Manypenny to Atchison, August 1853, *Daily National Intelligencer*, August 24, 1853.

44. "Expedition of Colonel Dodge," *New American State Papers, Military Affairs* 6: 135.

45. Pelzer, "Captain Ford's Journal," 564–565.

46. Ibid., 567; Perrine, ed., "Journal of Hugh Evans," 212.

47. Pelzer, "Captain Ford's Journal," 568.

48. "Expedition of Colonel Dodge," *New American State Papers, Military Affairs* 6: 143.

49. Ibid., 144.

CHAPTER 5

1. Chouteau to Sec. of War, March 3, 1834, LR/OIA, Western Creek Agency, NA.

2. Articles of a Treaty Made and Concluded at Fort Gibson, T494, Roll 8, NA.

3. Ibid.

4. Foreman, ed., "Journal of Proceedings," 395.

5. Fort Gibson Letterbook, 1834–1836, OHS.

6. Foreman, ed., "Journal of Proceedings," 396; *Army and Navy Chronicle*, October 1, 1835.

7. Mason to Arbuckle, July 2, 1835, M567, Reel 103, NA.

8. *Daily National Intelligencer*, September 2, 1835.

9. Foreman, ed., "Journal of Proceedings," 403.

10. Mason to Arbuckle, July 8, 1835, M567, Reel 103, NA.

11. Jones, ed., "Diary of Leonard McPhail," 285.

12. Ibid., 286.

13. Ibid.

14. Ibid., 288.

15. Mason to Arbuckle, July 8, 1835, M567, NA.

16. Jones, ed., "Diary of Leonard McPhail," 285.

17. Foreman, ed., "Journal of Proceedings," 411.

18. Jones, ed., "Diary of Leonard McPhail," 286–287.

19. Foreman, ed., "Journal of Proceedings," 416–417.

20. Ibid. Ascimke was paid $119, provided with a horse costing $65, and given $45 in goods for her services as an interpreter at the Camp Holmes treaty council. Ibid., 416–417.

21. Ibid., 418.

22. Ibid., 409–412; Kappler, ed., *Indian Treaties*, 435–439.

23. Foreman, ed., "Journal of Proceedings," 411.

24. Ibid., 412.

25. Ibid., 413.

26. Kappler, ed., *Indian Treaties*, 436–439.

27. Foreman, ed., "Journal of Proceedings," 415.

28. Ibid.

29. Ibid., 416.

30. Ibid.

31. P. L. Chouteau to Armstrong, February 1, 1837, LR/OIA, Western Suptcy., M234, Roll 922, NA; Stokes/Arbuckle to Cass, September 29, 1835, Lewis Cass

Papers, Box C-32, WHC/OU; Foreman, *Pioneer Days*, 226. See also Kavanagh, *Comanche Political History*, 241–242.

32. Chouteau to Stokes, April 19, 1836, Lewis Cass Papers, Box C-32, WHC/ OU.

33. Chouteau to Armstrong, February 1, 1837, LR/OIA, Western Suptcy., NA.

34. Chouteau to Armstrong, May 22, 1837, ibid. A witness of note was Capt. B.L.E. Bonneville, Seventh Infantry.

35. Stokes to Poinsett, September 8, 1837, LR/OIA, Western Suptcy., NA.

36. Chouteau to Armstrong, May 22, 1837, ibid.; Chouteau to Harris, September 8, November 25, December 8, 1837, ibid. The Delawares and Comanches made similar complaints against the Osages.

37. Chouteau to Harris, November 25, 1837, ibid.

38. Ibid.

39. Chouteau to Harris, January 3, 1838, ibid.

40. Chouteau to Harris, June 28, 1838, ibid.

41. Ibid.; *Daily National Intelligencer*, April 16, 1839. The affair has become known as the Battle of Wolf Creek.

42. Armstrong to Crawford, December 31, 1838, LR/OIA, Western Suptcy., NA.

43. Statement of Goods Furnished the Comanches and Kiowas, Lewis Cass Papers, Box C-32, WHC/OU.

44. Armstrong ltr., June 8, 1839, Foreman Transcript 1: MS/OHS.

CHAPTER 6

1. Kavanagh, *Comanche Political History*, 105.

2. Bolton, *Texas in the Middle Eighteenth Century*, 127; Richardson, *Comanche Barrier*, 70.

3. Hicks's Report, *Cherokee Advocate*, July 2, 1846.

4. Richardson, *Comanche Barrier*, 90–91.

5. Kavanagh, *Comanche Political History*, 235–237.

6. Deloria and DeMallie, *Documents* 1: 565–576.

7. McLean, *Robertson Papers* 16: 446–449.

8. May 30, 1838, cited in Kavanagh, *Comanche Political History*, 257.

9. Ibid., 573.10. Ibid., 572–574.

10. The final article of the treaty declared that "the Great Spirit has looked down and seen their actions. He will curse all Chiefs that tell a lie before his eyes. Their Women and Children cannot be happy."

11. Wooten, *Comprehensive History of Texas* 1: 344–346.

12. Richardson, *Comanche Barrier*, 104–105.

13. "The Treaty and Massacre," *Cherokee Advocate*, May 22, 1845.

14. Webb, *Texas Rangers*, 45–46.

15. Ibid.

16. Ibid., 70–72.

17. James, *The Raven*, 309.

18. Muckleroy, "Indian Policy of Texas," 199.

19. *Report of Messrs. Butler and Lewis*, 10–11. These Comanche divisions are given variously, but the report cited here appears to be a valid reflection of their organization in 1845.

20. Stroud, Williams, and Durst to Houston, September 4, 1843, in Winfrey and Day, eds., *Indian Papers of Texas* 1: 139.

21. Butler, a veteran military officer, had served in the Florida Seminole wars and as president of a bank before being elected governor of South Carolina in 1838. At the outbreak of the U.S.-Mexican War, he organized a volunteer unit and became its commanding colonel. Despite being wounded, he continued to lead the advance at Churubusco, Mexico, until he was killed on August 20, 1847.

22. Bushnell, "John Mix Stanley," 507–512; *Portraits of North American Indians*, 5–32.

23. Winfrey and Day, eds. *Indian Papers of Texas* 1: 150.

24. Ibid., 157.

25. Ibid., 160–161. This chief is identified as Ka-ka-katish, the Shooting Star, and his speech, although much the same in content and at times in phraseology, is given differently in *Portraits of North American Indians*, 50.

26. Winfrey and Day, *Indian Papers of Texas* 1: 153–155.

27. Ibid., 2: 251–272.

28. Eldridge to Houston, December 8, 1843, in ibid., 255.

29. Ibid.

30. "A keen, natty, little fellow who speaks Spanish and several Indian tongues and exercises great influence." *New Orleans Picayune*, May 23, 1846.

31. Winfrey and Day, eds., *Indian Papers of Texas* 2: 256.

32. Ibid., 257.

33. Ibid., 259.

34. Ibid., 260.

35. Ibid., 267–268; Hicks to Drew, March 17, 1846, John Drew Papers, Gilcrease Institute.

36. Winfrey and Day, eds., *Indian Papers of Texas* 2: 268.

37. Ibid., 269–271.

38. Ibid., 228–230, 272–273; Deloria and DeMallie, eds., *Documents* 1: 578–579.

39. Deloria and DeMallie, eds., *Documents* 1: 579–582; Winfrey and Day, eds., *Indian Papers of Texas* 1: 241–246.

40. *Arkansas Intelligencer*, December 30, 1843; January 6, 1844; Winfrey and Day, eds., *Indian Papers of Texas* 2: 64.

41. Bushnell, "John Mix Stanley," 507–512. Many of Stanley's paintings were destroyed in the Smithsonian fire on January 24, 1865.

42. Watson to Houston, May 4, 1844, in Winfrey and Day, eds., *Indian Papers of Texas* 2: 22–24.

43. Winn to Houston, May 4, 1844, in ibid., 25.

44. Western to Sloat, June 15, 1844, in ibid., 72.

45. Ibid., 115–119.

46. Minutes of the Council, October 7, 1844, cited in Webb, "Last Treaty of the Republic of Texas," 156, n. 8.

47. Winfrey and Day, eds., *Indian Papers of Texas* 2: 195.

48. Ibid., 194.

49. Ibid., 195.

50. Muckleroy, "Indian Policy of Texas," 197.

CHAPTER 7

1. Richardson, *Comanche Barrier*, 140.

2. Doyle, "robust and healthy, but much tanned," had been captured on the Colorado River in 1840. He was rescued by Delaware Bill Connor for $300 value in horse, rifles, and goods. Connor took him to Butler, who reimbursed the frontiersman $100 and promised to secure the remaining amount from officials in Washington. "Journal of Elijah Hicks," 70, n. 2.

3. *Report of Messrs. Butler and Lewis*, 1–3.

4. "Journal of Elijah Hicks," 70, n. 2.

5. *Cherokee Advocate*, May 28, 1846.

6. "She is quite an Amazon—wears a belt and dagger and shoots a rifle expertly, rides well on horseback and takes notes." "Journal of Elijah Hicks," 89.

7. Ibid., 69; *Arkansas Intelligencer*, January 24, February 7, 1846.

8. *Report of Messrs. Butler and Lewis*, 5–6.

9. Ibid., 6; Hicks's Report, *Cherokee Advocate*, July 2, 1846.

10. "Journal of Elijah Hicks," 83.

11. Ibid., 84.

12. Hicks's Report, *Cherokee Advocate*, July 2, 1846.

13. Ibid.

14. Ibid.

15. *Report of Messrs. Butler and Lewis*, 8; "Journal of Elijah Hicks," 73, 82, 94; Kendall Report, *New Orleans Picayune*, June 20, 1846.

16. *New Orleans Picayune*, June 20, 1846.

17. "Journal of Elijah Hicks," 95.

18. Ibid., 95–96.

19. *Report of Messrs. Butler and Lewis*, 9.

20. Bauer, *Zachary Taylor*, 119, 145–165.

21. "Journal of Elijah Hicks," 96–97.

22. Ibid., 95.

23. *New Orleans Picayune*, June 20, 1846.

24. Ibid., May 23, 1846.

25. *Niles' Register*, June 27, 1846.

26. *Report of Messrs. Butler and Lewis*, 13.

27. "Journal of Elijah Hicks," 98. Later in Washington, the costs listed by the commissioners were challenged on the question of just how much beef a tribesman would consume, estimated variously at six to fifteen pounds a day. *Report of Messrs. Butler and Lewis*, 18–20.

28. *Cherokee Advocate*, July 2, 1846.

29. Richardson, *Comanche Barrier*, 148.

30. Kappler, ed., *Indian Treaties*, 554–556.

31. Richardson, *Comanche Barrier*, 142, 150.

32. Kendall account, *New Orleans Picayune*, June 20, 1846.

33. *Daily National Intelligencer*, June 29, 1846.

34. Quaife, ed., *Diary of James K. Polk* 2: 3.

35. Ibid.

36. Ibid., 4.

37. *Cherokee Advocate*, August 6, 1846; *Columbian Fountain* (Washington, D.C.), August 13, 1846; *Alexandria Gazette*, July 3, 4, 1846; *Daily National Intelligencer*, July 8, 1846; *New York Herald*, July 24, 1846.

38. Quaife, ed., *Diary of James K. Polk* 2: 46.

39. Williams and Barker, *Writings of Sam Houston* 8: 40–41.

40. Harmon, "United States Indian Policy in Texas," 380–381.

41. Richardson, *Comanche Barrier*, 146.

42. Biesele, "Relations Between the German Settlers and the Indians in Texas," 118–123.

43. Ibid., 125.

44. *CofIA Report, 1848*, 588; Richardson, *Comanche Barrier*, 150.

45. Richardson, *Comanche Barrier*, 156.

46. Frazer, *Forts of the West*, 139–164.

47. Rollins to Lea, October 30, 1850, Documents Relating to Indian Treaties, T494, NA.

48. Ibid.

49. Richardson, *Comanche Barrier*, 159.

50. Rollins to Lea, November 2, 1850, Documents Relating to Indian Treaties, T494, NA; *CofIA Report, 1850*, 587.

51. Winfrey and Day, eds., *Indian Papers of Texas* 3: 130–137.

52. Rollins to Lea, December 22, 1850, Documents Relating to Indian Treaties, T494, NA.

53. Ibid.

54. Williams and Barker, *Writings of Sam Houston* 5: 345, n. 3.

55. Winfrey and Day, eds., *Indian Papers of Texas* 3: 134. Rollins had a stone marker erected to mark the treaty site. Richardson, *Comanche Barrier*, 162.

56. Deloria and DeMallie, *Documents* 2: 1293–1296.

57. Smith, *Old Army in Texas*, 17–18.

58. *New York Times*, September 17, 1852.

59. Richardson, *Comanche Barrier*, 212.

60. *Daily National Intelligencer*, May 10, August 17, 1853; Simons to Davis, November 12, 1853, LR/OIA, Texas Agency, M234, NA; Mix to Drew, May 26, 1853, LR/OIA, Southern Suptcy., M234, NA.

61. Richardson, *Comanche Barrier*, 214.

62. Ibid., 216–218.

63. Ford to Runnels, May 22, 1858, *HR Ex. Doc. 27*, 18–19; John S. Ford Memoirs, Barker Historical Collection 4: 676ff.

64. Harmon, "United States Indian Policy in Texas," 398.

65. Thoburn, "Battle With Comanches," 22–28; Van Dorn Report, *HR Ex. Doc. 27*, 50–53.

66. Thoburn, "Indian Fight in Ford County, Kansas," 312–329; *Dallas Herald*, June 15, 1859.

67. Richardson, *Comanche Barrier*, 245–259.

68. Chapman, "Wichita Reservation," 1048; Wright, "Fort Cobb," 54–55; Richardson, *Comanche Barrier*, 257.

CHAPTER 8

1. Mattes, *Great Platte River Road*, 484, 516.

2. Ibid.; Clarke, *Stephen Watts Kearny*, 92. Kearny's force included two officers of particular note: Lt. Philip Kearny and Lt. Philip St. George Cooke.

3. Clarke, *Stephen Watts Kearny*, 94.

4. Grinnell, *Fighting Cheyennes*, 100–101.

5. Mitchell to Lea, November 11, 1851, KHS, Clark Papers 9: 359–361; Lowe, *Five Years a Dragoon*, 62.

6. *CofIA Report, 1851*, 333; *New York Times*, October 14, 1851.

7. Lowe, *Five Years a Dragoon*, 60–61.

8. *Missouri Republican*, October 24, 1851.

9. Chittenden and Richardson, *Life, Letters, and Travels of Father De Smet* 2: 58.

10. *Missouri Republican*, October 29, 1851. Lowe remembered the incident a bit differently, saying it was a Sioux who committed the crime. Lowe, *Five Years a Dragoon*, 64.

11. *Missouri Republican*, October 29, 1851.

12. Chittenden and Richardson, *Life, Letters, and Travels of Father De Smet* 2: 673–674.

13. *Missouri Republican*, October 24, 27, 29, 1851.

14. Ibid., October 24, 1851.

15. Chittenden and Richardson, *Life, Letters, and Travels of Father De Smet* 2: 675.

16. *Missouri Republican*, October 27, 1851.

17. Ibid.

18. Ibid.

19. Lowe, *Five Years a Dragoon*, 70.

20. *Missouri Republican*, November 3, 1851.

21. Ibid.

22. Ibid.

23. Ibid.

24. Ibid.

25. Ibid.

26. Ibid., November 10, 1851.

27. Ibid.

28. Ibid.

29. Original Document, Treaty of 1851, NA.

30. Amended Treaty of Fort Laramie, Ratified Indian Treaties, M668, Roll 10, NA.

31. Chittenden and Richardson, *Life, Letters, and Travels of Father De Smet* 2: 683.

32. Lowe, *Five Years a Dragoon*, 70; *New York Times*, October 30, 1851.

33. *New York Times*, October 30, 1851.

34. Chittenden and Richardson, *Life, Letters, and Travels of Father De Smet*, 2: 687.

35. Ibid.; *St. Louis Intelligencer*, November 1, 1851.

36. *Daily National Intelligencer*, November 19, December 1, 1851.

37. Ibid., January 7, 1852.

38. *New York Times*, December 17, 1852.

39. *Daily National Intelligencer*, February 21, 1852.

40. Ibid., August 22, 23, 1853.

41. Ibid., August 22, 24, 1853.

42. Kappler, ed., *Indian Treaties*, 595.

43. Sunder, *Fur Trade on the Upper Missouri*, 143.

CHAPTER 9

1. *Niles' Register*, October 19, 1816: 127; *New American State Papers: Foreign Relations* 4: 211–213.

2. *Niles' Register*, October 22, 1825, 127; Kappler, ed., *Indian Treaties*, 246–247.

3. Kappler, ed., *Indian Treaties*, 248–250.

4. Young, *First Military Escort*, 108–117; Cooke, "Journey on the Santa Fe Trail," 283–291.

5. James, *Three Years Among the Mexicans and Indians*, 227.

6. Most accounts rely on George Bird Grinnell, who gave the date of this meeting as 1840 in *Fighting Cheyennes*, 63ff. Evidence of record, however, indicates the event occurred during the summer of 1841. See Smither, ed., *Journals of the Sixth Congress of the Republic of Texas, 1841–1842* 3: 439.

7. Grinnell, *Fighting Cheyennes*, 64–69; Grinnell, *Bent's Old Fort and Its Builders*, 43.

8. Grinnell, *Bent's Old Fort and Its Builders*, 42–44; *Daily National Intelligencer*, April 16, 1839.

9. Hallock, "Siege of Fort Atkinson," 638–648.

10. *New York Times*, August 18, 1852.

11. *CofIA Report, 1853*, 384; *Daily National Intelligencer*, May 3, 1853.

12. Fitzpatrick to CofIA, November 19, 1853, Documents Relating to Indian Treaties, T494, NA.

13. Ibid.

14. Ibid.

15. Lowe, *Five Years a Dragoon*, 106.

16. Kappler, ed., *Indian Treaties*, 600–602.

17. Ibid.

18. *CofIA Report, 1853*, 364.

19. Amended Treaty of Fort Laramie, Ratified Indian Treaties, M668, Roll 10, NA.

20. *Daily National Intelligencer*, August 2, 1853.

21. *CofIA Report, 1853*, 366–367.

22. Validity of the amendment has been challenged on the grounds that only four of the original six Sioux chiefs, one of whom was by that time deceased and the other absent at Fort Laramie, signed the significant alteration. The marks of other Sioux leaders were obtained at Fort Pierre by Major Alfred Vaughan, agent for the Upper Missouri. For a fuller discussion, see Anderson, "Controversial Sioux Amendment to the Fort Laramie Treaty of 1851," 201–220.

23. Kappler, ed., *Indian Treaties*. 600–602, Article 10.

24. *CofIA Report, 1854*, 299.

25. *CofIA Report, 1853*, 367.

26. *CofIA Report, 1855*, 179.

27. Ibid.

CHAPTER 10

1. Kappler, ed., *Indian Treaties*, 594–596.

2. Grinnell, *Fighting Cheyennes*, 112–113; Chalfant, *Cheyennes and Horse Soldiers*, 39–41.

3. For a detailed account of the Sumner fight, see Chalfant, *Cheyennes and Horse Soldiers*.

4. *CofIA Report, 1858*, 450.

5. *CofIA Report, 1859*, 507.

6. Ibid., 506.

7. Root, "Extracts From Diary," 207–208.

8. Sturgis Report, June 10, 1860, LR/CofIA, Southern Suptcy., M234, NA; *Daily National Intelligencer*, August 25, 1860.

9. *Western Mountaineer* (Golden, Colorado), October 4, 1860.

10. *Leavenworth Daily Times*, October 23, 1860.

11. *Western Mountaineer*, October 4, 1860.

12. Ibid.

13. *Correspondence of John Sedgwick* 2: 18–19.

14. *CofIA Report, 1860*, 453.

15. Ibid. On this, Arapaho chief Little Raven said: "Another thing: tell the President if he treats for their lands he must give a good price, as they are digging gold on our land. [We] knew it was wrong, but never troubled the whites, thinking the government would make it up." *CofIA Report, 1865*, 708.

16. *Leavenworth Daily Times*, October 23, 1860.

17. Boone to Robinson, February 18, 22, 1861, Documents Relating to Indian Treaties, T494, NA; Kappler, ed., *Indian Treaties*, 807–810.

18. Kappler, ed., *Indian Treaties*, 807–810; Amendment to Treaty of Fort Wise, Documents Relating to Indian Treaties, M668, NA.

19. *Leavenworth Times*, March 13, 1863.

20. *Washington Evening Star*, March 27, 1863.

21. Ibid.

22. *New York Times*, April 8, 11, 13, 16, 1863.

23. Articles of Agreement & Convention Made and Concluded at the City of Washington, T494, Roll 8, NA; Deloria and DeMallie, *Documents* 2: 867–869.

24. *New York Times*, April 6, 1863.

25. *Official Records* I, 12/2: 214, 400–401; I, 34/3: 167; I, 34/4: 402–404; I, 34/1: 883–888; I, 41/3: 798–799; *CofIA Report, 1863*, 242.

26. *CofIA Report, 1863*, 247–248.

27. *Official Records* I, 24/4: 402–404; *Sen. Rep. 156*, 39/2, "The Chivington Massacre," 75.

28. See Hoig, *Sand Creek Massacre*, for a full account of the meeting and events prior to and following.

29. *Sen. Ex. Doc. 26*, "Sand Creek Massacre," 39/2: 91.

CHAPTER 11

1. Ware, *Indian War of 1864*, 3.

2. Report of Lt. Col. William H. Emory, May 19, 1861, *Official Records* I, 1: 648–649; Report of Lt. W. M. Averell, April 17, 1861, *Official Records* I, 1: 493–496.

3. Pike, "Narrative of a Journey in the Prairie," *Arkansas Advocate* (Little Rock), April 14, 17, May 1, 8, 15, 22, 29, June 5, 19, 1835.

4. *Galveston Weekly News*, September 3, 1861, Barker Historical Collection.

5. Pike, *Report on Mission to the Indian Nations*, 8–20.

6. Ibid., 28–29.

7. Ibid., 21.

8. Articles of a Convention, *Official Records* 4, 1: 542–554.

9. Ibid., 543.

10. Pike, *Report on Mission to the Indian Nations*, 23.

11. *Official Records* IV, 2: 356. The chief who signed the treaty on July 4, 1862, was identified as Tes-toth-cha, whose band resided on Elk Creek in the Wichita Mountains.

12. Abel, *The American Indian as a Participant in the Civil War*, 13–26.

13. Page to Johnson, May 6, 1862, Special Collections, University of Arkansas Libraries.

14. Leeper to Pike, April 13, 1862, cited in Abel, *The American Indian as a Participant in the Civil War*, 348–350.

15. Pike to Davis, July 31, 1862, with P.S., August 3, 1862, *Official Records* 1, 8: 868–869.

16. Trickett, "Civil War," 268.

17. Abel, *The American Indian as a Participant in the Civil War*, 183.

18. *Emporia News*, December 6, 1862.

19. Deloria and DeMallie, *Documents* 1: 642–649; Pike, *Report on Mission to the Indian Nations*, 27.

20. Deloria and DeMallie, *Documents* 1: Article 38, 647.

21. *CofIA Report, 1863*, 324–325; Bartles, "Massacre of Confederates," 62–66.

22. Deloria and DeMallie, *Documents* 2: 1031–1036. Although Deloria and DeMallie present the treaty and ensuing revisions by Congress as having been duly signed and approved, the authors indicate that the Osages rejected the agreement. Nonetheless, the government went ahead with relocation of other tribes on the Osage land.

23. Lewis, "Camp Napoleon," 361–362.

24. Dale, "Additional Letters of General Stand Watie," 140–141.

25. *St. Louis Democrat*, September 6, 1865.

26. *Proceedings, War and Reconstruction*, 3–4; *Kansas Daily Tribune*, September 16, 1865; Gibson, *Oklahoma*, 128.

27. *Proceedings, War and Reconstruction*, 3–4,

28. Gibson, *Oklahoma*, 129.

CHAPTER 12

1. *Kansas Daily Tribune*, September 1, 1865.

2. Cited in ibid., September 1, 3, 8, 27, 1865.

3. Ibid., August 24, 1865.

4. Chisholm to Leavenworth, August 1, 1865, LR/OIA, Kiowa Agency, 1864–1868, M234, NA.

5. Kappler, ed., *Indian Treaties*, 892–895.

6. "Diary of Samuel A. Kingman," 445.

7. Ibid., 446.

8. *CofIA Report, 1866*, 704; Documents Relating to Indian Treaties, T494, Roll 7, NA.

9. *CofIA Report, 1866*, 706.

10. Ibid., 709.

11. Ibid., 708.

12. Kappler, ed., *Indian Treaties*, 888.

13. *CofIA Report, 1866*, 720; Schmeckebier, *Office of Indian Affairs*, 92–93; Documents Relating to Indian Treaties, T494, Roll 7, NA.

14. "Diary of Samuel A. Kingman," 448.

15. Kappler, ed., *Indian Treaties*, 887–892.

16. *CofIA Report, 1866*, 713; Documents Relating to Indian Treaties, T494, Roll 7, NA.

17. *CofIA Report, 1866*, 715; Documents Relating to Indian Treaties, T494, Roll 7, NA.

18. *CofIA Report, 1866*, 715; Documents Relating to Indian Treaties, T494, Roll 7, NA.

19. *CofIA Report, 1866*, 715; Documents Relating to Indian Treaties, T494, Roll 7, NA.

20. Kappler, ed., *Indian Treaties*, 892–895.

21. Richardson, *Comanche Barrier*, 292; Harmon, "United States Indian Policy in Texas, 1845–1860," 383.

22. "Diary of Samuel A. Kingman," 447, 450.

23. Ibid.

24. *CofIA Report, 1866*, 720.

25. Ibid.

26. McCusker to Murphy, November 15, 1867, LR/OIA, Wichita Agency, M234, NA.

27. *Leavenworth Daily Conservative*, September 27, 1867.

28. Ibid.

29. Gibson, *Oklahoma*, 143.

30. Report of a Council Held at Fort Zarah, Kansas, Nov. 10th, 1866, With the Arapaho & Cheyenne Indians, T494, Roll 7, NA.

31. Ibid.

32. Report of Bogy and Irwin, December 1, 1866, T494, Roll 7, NA.

33. Bogy Report, December 1, 1866, T494, Roll 11, NA.

34. Report of a Council Held at Fort Zarah, Kansas, Nov. 10th, 1866, With the Arapaho & Cheyenne Indians, T494, Roll 7, NA.

35. Irwin Report, n.d., T494, Roll 7, NA.

36. Bent Report, n.d., T494, Roll 7, NA; Bogy Report, December 1, 1866, T494, Roll 11, NA.

37. Proceedings of a Council Held at Fort Zarah, Kansas, Nov. 20th, 1866, With the Dog Soldiers of the Cheyennes, T494, Roll 7, NA.

CHAPTER 13

1. *Daily National Intelligencer*, September 18, 1854; Hyde, *Red Cloud's Folk*, 75.

2. Harney Report, *Daily National Intelligencer*, October 4, 1855; Hyde, *Red Cloud's Folk*, 79–80.

3. Mattes, *Great Platte River Road*, 18–20, 94, 98.

4. Commissioner James W. Denver, a Kansas governor and namesake of Denver, Colorado, had secured land cessions from the four confederated Pawnee bands at Table Creek, Nebraska, on September 24, 1858. Articles of Agreement and Convention Made This Twenty Fourth Day of September A.D. 1858 at Table Creek, Nebraska Territory, T494, Roll 8, NA. The Ponca likewise ceded claims to territory along the Platte at Washington in March 1858.

5. Ware, *Indian War of 1864*, 68.

6. Mattes, *Great Platte River Road*, 20.

7. Ware, *Indian War of 1864*, 98.

8. Ibid., 274–275.

9. Ibid., 110.

10. Ibid., 112–114.

11. Ibid., 111–112.

12. Ibid., 115.

13. Ibid.

14. Ibid., 158–168.

15. Ibid., 160–165.

16. Grinnell, *Fighting Cheyennes*, 216–229.

17. Vaughn, *Battle of Platte Bridge*, 60, 94.

18. *Kansas Daily Tribune*, September 3, 1865.

19. *Official Records* 1: 48, 2: 1217, 1236–1237; *St. Louis Democrat*, October 3, 1865; Grinnell, *Fighting Cheyennes*, 204–215. Another arm of the campaign under Col. N. Cole that drove westward from Nebraska not only failed to find Indians to fight but suffered near disaster from the elements and the perils of a difficult march. Ibid., 212. A participant's account appears in the *St. Louis Democrat*, October 13, 17, 1865.

20. Johnson directive, August 15, 1865, Documents Relating to Indian Treaties, T494, Roll 7, NA. Other treaty parties were even then effecting treaties with the southern tribes at the Little Arkansas and with those of eastern Indian Territory at Fort Smith.

21. Harlan to Commission, August 18, 1865, T494, Roll 7, NA.

22. Ibid.

23. Ibid.

24. Witness account, *St. Louis Democrat*, October 11, 1865.

25. Ibid.

26. Commission Report, October 21, 1865, T494, Roll 7, NA.

27. Ibid.; *St. Louis Democrat*, October 25, 1865.

28. Kappler, ed., *Indian Treaties*, 896–908.

29. Commission to Harlan, October 21, 1865, T494, Roll 7, NA.

30. Ibid.

31. Curtis to Harlan, December 20, 1865, T494, Roll 7.

32. Articles of a Treaty Made and Concluded at Fort Laramie, June 27, 1866, T494, Roll 9, NA.

33. *Kansas Daily Tribune*, June 28, 1866.

34. Ibid., July 26, 1866.

35. Ibid., August 2, 1866.

36. Deloria and DeMallie, *Documents* 2: 1368–1370.

37. Ibid., 1369, 1371.

38. Ibid., 1370–1373.

39. Report of Commissioners to Treat With the Indians at Fort Laramie, n.d., T494, Roll 7, NA.

40. Ibid.

41. *Kansas Daily Tribune*, August 24, 1866. See also Carrington, *Ab-sa-ra-ka*, 122–123.

42. *Kansas Daily Tribune*, August 24, 1866.

43. Hebard and Brininstool, *Bozeman Trail* 1: 266–277; Frazer, *Forts of the West*, 84, 103.

44. Carrington, *Ab-sa-ra-ka*, 200–210; Hebard and Brininstool, *Bozeman Trail* 1: 337–339.

CHAPTER 14

1. *New York World*, July 22, 1867.

2. Hoig, *Battle of the Washita*, 23.

3. Jones, *Treaty of Medicine Lodge*, 17–19; Official Report of the Peace Commission, *Missouri Democrat*, January 11, 1868.

4. Official Report of the Peace Commission, *Missouri Democrat*, January 11, 1868.

5. Jones, *Treaty of Medicine Lodge*, 25.

6. *Missouri Democrat*, October 19, 1867.

7. *Missouri Republican*, October 18, 1867.

8. *Chicago Times*, October 25, 1867.

9. Ibid., October 13, 1867.

10. Jones, *Treaty of Medicine Lodge*, 59.

11. *Leavenworth Daily Conservative*, September 9, 1867; *Chicago Tribune*, September 30, 1867.

12. *Missouri Democrat*, October 23, 1867; *Missouri Republican*, October 24, 1867.

13. *New York Tribune*, October 23, 1867.

13. Ibid.

14. *Chicago Times*, October 29, 1867.

15. *New York Times*, October 30, 1867. See also *Cincinnati Gazette*, October 26, 1867.

16. *Chicago Times*, October 29, 1867; *Cincinnati Gazette*, October 28, 1867; *Cincinnati Commercial*, October 28, 1867.

17. *Kansas Weekly Tribune*, October 31, 1867.

18. *Chicago Tribune*, October 29, 1867.

19. *Kansas Weekly Tribune*, November 14, 1867.

20. *Leslie's Illustrated Newspaper*, November 23, 1867; Jones, *Treaty of Medicine Lodge*, 136; Stanley, "A British Journalist Reports," 292.

21. *Missouri Democrat*, November 2, 1867.

22. *Cincinnati Gazette*, November 4, 1867.

23. Stanley, *My Early Travels*, 258.

24. *Cincinnati Commercial*, November 4, 1867,

25. *Kansas Weekly Tribune*, November 11, 1867. See also *New York Tribune*, November 8, 1867; *Missouri Democrat*, November 2, 1867; *Cincinnati Commercial*, November 4, 1867; *Chicago Tribune*, November 4, 1867; *Missouri Republican*, November 2, 1867.

26. *Cincinnati Commercial*, November 4, 1867.

27. *New York Tribune*, November 8, 1867.

28. *Chicago Tribune*, November 4, 1867.

29. *Cincinnati Commercial*, November 4, 1867; *New York Tribune*, November 8, 1867; *Kansas Weekly Tribune*, November 11, 1867.

30. Kappler, ed., *Indian Treaties*, 989.

31. *Kansas Weekly Tribune*, November 11, 1867. Stanley, however, failed to make this charge in his report of the treaty signing for newspaper readers in Henderson's home state. *Missouri Democrat*, November 2, 1867.

32. Kappler, ed., *Indian Treaties*, 984–989.

33. Hagan, *United States–Comanche Relations*, 42.

CHAPTER 15

1. Official Report of the Peace Commission, *Missouri Democrat*, January 11, 1868.

2. Green, ed., "Lt. Palmer Writes From the Bozeman Trail, 1867–68," 24.

3. Stanley, *My Early Travels*, 268. Stanley, who was present, said that a treaty was signed with the Crows at this time. Ibid., 274. Deloria and DeMallie, however, list none such, ratified or unratified, in their *Documents of American Indian Diplomacy*.

4. *Washington Evening Star*, April 10, 1868.

5. Green, ed., "Lt. Palmer Writes From the Bozeman Trail, 1867–68," 27–30.

6. Stanley, *My Early Travels*, 283.

7. Athearn, *William Tecumseh Sherman and the Settlement of the West*, 196.

8. *Leavenworth Daily Conservative*, April 9, 1868.

9. Hyde, *Red Cloud's Folk*, 164.

10. Hedren, *Fort Laramie and the Great Sioux War*, 2; *Washington Evening Star*, April 23, 1868.

11. Sanborn to Sherman, April 28, 1868, *Missouri Democrat*, May 7, 1868; William T. Sherman Papers 23, Library of Congress.

12. Kappler, ed., *Indian Treaties*, 1012–1015.

13. *New York Times*, May 15, 1868.

14. Ibid.

15. Kappler, ed., *Indian Treaties*, 998–1003.

16. Olson, *Red Cloud and the Sioux Problem*, 70–71.

17. Ibid., 75; Crawford, *Rekindling Camp Fires*, 161.

18. Chittenden and Richardson, *Life, Letters, and Travels of Father De Smet* 3: 903.

19. Ibid., 910–912.

20. Ibid., 921.

21. Crawford, *Rekindling Camp Fires*, 158.

22. Ibid., 165.

23. Ibid., 170.

24. Kappler, ed., *Indian Treaties*, 998–1007. These signings were secured at Fort Rice, although such is not indicated on the 1868 Fort Laramie treaty document.

25. Augur Report, October 14, 1868, *Annual Report, Secretary of War, 1868*, 21–24; Olson, *Red Cloud and the Sioux Problem*, 76; Grinnell, *Fighting Cheyennes*, 244; Frazier, *Forts of the West*, 184.

26. Athearn, *William Tecumseh Sherman and the Settlement of the West*, 228.

27. Proceedings of the Peace Commission, *New York Times*, October 13, 1868.

28. Ibid.

29. Olson, *Red Cloud and the Sioux Problem*, 77–78; Athearn, *William Tecumseh Sherman and the Settlement of the West*, 228–229.

30. Dye to Ruggles, November 20, 1868, Upper Platte Agency, M234, NA.

31. Olson, *Red Cloud and the Sioux Problem*, 80–81.

32. Prucha, *American Indian Policy in Crisis*, 113–114.

CHAPTER 16

1. Hutton, *Phil Sheridan and His Army*, 180.

2. Sheridan to Sherman, September 26, 1868, *Record of Engagements*, 8.

3. Sheridan to Sherman, November 1, 1869, *Report of the Secretary of War, 1869–1870*.

4. Sheridan to Sherman, September 26, 1868, ibid., 12.

5. Hurst, "Beecher's Island Fight," 533, 534; *New York Tribune*, October 5, 1868; *New York Herald*, October 12, 1868; Forsyth, *Thrilling Days in Army Life*, 54–55; Hoig, *Battle of the Washita*, 54–68.

6. Sully to McKeever, September 16, 1868, Records of U.S. Army Commands, Selected Letters, 1868–1872, NA. See also Hoig, *Battle of the Washita*, 69–74.

7. Hyde, *Life of George Bent*, 316–317; Ediger and Hoffman, "Some Reminiscences," 140. For a full account of the Washita campaign, see Hoig, *Battle of the Washita*.

8. Sheridan to Sherman, November 1, 1869, *Report of the Secretary of War, 1869–1870*.

9. Manypenny, *Our Indian Wards*, 246–247.

10. Rister, "Evans' Christmas Day Indian Fight," 275–301; Hoig, *Tribal Wars of the Southern Plains*, 264–268.

11. Hyde, *Life of George Bent*, 331–334.

12. Prucha, *American Indian Policy in Crisis*, 73–77.

13. Utley, "Peace Policy of General Grant," 126.

14. Sherman ltr., May 14, 1871, LR/OIA, Kiowa Agency, NA; Tatum, *Red Brothers*, 116; Hoig, *The Kiowas and the Legend of Kicking Bird*, 155–160.

15. *Friend's Review* 26 (November 2, 1872), 166; *New York Times*, October 12, 23, 1872; *Washington Evening Star*, October 17, 23, 1872; Hoig, *The Kiowas and the Legend of Kicking Bird*, 174–177, 193.

16. Hoig, *The Kiowas and the Legend of Kicking Bird*, 213–226.

17. For a full account, see Pratt, *Battlefield and Classroom*.

18. Prucha, *American Indian Policy in Crisis*, 181.

19. Ibid., 86–87.

20. *U.S. Statutes at Large* 16: 566. The clause went on to say that all previous treaties that had been lawfully made and ratified would remain valid.

21. Prucha, *American Indian Policy in Crisis*, 69–71.

CHAPTER 17

1. *CofIA Report, 1868*, 250–252.

2. Sherman to Augur, December 4, 1868, LR, Dept./Platte, NA; cited in Olson, *Red Cloud and the Sioux Problem*, 85.

3. Olson, *Red Cloud and the Sioux Problem*, 85.

4. Ibid., 94–99.

5. *Twenty-Fifth Annual Report of the Board of Indian Commissioners, 1893*, 3–15; cited in Olson, *Red Cloud and the Sioux Problem*, 105.

6. Olson, *Red Cloud and the Sioux Problem*, 107–108.

7. Ibid.

8. Quintin to Sanbourne, May 19, 1871, LR, Montana Suptcy., M234, RG 75, NA.

9. Report of the U.S. Special Commission, August 22, 1870–October 10, 1870, Wm. Fayell, LR, Upper Platte Agency, RG 75, NA; Brunot/Campbell to Sec. of Interior, October 29, 1870, in *CofIA Report, 1870*, 384–388.

10. Hyde, *Red Cloud's Folk*, 189–204.

11. Utley, *Frontier Regulars*, 237.

12. Hyde, *Red Cloud's Folk*, 198.

13. Kappler, ed., *Indian Treaties*, 1002–1003.

14. Utley, *Frontier Regulars*, 242–243.

15. Briggs, "Black Hills Gold Rush," 71–99.

16. Wemett, "Custer's Expedition," 292–301; McLaird and Turchen, "Exploring the Black Hills," 404–437.

17. Prucha, *American Indian Policy in Crisis*, 170–171.

18. Hyde, *Red Cloud's Folk*, 241–244.

19. McLaird and Turchen, "Exploring the Black Hills," 415–416.

20. Article 12 of the treaty specified: "No treaty for the cession of any portion or part of the reservation herein described which may be held in common shall be of any validity or force as against the said Indians, unless executed and signed by at least three-fourths of all the adult male Indians, occupying or interested in the same." Kappler, ed., *Indian Treaties*, 1002.

21. Sherman to Hitchcock, February 11, 1873, Sherman Papers 90: 308–310, Library of Congress.

22. Utley, *Frontier Regulars*, 247.

23. Utley, "Peace Policy of General Grant," 140–141.

24. *HR Ex. Doc. 184*, 44/1: 8–9; Olson, *Red Cloud and the Sioux Problem*, 216.

25. Utley, *Frontier Regulars*, 248.

26. Report and Journal of the Commission to Obtain Certain Concessions From the Sioux Indians, December 18, 1876, *Sen. Ex. Doc. 9*, 44/2: 4. See also Prucha, *American Indian Policy in Crisis*, 171–172; Olson, *Red Cloud and the Sioux Problem*, 228.

27. Olson, *Red Cloud and the Sioux Problem*, 228.

28. Kappler, ed., *Indian Treaties*, 998.

29. Deloria and DeMallie, *Documents* 2: 1530–1534.

30. Utley, "Peace Policy of General Grant," 121.

31. *Fourth Annual Report of the Board of Indian Commissioners, 1872*, 4.

32. Prucha, *American Indian Policy in Crisis*, 68–69; Utley, "Peace Policy of General Grant," 131.

33. *U.S. Statutes at Large* 16: 566.

34. Utley, "Peace Policy of General Grant," 132.

35. Deloria and DeMallie, *Documents*, 1: 233–248, provide a discussion of the end to U.S. treaty making and the Senate debate on the matter.

Bibliography

ARTICLES

Anderson, Harry. "The Controversial Sioux Amendment to the Fort Laramie Treaty of 1851." *Nebraska History* 37 (September 1956).

————. "Indian Peace-Talkers and the Conclusion of the Sioux War of 1876." *Nebraska History* 44 (December 1963).

Bartles, W. L. "Massacre of Confederates by Osage Indians in 1863." *Collections of the Kansas State Historical Society* 8 (1903–1904).

Biesele, R. L. "Relations Between the German Settlers and the Indians in Texas, 1844–1860." *Southwestern Historical Quarterly* 31 (October 1927).

Briggs, Harold E. "The Black Hills Gold Rush." *North Dakota Historical Quarterly* 5 (1930–1931).

Bushnell, David I., Jr. "John Mix Stanley, Artist-Explorer." *Smithsonian Annual Report* (1924).

Chapman, Berlin B. "Establishment of the Wichita Reservation." *Chronicles of Oklahoma* 11 (December 1933).

Cooke, Philip St. George. "A Journey on the Santa Fe Trail," William E. Connelley, ed. *Mississippi Valley Historical Review* 12 (September 1925).

Dale, E. E. "Additional Letters of General Stand Watie." *Chronicles of Oklahoma* 1 (October 1921).

"Diary of Samuel A. Kingman." *Kansas Historical Quarterly* 1 (November 1932).

Ediger, Theodore A., and Vinnie Hoffman. "Some Reminiscences of the Battle of the Washita." *Chronicles of Oklahoma* 33 (Summer 1955).

"Extracts From the Diary of Major Sibley." *Chronicles of Oklahoma* 5 (June 1927).

Foreman, Carolyn. "Colonel James B. Many, Commandant at Fort Gibson, Fort Towson, and Fort Smith." *Chronicles of Oklahoma* 19 (June 1940).

Foreman, Grant, ed. "Journal of Proceedings at Our First Treaty With the Wild Indians." *Chronicles of Oklahoma* 14 (December 1936).

Green, Jerome A., ed. "Lt. Palmer Writes From the Bozeman Trail, 1867–68." *Montana Magazine* 28 (July 1978).

Gregg, Kate L. "The History of Fort Osage." *Missouri Historical Review* 34 (July 1940).

Grinnell, George Bird. "Bent's Old Fort and Its Builders." *Collections of the Kansas State Historical Society, 1919–1922* 15 (1923).

Hallock, Charles. "The Siege of Fort Atkinson." *Harper's New Monthly Magazine* 15 (October 1857).

Harmon, George D. "The United States Indian Policy in Texas, 1845–1860." *Mississippi Valley Historical Review* 17 (October 1930).

Hurst, John. "The Beecher's Island Fight." *Collections of the Kansas State Historical Society, 1919–1922* 15 (1923).

Jones, Harold W., ed. "The Diary of Assistant Surgeon Leonard McPhail on His Journey to the Southwest in 1835." *Chronicles of Oklahoma* 18 (September 1940).

"Journal of Elijah Hicks." *Chronicles of Oklahoma* 13 (March 1935).

Lewis, Ann. "Camp Napoleon." *Chronicles of Oklahoma* 9 (December 1931).

McLaird, James P., and Lesta V. Turchen. "Exploring the Black Hills, 1855–1875." *South Dakota History* 4 (Fall 1974).

Muckleroy, Anna. "The Indian Policy of Texas." *Southwestern Historical Quarterly* 26 (January 1923).

Pelzer, Louis, ed. "Captain Ford's Journal of an Expedition to the Rocky Mountains." *Mississippi Valley Historical Review* 12 (March 1926).

Perrine, Fred S., ed. "The Journal of Hugh Evans, Covering the First and Second Campaigns with the United States Dragoon Regiment in 1834 and 1835." *Chronicles of Oklahoma* 3 (September 1925).

Reid, Russell, and Clell G. Gannon, eds. "Journal of the Atkinson-O'Fallon Expedition." *North Dakota Historical Quarterly* 4 (October 1929).

Rister, Carl Coke, ed. "Colonel A. W. Evans' Christmas Day Indian Fight (1868)." *Chronicles of Oklahoma* 16 (September 1938).

Root, George A., ed. "Extracts From the Diary of Captain Lambert Bowman Wolf." *Kansas Historical Quarterly* 1 (May 1932).

Stanley, Henry M. "A British Journalist Reports the Medicine Lodge Peace Councils of 1867." *Kansas Historical Quarterly* 33 (Autumn 1967).

Thoburn, Joseph B. "Battle With Comanches." *Sturm's Oklahoma Magazine* 10 (August 1910).

————. "Indian Fight in Ford County, Kansas." *Collections of the Kansas State Historical Society* 12 (1911–1912).

"A Treaty Between Virginia and the Catawbas and Cherokees, 1756." *Virginia Magazine of History and Biography* 13 (January 1906).

Trickett, Dean. "The Civil War in the Indian Territory." *Chronicles of Oklahoma* 18 (September 1940).

Utley, Robert M. "The Celebrated Peace Policy of General Grant." *North Dakota History* 20 (July 1953).

Walker, Francis A. "The Indian Question." *North American Review* 116 (April 1873).

Webb, W. P. "The Last Treaty of the Republic of Texas." *Southwestern Historical Quarterly* 25 (January 1922).

Wemett, W. M. "Custer's Expedition to the Black Hills in 1874." *North Dakota Historical Quarterly* 6 (October 1931–July 1932).

Whipple, Henry B. "The Indian System." *North American Review* 99 (October 1864).

Williams, Samuel C. "Tatham's Characters Among the North American Indians." *Tennessee Historical Magazine* 7 (October 1921).

Wright, Muriel H. "A History of Fort Cobb." *Chronicles of Oklahoma* 34 (Spring 1956).

Young, Otis E. "The United States Mounted Ranger Battalion, 1832–33." *Mississippi Valley Historical Review* 41 (December 1954).

BOOKS

Abel, Annie Heloise. *The American Indian as a Participant in the Civil War*. Cleveland: Arthur H. Clark, 1919.

————. *The American Indian as a Slaveholder and Secessionist*. Cleveland: Arthur H. Clark, 1915.

Athearn, Robert G. *William Tecumseh Sherman and the Settlement of the West*. Norman: University of Oklahoma Press, 1956.

Barry, Louise. *The Beginning of the West: Annals of the Kansas Gateway to the American West, 1540–1854*. Topeka: Kansas State Historical Society, 1972.

Bartles, W. L. "Massacre of Confederates by Osage Indians." *Kansas State Historical Collections*, 8 (1903–1904).

Bauer, Jack. *Zachary Taylor*. Baton Rouge: Louisiana State University Press, 1985.

Berthrong, Donald J. *The Southern Cheyennes*. Norman: University of Oklahoma Press, 1963.

Blaine, Martha Royce. *Pawnee Passage: 1870–1875*. Norman: University of Oklahoma Press, 1990.

Bolton, Herbert E. *Texas in the Middle Eighteenth Century*. New York: Russell and Russell, 1962.

Carrington, Margaret. *Ab-sa-ra-ka, Home of the Crows*. Philadelphia: J. B. Lippincott, 1869.

Catlin, George. *Letters and Notes on the Manners, Customs, and Conditions of the North American Indians.* 2 vols. Reprint, New York: Dover, 1973.

———. *North American Indians.* 2 vols. Edinburgh: John Grant, 1956.

Chalfant, William Y. *Cheyennes and Horse Soldiers.* Norman: University of Oklahoma Press, 1989.

Chittenden, Hiram Martin, and Alfred Talbot Richardson. *Life, Letters, and Travels of Father Pierre Jean De Smet, S. J., 1801–1873.* 4 vols. New York: F. D. Harper, 1905.

Clarke, Dwight L. *Stephen Watts Kearny, Soldier of the West.* Norman: University of Oklahoma Press, 1961.

Cohen, Felix S. *Handbook of Federal Indian Law.* Albuquerque: University of New Mexico Press, 1971.

Correspondence of John Sedgwick, Major General, 2 vols. New York: De Vinne, 1902–1903.

Coues, Elliott, ed. *New Light on the Early History of the Greater Northwest, the Manuscript Journals of Alexander Henry, Fur Trader for the Northwest Company, and of David Thompson, Official Geographer and Explorer of the Same Company, 1799–1814.* New York: Francis P. Harper, 1897.

Crawford, Lewis F., ed. *Rekindling Camp Fires.* Bismarck: State Historical Society of North Dakota, 1926.

Deloria, Vine, Jr. *Behind the Trail of Broken Treaties: An Indian Declaration of Independence.* New York: Delacorte, 1974.

Deloria, Vine, Jr., and Raymond J. DeMallie. *Documents of American Indian Diplomacy, Treaties, Agreements, and Conventions, 1775–1979.* 2 vols. Norman: University of Oklahoma Press, 1999.

Dodge, R. I. *Our Wild Indians.* Hartford, Connecticut: A. D. Worthington and Co., 1882.

Fehrenbach, T. R. *Comanches, the Destruction of a People.* New York: Alfred A. Knopf, 1974.

Foley, Wiliam E., and C. David Rice. *The First Chouteaus, River Barons of Early St. Louis.* Urbana: University of Illinois Press, 1983.

Foreman, Grant. *Pioneer Days in the Early Southwest.* Cleveland: Arthur H. Clark, 1926.

Forsyth, Gen. George A. *Thrilling Days in Army Life.* New York: Harper & Brothers, 1901.

Frazer, Robert M. *Forts of the West.* Norman: University of Oklahoma Press, 1965.

Ghent, W. J. *The Early Far West, a Narrative Outline, 1540–1850.* New York: Longmans, Green, 1931.

Gibson, Arrell Morgan. *Oklahoma, a History of Five Centuries.* Norman: University of Oklahoma Press, 1981.

Gregg, Josiah. *Commerce of the Prairies.* Norman: University of Oklahoma Press, 1990.

Grinnell, George Bird. *Bent's Old Fort and Its Builders.* Topeka: Kansas State Historical Society, 1922.

————. *The Fighting Cheyennes*. Norman: University of Oklahoma Press, 1958.

Hagan, William T. *The Indian Rights Association: The Herbert Welsh Years, 1882–1904*. Tucson: University of Arizona Press, 1985.

————. *Taking Indian Lands: The Cherokee (Jerome) Commission, 1889–1893*. Norman: University of Oklahoma Press, 2003.

————. *United States–Comanche Relations: The Reservation Years*. New Haven: Yale University Press, 1976.

Hebard, Grace, and E. A. Brininstool. *The Bozeman Trail*. 2 vols. Cleveland: Arthur H. Clark, 1922.

Hedren, Paul L. *Fort Laramie and the Great Sioux War*. Lincoln: University of Nebraska Press, 1988.

Heitman, Francis B. *Historical Register and Dictionary of the United States Army*. Washington, D.C.: Government Printing Office, 1903.

Hildreth, James. *Dragoon Campaigns to the Rocky Mountains*. New York: Wiley and Long, 1936.

Hoig, Stan. *The Battle of the Washita*. New York: Doubleday, 1976.

————. *The Kiowas and the Legend of Kicking Bird*. Boulder: University Press of Colorado, 2000.

————. *The Sand Creek Massacre*. Norman: University of Oklahoma Press, 1961.

————. *Tribal Wars of the Southern Plains*. Norman: University of Oklahoma Press, 1993.

Hoopes, Alban W. *Indian Affairs and Their Administration*. Philadelphia: University of Pennsylvania Press, 1932.

Horsman, Reginald. *Race and Manifest Destiny: The Origins of American Racial Anglo-Saxonism*. Cambridge: Harvard University Press, 1981.

Hutton, Paul Andrew. *Phil Sheridan and His Army*. Foreword by Robert M. Utley. Norman: University of Oklahoma Press, 1985.

Hyde, George E. *Life of George Bent*. Edited by Savoie Lottinville. Norman: University of Oklahoma Press, 1968.

————. *Red Cloud's Folk: A History of the Oglala Sioux Indians*. Norman: University of Oklahoma Press, 1975.

Irving, Washington. *Adventures of Captain Bonneville: U.S.A. in the Rocky Mountains and the Far West*. Norman: University of Oklahoma Press, 1961.

Israel, Fred L., ed. *The State of the Union Messages of the Presidents, 1790–1966*. 3 vols. New York: Chelsea House, 1966.

Jackson, Helen Hunt. *A Century of Dishonor: A Sketch of the United States Government's Dealing With Some of the Indian Tribes*. New York: Harper and Brothers, 1881.

Jacobs, Wilbur. *Dispossessing the American Indian: Indians and Whites on the Colonial Frontier*. New York: Charles Scribner's Sons, 1972.

James, Edwin. *An Account of an Expedition From Pittsburgh to the Rocky Mountains*. 2 vols. Ann Arbor: University Microfilms, 1966.

James, Marquis. *The Raven*. Indianapolis: Bobbs Merrill, 1929.

James, Thomas. *Three Years Among the Mexicans and Indians*. Chicago: Rio Grande, 1962.

Jones, Douglas C. *The Treaty of Medicine Lodge*. Norman: University of Oklahoma Press, 1966.

Kappler, Charles J., comp. and ed. *Indian Treaties*. New York: Interland, 1972.

Kavanagh, Thomas W. *Comanche Political History: An Ethnohistorical Perspective, 1706–1875*. Lincoln: University of Nebraska Press, 1996.

Lester, C. Edwards. *Sam Houston and His Republic*. New York: Burgess, Stringer, 1846.

Lewis, J. O. *Aboriginal Port Folio*. Philadelphia: J. O. Lewis, 1835(–1836).

Lowe, Percival G. *Five Years a Dragoon ('49 to '54) and Other Adventures on the Great Plains*. Norman: University of Oklahoma Press, 1965.

Manypenny, George W. *Our Indian Wards*. Cincinnati: Robert Clarke, 1880.

Mattes, Merrill J. *The Great Platte River Road*. Lincoln: Nebraska State Historical Society, 1969.

McLean, Malcolm. *Papers Concerning Robertson's Colony*. 18 vols. Austin: University of Texas Press, 1974–1993.

Nichols, Roger L. *General Henry Atkinson: A Western Military Career*. Norman: University of Oklahoma Press, 1965.

Olson, James C. *Red Cloud and the Sioux Problem*. Lincoln: University of Nebraska Press, 1965.

Pike, Albert. *Report on Mission to the Indian Nations*. Washington, D.C.: Masonic Order, facsimile reprint, 1968, Gibson File, Western History Collection, University of Oklahoma.

Portraits of North American Indians, With Sketches of Scenery, etc. Painted by J. M. Stanley. Washington, D.C.: Smithsonian Institution, December 1852.

Pratt, Richard Henry. *Battlefield and Classroom: Four Decades With the American Indian, 1867–1904*. Edited by Robert Utley. New Haven: Yale University Press, 1966.

Price, Monroe E. *Law and the American Indian: Readings, Notes, and Cases*. New York: Bobbs Merrill, 1973.

Prucha, Francis Paul. *American Indian Policy in Crisis: Christian Reformers and the Indian, 1865–1900*. Norman: University of Oklahoma Press, 1976.

———. *American Indian Policy in the Formative Years: The Indian Trade and Intercourse Acts, 1790–1834*. Cambridge: Harvard University Press, 1962.

———. *The Great Father: The United States Government and the American Indians*. 2 vols. Lincoln: University of Nebraska Press, 1984.

———. *Indian Policy in the United States*. Lincoln: University of Nebraska Press, 1981.

Quaife, Milo Milton, ed. *The Diary of James K. Polk*. 4 vols. Chicago: A. C. McClurg, 1910.

Richardson, Rupert Norval. *The Comanche Barrier to South Plains Settlement*. Glendale: Arthur H. Clark, 1933.

Royce, Charles C. *The Cherokee Nation of Indians*. Chicago: Smithsonian Institution Press, 1875.

Satz, Ronald N. *American Indian Policy in the Jacksonian Era*. Lincoln: University of Nebraska Press, 1975.

Schmeckebier, Laurence F. *The Office of Indian Affairs, Its History, Activities, and Organization*. Baltimore: Johns Hopkins University Press, 1927.

Schoolcraft, H. R. *Personal Memoirs of a Residence of Thirty Years With the Indian Tribes, 1812–1842*. Philadelphia: Grambo, 1851.

Slattery, Charles Lewis. *Felix Reville Brunot, 1820–1898; A Civilian in the War for the Union, President of the First Board of Indian Commissioners*. New York: Longmans, Green, 1901.

Smith, Thomas T. *The Old Army in Texas*. Austin: Texas State Historical Association, 2000.

Smither, Harriett, ed. *Journals of the Sixth Congress of the Republic of Texas*. 3 vols. Austin: Von Boeckmann-Jones, 1940–1945.

Stanley, Henry M. *My Early Travels in America*. Lincoln: University of Nebraska Press, 1982. Original printing as Vol. 1 of *My Early Travels and Adventures in America and Asia*. New York: Scribner, 1895.

Sunder, John E. *The Fur Trade on the Upper Missouri, 1840–1865*. Norman: University of Oklahoma Press, 1965.

Tatum, Lawrie. *Our Red Brothers and the Peace Policy of President Ulysses S. Grant*. Lincoln: University of Nebraska Press, 1970.

Thwaites, Reuben Gold, ed. *James' Account of the S. H. Long Expedition, 1819–20, Early Western Travels, 1748–1846*. Vol. 16. Cleveland: Arthur H. Clark, 1905.

Unrau, William E. *The Kansa Indians, a History of the Wind People, 1673–1873*. Norman: University of Oklahoma Press, 1971.

Utley, Robert M. *Frontier Regulars, the United States Army and the Indian, 1866–1891*. New York: Macmillan, 1973.

Vaughn, J. W. *The Battle of Platte Bridge*. Norman: University of Oklahoma Press, 1963.

Ware, Eugene F. *The Indian War of 1864*. New York: St. Martin's, 1960. Original publication Topeka: Crane, 1911.

Webb, Walter Prescott. *The Texas Rangers*. Austin: University of Texas Press, 1965.

Williams, Amelia, and Eugene C. Barker. *The Writings of Sam Houston, 1793–1863*. 8 vols. Austin: University of Texas Press, 1938–1943.

Williams, Samuel Cole. *Henry Timberlake's Memoirs, 1756–1765*. Marietta, Ga.: Continental Book Co., 1948.

Winfrey, James H., and James M. Day, eds. *Indian Papers of Texas and the Southwest, 1825–1916*. 4 vols. Austin: Pemberton, 1966.

Wooster, Robert. *The Military and United States Indian Policy, 1865–1903*. New Haven: Yale University Press, 1988.

Wooten, Dudley Goodall, ed. *A Comprehensive History of Texas*. 2 vols. Dallas: W. G. Scarff, 1898.

Young, Otis E. *The First Military Escort on the Santa Fe Trail, 1829*. Glendale: Arthur H. Clark, 1952.

COLLECTIONS

Gilcrease Institute, Tulsa, Oklahoma
    John Drew Papers
Kansas Historical Society, Topeka
    Clark Papers
Library of Congress, Washington, D.C.
    William T. Sherman Papers
Oklahoma Historical Society Research Division, Oklahoma City
    Foreman Transcript
    Fort Gibson Letterbook, 1834–1836
    T. H. Barrett Collection
University of Arkansas Libraries, Fayetteville
    Special Collections
University of Central Oklahoma, Edmond
    Archives and Special Collections
University of Oklahoma Libraries, Norman
    Western History Collection
    Lewis Cass Papers
University of Texas, Austin
    Barker Historical Collection, Ford Memoirs

GOVERNMENT DOCUMENTS—PUBLISHED

Annual Report, Secretary of War, 1868
Board of Indian Commissioners, Annual Reports
Carter, Clarence E., ed. *The Territorial Papers of the United States.* 27 vols. Washington, D.C.: U.S. Printing Office, 1934–48.
Commissioner of Indian Affairs, Annual Reports, 1848, 1850, 1851, 1853, 1854, 1855, 1858, 1859, 1860, 1863, 1864, 1865, 1866, 1867, 1868, 1870, 1872
Compilation of the Official Records of the Union and Confederate Armies, War of the Rebellion, 1880–1891. 128 vols. Washington, D.C.: GPO, 1880–1891.
"Expedition of Colonel Dodge." *Senate Report No. 654, 24/1.*
HR Ex. Doc. 1, 19/1.
HR Ex. Doc. 27, 35/2.
HR Ex. Doc. 184, 44/1.
New American State Papers, Foreign Relations
New American State Papers, Indian Affairs
New American State Papers, Military Affairs
Portraits of North American Indians With Sketches of Scenery, Etc., Painted by J. M. Stanley, Deposited With the Smithsonian Institution. Washington, D.C.: Smithsonian Institution, 1852.
Proceedings: War and Reconstruction in Indian Territory: a History Conference in Observance of the 130th Anniversary of the Fort Smith Council. Fort Smith: National Park Service at Fort Smith, 1995.

Record of Engagements With Hostile Indians Within the Military Division of the Missouri From 1868 to 1882. Chicago: Military Division of the Missouri, 1882.

Report of Messrs. Butler and Lewis, Commissioners to Treat With the Camanches and Other Prairie Indians Under Instructions From the War Department, September 13, 1845. Washington, D.C.: GPO, 1846.

Report of the Secretary of War, 1868, 1869, 1870

Sen. Ex. Doc. 1, 23/2, Dodge Report.

Sen. Ex. Doc. 1, 23/1, Wheelock Report.

Sen. Ex. Doc. 9, Report and Journal of the Commission to Obtain Concessions From the Sioux Indians, Dec. 18, 1876.

Sen. Ex. Doc. 26, 39/2, Sand Creek Massacre.

Sen. Ex. Doc. 34, 46/3, CofIA Report, 1881.

Sen. Rep. 156, 39/2, The Chivington Massacre.

U.S. Statutes at Large

GOVERNMENT DOCUMENTS—UNPUBLISHED

Original Document, Treaty of 1851, NA.

M567—LR by Office of the Adjutant General (Main Series), NA.

M234—LR, Office of Indian Affairs, Kiowa Agency, NA.

M234—LR, Office of Indian Affairs, Montana Suptcy., NA.

M234—LR, Office of Indian Affairs, Southern Suptcy., NA.

M234—LR, Office of Indian Affairs, Texas Agency, NA.

M234—LR, Office of Indian Affairs, Upper Platte Agency, NA.

M234—LR, Office of Indian Affairs, Western Creek Agency, NA.

M234—LR, Office of Indian Affairs, Western Suptcy., NA.

M234—LR, Office of Indian Affairs, Wichita Agency, NA.

M668—Records Relating to Indian Treaties, Ratified Indian Treaties, 1722–1869, NA.

RG75—Proceedings of a Council Held at Fort Gibson, Sept. 1834, NA.

RG98—LR, Dept. of the Platte.

RG393—Records of U.S. Army Commands, 1821–1920, Selected Ltrs., NA.

T494—Articles of Agreement and Convention Made and Concluded at the City of Washington, Roll 8, NA.

T494—Articles of a Treaty Made and Concluded at Fort Gibson, NA.

T494—Documents Relating to the Negotiation of Ratified and Unratified Treaties With Various Indian Tribes, NA.

T494—Articles of Agreement and Convention Made This Twenty-Fourth Day September A.D. 1858 at Table Creek, Nebraska Territory, Roll 8, NA.

T494—Report of a Council Held at Fort Zarah, Kansas, Roll 7, NA.

PERIODICALS

Alexandria Gazette (Virginia)
American Magazine (1760)
Arkansas Advocate (Little Rock)
Arkansas Intelligencer (Van Buren)
Army and Navy Chronicle
Cherokee Advocate (Tahlequah, I.T.)
Chicago Times
Chicago Tribune
Cincinnati (Ohio) *Commercial*
Cincinnati (Ohio) *Gazette*
Columbian Fountain (Washington, D.C.)
Daily National Intelligencer (Washington, D.C.)
Dallas Herald
Emporia (Kansas) *News*
Frank Leslie's Illustrated Newspaper
Friends' Review
Galveston (Texas) *Weekly News*
Harper's Illustrated Weekly
Harper's Weekly
Kansas City Times
Kansas Daily Tribune (Lawrence)
Kansas Weekly Tribune (Lawrence)
Leavenworth (Kansas) *Daily Conservative*
Leavenworth (Kansas) *Daily Times*
Missouri Democrat (St. Louis)
Missouri Republican (St. Louis)
Nebraska Republican (Omaha)
New Orleans Picayune
New York Herald
New York Times
New York Tribune
New York World
Niles' Register
St. Louis Democrat
St. Louis Intelligencer
Washington Evening Star
Western Mountaineer (Golden, Colorado)

Index

Page numbers in italics indicate illustrations

Abbay, George C.: captured by Indians, 35–36, 40; death of, 41
Abert, James (Lt.), topographical party of, 86
Absentee Shawnee Indians, deaths of, 129
Acaquash (Ecoquash, Waco chief), 57, 62–63, 66–67
Adelsverein, German nobleman society, 77
Adobe Walls, 1874 battle of, 170
African-Americans, subjugation of, xiv, 184
Alamo, 58, 60, 83
Alasares (Wichita chief), 99
Alerdice, Susanna, death of, 169
Alights on the Cloud (Cheyenne chief), 94–95
Allison, W. B. (Sen.), 176
American Indians, societal existence of, 184
Anadarko Indians, 62–63, 65, 67, 74, 81–82, 117, 129; treaty of with South, 117; U.S. Indian treaties, 185
Anglo-Saxon, presumed superiority of, xiv
Antelope Hills, 82, 166
Anthony, Scott J. (Maj.), orders Cheyennes to Sand Creek camp, 114

Apache Indians, 102. *See also* Plains Apache Indians
Arapaho Indians, 35, 86–87, 93, 96, 98–100, 102, 108–10, 126–28, 130–31, 134, 139, 151, 161, 165, 167, 172; attack on Comanche camp, 55–56; Barnum display of, 112; Dodge contact with, 44; effect of Colorado events on, 114; Fort Laramie council attended by, 88; Medicine Lodge council attended by, 125, 146–47, 150; reservation for, 152; territory assigned to, 106–07; treaties of, 185; village attacked, 138. *See also* Northern Arapaho Indians, Southern Arapaho Indians
Arbuckle, Matthew (Gen.), 49–53, 58; appointed treaty commissioner, 48
Arikara Indians, 36, 44–45, 93; Atkinson/O'Fallon visit to, 22; Dodge contact with, 44; Fort Laramie council attended by, 88; treaties of, 185; troubles of, 16–17
Arikaree Fork, battle of, 166
Arkansas, 31–32, 47, 116

Arkansas River, 28, 31, 35, 37, 44, 54, 56, 58, 86, 88, 98, 100–101, 106, 109, 111, 113, 116, 118, 127–29, 131, 151–53, 164–66, 194; Comanche camps on, 108; Osage range of, 27; road on, 106, 113; traders operating on, 98

Arkansas Territory, Osage land titles of ceded to U.S., 31

Armstrong, William (Capt.), 18, 56

Armstrong, F. W., 37, 43; appointment as treaty commissioner, 48; Fort Gibson council attended by, 42; illness and death of, 48; Osage treaty initiated by, 47

Arra-tu-resash (Big Robber, Crow chief), 93

Ascimke (Wichita captive girl), 51

Ash Hollow, Nebraska, 133

Ashley, William, 17, 24

Assiniboine Indians, 24, 93–94; Fort Laramie council attended by, 88; treaties of, 186

Atkinson, Henry (Col.): Arikara meeting of, 22; O'Fallon conflict with, 23; river craft experiment of, 18; Yellowstone expedition of, 15–19, 24, 35–36

Augur, C. C. (Maj. Gen.), 144, 157, 172; role as commissioner, 145

Austin, Texas, 58, 61, 73

Auton-ish-eh (Arapaho chief), Fort Laramie speech of, 92

Axe (Pawnee Loup chief), 45

Bad Hand (Sioux), treaty proposal by, 140

Baldwin, Frank (Lt.), 170

Barbour, James (Sec. of War), 24; pledge to Indians, 4

Barnard, George, 74

Barnard's trading house, 72

Barnum, P. T., Indians displayed in museum of, 112

Battles of: Adobe Walls (1874), 170; Arikaree Fork, 166; Chouteau's Island, 98; Little Robe Creek, 82; New Orleans, 91; Palo Alto, 73; Palo Duro Canyon, 170; Pea Ridge, Arkansas, 115; Platte River Bridge, 137; Plum Creek, 60; the Rosebud, 178; Summit Springs, 169; the Washita, 167–68; Wichita Agency, 120; Wilson's Creek, 118; Wolf Creek, 99

Baylor, Agent John R., 83

Bean, Jesse, 34

Bear Blanket (Sioux), 140

Bear's Feather (Old Bark, Cheyenne chief), Fort Laramie speech of, 92

Bear's Tooth (Crow chief), speech of, 154–55

Beatte (Beatie), Pierre, 37, 40

Becknell, William, Santa Fe trade route opened by, 35

Beecher, Lt. Frederick, 166

Beka-chebetcha (Cut Nose, Arapaho chief), 92

Belknap, Sec. of War William, 176

Bent, George, 151

Bent, Robert, 109, 125, 130; land awarded to, 110

Bent, William, 10, 101, 109, 111, 126, 131; role as agent for Cheyennes and Arapahos, 107–08; at Fort Zarah council, 130; trade caravan of, 98; treaty commissioner role of, 125

Bent's Fort, 35, 44, 51, 107; intertribal peace council at, 99

Bent's New Fort, description of, 108

Big Wichita River, 64

Big Bow (Kiowa chief), 125

Big Cheyenne River, 173

Big Fatty (Pawnee chief), 94

Big Hill (Osage) band, 121

Big Mandan (Brulé orator), complaints of white misdeeds, 135

Big Mouth (Arapaho chief), 110, 125

Big Mouth (Sioux chief), 140–41

Big Robber (Arra-tu-resash, Crow chief), 93

Big Tree (Kiowa), 169–70

Big Yancton (Sioux chief), complaint of, 92

Bighorn Mountains, 142, 157, 174

Bighorn River, 142, 161, 155, 176

Biloxi Indians, 65, 74

Bintah (Caddo chief), 62

Bird's Fort, 63, 65

Bismarck, North Dakota, 22, 175

Black, J. S., 62

Black Bear (Arapaho chief), 138

Black Bear (Cheyenne chief), 157

Black Bear (Otoe chief), 94, 95

Black Beaver, Indian Territory evacuation led by, 116

Black Dog (Shone-ta-sah-ba, Osage chief), 50, 53, 120

Black Hawk (Oglala chief), 93
Black Hill Expedition, 175
Black Hills, 174–77, 184
Black Kettle (Cheyenne chief), 110, *111*, 114, 128, 130, 132, 143–44, 147, 149, 183; death of, 168; depredations by band of, 165; at Fort Wise council, 109; at Little Arkansas council, 125; peace overture by, 113; peaceful position of, 146; speech of, 124, 126; takes band south, 131; Washita village of attacked, 167
Black Nable (Sioux leader), 140
Blackfoot Indians, 17, 44; treaty hopes of fail, 24
Blackfoot Sioux, 87, 139, 157
Blah-at-sah-ah-kak-che (Little Owl, Arapaho chief), 92
Blinn, Mrs. Clara, 168
Board of Indian Commissioners, 178–79
Bogy, Capt. Charles, 130
Bogy, Commissioner Lewis V., 130; empty promise of, 131
Boone, Albert G., conducts Treaty of Fort Wise, 109–10
Boone, Daniel, 36, 109
Boone, Lt. Nathan, 36
Bowles (Duwali, Cherokee chief), death of, 59; friendship of with Sam Houston, 61
Bozeman Trail, 155, 158, 160, 162; ignored in 1866 pact, 141
Brant, Thomas, 53
Brazos River, 65, 70–71, 73, 81; peace council on, 61–63
Brazos reservations, 81–82, 104; removal of tribes from, 83–84
Bridger, Jim, 10, 87, 89, 93
British crown, Indian treaty system of, 1
Brown, B. Gratz, 87, 101; Treaty of Fort Laramie (1851) reported by, 88, 91
Brown, George, 145; describes Dog Soldiers, 150
Brulé Sioux Indians, 87, 92, 133–34, 139–41, 155–57
Brunot, Commissioner Felix, 174; criticizes treaty system, 2
Buchanan, James (President), likeness of, 108
Bucksnort, Texas, 73
Budd, H. J., 145
Buell, Lt. Col. George W., 170

Buffalo Chief (Arapaho chief), speech of, 151–52
Buffalo Hump (Po-char-na-quar-hip, Comanche chief), 82, 119; at Council Springs meeting, 67; depredations denied by, 79; depredations of, 119; Gulf Coast raid of, 60, 75, 78, 81–82, 118, 125; meeting of with Pike, 117; portrait of painted, 66; presence at Comanche Peak, 71; raid into Mexico, 77; speech of, 72
Bull Bear (Cheyenne chief), 131–32; leads Dog Soldiers to war, 113; signs Medicine Lodge treaty, 152
Bullet (Delaware chief), 37, 40
Bureau of Indian Affairs, 161, 169
Burrow, James (Kiowa captive), 128
Butler, Pierce M., 74, 76; appointment of as Indian commissioner, 69; at Comanche Peak, 70; peace expedition of, 65–66; presence of at Texas treaty, 62
Butte des Morts, 12; treaty site of, *26*

Cache Creek, 64, 66, 68
Caddo Indians: at Bird's Fort, 61, 65, 67, 74–75, 79, 81; at Council Springs, 67; at Fort Smith council, 123; Civil War refuge of, 120; deaths of, 129; language of, 10; treaties of, 186
Calhoun, John C. (Sec. of War), 11; actions on the Upper Missouri, 15
California, 18, 86–87, 134, 175
California Gold Rush, 78, 100; trail drive to, 101
Camp Connor, renaming of as Fort Reno, 142
Camp Holmes, 51, 53; treaty site of, 49. *See also* Camp Mason
Camp Leavenworth, 38
Camp Mason, 55–56. *See also* Camp Holmes
Camp Napoleon, intertribal council at, 122
Camp Radziminski, 82
Camp (Fort) Robinson, 174
Camp Supply. *See* Fort Supply
Camp Washita, 38
Camp Weld, peace talks at, 113
Campbell, Robert, 94; at Fort Laramie council, 89
Canada, 178; fur trade of, 15
Canadian River, 35, 37–38, 48, 70, 117

Canby, Edward (Gen.), murder of, 171
Cantonment (Camp) Barbour, founding
    of, 24
Cantonment Missouri, as early redoubt, 15–
    16
Capron, Horace, 81
captives, 51, 55, 63, 65, 69, 73–74, 127–28, 130,
    169
Carlisle Indian School, 171
Carr, A. E. (Maj.), 169
Carrington, Henry B. (Brig. Gen.),
    Bozeman Trail posts built by, 142
Carson, Kit, treaty commissioner role of, 125
Casper, Wyoming, 137
Cass, Lewis, 12; observation regarding treaty
    making, 11; treaty efforts of, 25–26
Catawba Indians, 5
Catlin, George, 37; illness of, 40; Indians
    view paintings of, 76; member of
    Leavenworth Expedition, 38; march
    ordeal recorded by, 42; sketches Indian
    leaders, 42
Central Plains, 14, 110, 164; destiny of, 123;
    first treaty experience of, 18; Indian
    barrier across, 33; intertribal warring on,
    44, 96; national title to, 180; problems of
    contact on, 12; proprietorship on, xiii;
    U.S. expansion across, 85; white
    intrusion onto, 97
Central Superintendency, 169
Chambers, Adam B., 86, 89, 95
Chandler, Zachariah (Sec. of Int.), 176–77
Chapman, Amos, 166
Charaterish (Pawnee chief), 14
Cherokee County, Texas, Indian massacre
    in, 58
Cherokee Indians, xii, 4, 13, 37, 41, 43, 47,
    51–52, 58, 65, 70–71, 74, 113, 116, 129–30;
    at Camp Holmes treaty, 49; Civil War
    position of, 116; council houses of, 5;
    ejection from Texas, 59; leadership issue
    of, 123; pro-Rebel forces of attack
    loyalists, 118; relocation of, 31; Texas
    removal of, 81; treaty with, 9; Wilson's
    Creek action of, 118
Cherokee Nation, 127; Southern alignment
    of, 118; Plains Indian council sponsored
    by, 101
Cherokee Outlet, 130; creation of, 127

Cherokee Treaty of 1828, 127
Cherryvale, Kansas, 121
Cheyenne Indians, 35, 44, 51, 55, 86–87, 90,
    92–96, 98–100, 103, 106–10, 113, 125–28,
    130–32, 134, 137, 139, 141–42, 151, 154–56,
    161, 165, 168, 183; attack at Arikaree Fork,
    166; Chivington attack on, 113; display
    of by Barnum, 112; ear-cutting cer-
    emony of, 91; effect of Colorado events
    on, 114; Fort Laramie council attended
    by, 88; Fort Wise council attended by,
    109; Fort Wise treaty refuted by, 113;
    Little Arkansas treaty signed by, 128;
    massacre of Comanche camp, 55–56; at
    Medicine Lodge, 146–47, 150; and
    meeting with Atkinson, 21; Pawnee/
    Arikara meeting of, 45; Sacred Medicine
    Arrow Ritual of, 147, 149; territory
    assigned to by Fort Laramie treaty, 106;
    treaties of, 186. See also Cheyenne Dog
    Soldiers, Northern Cheyenne Indians,
    Southern Cheyenne Indians, Suhtai
    band
Cheyenne/Sioux village, 143; Hancock's
    burning of, 147
Cheyenne Dog Soldiers, 11, 122, 125, 127,
    131, 143, 146, 151–54, 165, 168, 183; arrival
    of at Medicine Lodge, 150; difficult
    problem posed by, 149; domination of
    western Kansas, 143; hostility of, 147;
    post–Sand Creek attacks of, 113
Chicago, Illinois, 161, 164–65
Chickasaw Council House, Cherokee treaty
    at, xii
Chickasaw Indians, 4, 37, 65, 70, 83, 116, 130;
    Civil War alignment of, 117; pro-Rebel
    forces of attack loyalists, 118; scouts of,
    70; stickball contest of, 56
Chi-sho-hung-ka (Osage chief), 120
Chisholm, George, 56
Chisholm, Jesse, 10, 37, 43, 56, 61, 66, 73–76,
    79, 122, 125, 127
Chisholm, Thomas (Cherokee chief), death
    of, 52; role of at Fort Gibson council, 42–
    44
Chivington, John M. (Col.), 106, 126, 144;
    Sand Creek attack of, 113
Choctaw Indians, 4, 37, 44, 47–48, 51, 53, 56,
    83, 91, 116, 130; burial of Pushmataha in

Congressional Cemetery, 113; Civil War position of, 117; pro-Rebel forces of attack loyalists, 118; stickball contest of, 56

Chom-o-pard-u-a (Comanche chief), 67

Chouteau, A. P. (Col.), death of, 56; Indian delegation visit to Washington postponed by, 55; loss of Osage land denounced by, 47; Pawnee attack on, 98; role as treaty commissioner, 54; relocation of Osages by, 30; trading post of, 53–54; treaty expedition accompanied by, 48

Chouteau, Auguste, 15–16

Chouteau, Edward, 54–55, 88

Chouteau, Jean Pierre, persuades Osages to sign treaty, 29–30

Chouteau, Paul Liguest (Maj.), 53–54

Chouteau's Island, 98

Church humanitarians, challenge to U.S. treaty system, 1–2; Indian policy control sought by, xiv

Cimarron Crossing, 124–25

Cimarron Cutoff, 35, 100

Cimarron River, 64, 153; saline visited by Osages, 28

Civil War, xiv, 110, 118, 122, 134–35, 164–65

Civil John (Seneca chief), 44; at Fort Gibson council, 42

Clark, William (Gov.), 14–16, 28, 30; Osage fort proposed by, 28; Osage treaty conducted by, 29–30; promise to Indians, 26; speech of, 25; treaty expedition of, 25

Clark, Ben, 166

Clear Fork of Brazos, 65, 79

Clermont (Osage chief), 50–51, 54; at Fort Gibson council; 43; band of, 120; doubts of U.S. promises expressed by, 47–48; 1825 delegation led by, 31; speech of, 34

Coffee, Holland, 48–49

Coffee's trading post, 49, 70

Cohen, Felix S., xi

Coles, William, as 1825 treaty commissioner, 31

Colley, Samuel G., 111

Collins, Caspar, death of, 137

Colorado, 35, 98, 131, 140, 144, 151, 165–66, 175. See also Colorado Territory

Colorado River, 54, 60, 66, 70–71, 73, 77, 80–81; gold discovered in, 107

Colorado Territory, 107, 110–11, 121

Comanche Indians, 35–37, 41–42, 44, 48–52, 54–56, 63, 65, 68, 70, 73, 75–76, 79, 81–84, 98–104, 107–8, 117–19, 123–25, 127, 149, 152, 161, 167–68, 170; anger of over San Antonio affair, 64; Cache Creek treaty council of, 66; Camp Holmes treaty recanted by, 53; captives held by, 69; Comanche Peak meeting of, 68–72; conditions set by Texas treaty, 59; contact with sought, 34; Council Springs council attended by, 66–67; courthouse massacre of, 60; depredations of, 113, 122; divisions of, 61; dragoon meeting with, 39; friendly meeting with, 39; Leavenworth expedition met by, 38; Medicine Lodge attended by, 146–48; Parker's Fort raided by, 58; presence at Fort Smith council, 123; raiding into Mexico, 77, 169; reservation assigned to, 128; Texas peace commission hosted by, 65; Texas Ranger attack on, 61; Texas treaties with, 57–58, 62, 74, 80; treaty of German settlement, 78; U.S. treaties with, 186–87; Washington treaty with, 112; woeful condition of, 81. See also Hoish Comanches, Kotsoteka Comanches, Nokoni Comanches, Noon-ah Comanches, Penetaka Comanches, Ten-nay-wash Comanches, Yamparica Comanches

Commissioner of Indian Affairs, role of in treaty making, 2

Confederacy, 115–118; Indian treaties with, 118–23. See also South

Congressional Cemetery, Indian delegates buried at, 7, 113

Connor, John (Delaware leader), 56, 61, 63–64, 66, 75, 79; Texas Indians removed by, 81

Connor, Patrick E. (Gen.), Arapaho village attacked by, 137–38

Coodey, Shorey (Judge) (Cherokee speaker), 70–71, 123

Cooley, Dennis N. (Commissioner), 122

Cooper, Samuel (Col.), 89

Corn Tassel (Cherokee chief), lecture of to commissioners, 6

Cottonwood Springs, Nebraska, 135

Council Bluffs, Iowa, 15; as treaty site, 24

Council at Fort Zarah, Kansas (1866), 130–32

Council at mouth of Cache Creek (1843), 66

Council on North Fork, Red River (Texas, 1843), 64

Council Springs (Texas), 66, 71, 73, 76; council of, 67; council of 1843 at, 62; council of 1844 at, 66–67; council of 1845 at, 68; council of 1846 at, 71–73

Cox, Jacob D. (Sec. of Int.), 173

Coy (Kiowa woman), 111

Crawford, Samuel (Gov.): military force supported by, 146; interview of, 144

Crazy Horse (Sioux chief), 174, 184

Crazy Woman's Fork, 142

Creek Indians, 4, 13, 37, 41, 44, 47–48, 51, 53–54, 70–71, 116, 118, 130; Camp Holmes treaty presence of, 49; ceded lands of, 123; Civil War position of, 116; council with Pike, 117; retreat of loyalists to Kansas, 118

Crook, George (Gen.), 164, 176; campaign of, 178

Cross Timbers, 42, 49, 52

Crow Agency, 157

Crow Indians, 86, 94–95, 154–55; at Fort Laramie council, 91, 93; 1825 treaty of, 23–24

Culbertson, Alexander, 88

Culver, Agent F. B., 109

Curtis, Samuel R. (Maj. Gen.), role as treaty commissioner, 138–39

Custer, George Armstrong (Lt. Col.), 163–64, 166, 169; appointment as Seventh Cavalry commander, 143; Black Hills Expedition of, 175, 184; courtmartial of, 144; Kansas campaign of, 144; Little Bighorn defeat of, 178; Washita campaign of, 167–68

Cut Nose (Arapaho chief). See Beka-chebetcha

Cut Nose (Cheyenne chief), 140

Cuthead Sioux, 157, 160

Dakota Territory, 134, 138–39, 157–58, 172, 175, 178

Daniels, N. H. (Lt.), 141

Darlington, Brinton, 168

Darlington Agency, 168, 171

Davidson, John W. (Lt. Col.), 170

Davis, Edmund J. (Gov.), 170

Davis, Jefferson (1st Lt.), 36, 117, 120

Dawes Commission, 171

De Smet, Father Pierre Jean, 88, 93–94, 158, 160, 162; Cheyenne ear-notching described by, 91; interview of, 144; peace commission joined by, 156; report on Horse Creek council by, 89, 91

Dearborn, Henry (Sec. of War), 28

Delaware Indians, 33, 63–65, 79, 108, 116–17, 170; Civil War refuge of, 120; Texas removal of, 81; treaty councils attended by, 62, 67, 72

Deloria, Vine, Jr., xii; treaty method described by, 2

DeMallie, Raymond, J., xii; treaty method described by, 2

Denver, 110–11, 121; peace talks held at, 113

Dodge, Henry (Lt. Col.), 10, 15, 36, 43, 45, 76; peace talks conducted by, 38–41; Indian delegation recruited by, 42; mountain expedition of, 44–46, 51; takes command of Leavenworth Expedition, 38–39

Dodge City, Kansas, 100

Dole, William P. (Commissioner), 121

Doublehead (Cherokee), 70, 73

Doudna, Willoughby (Capt.), 121

Dougherty, John, 44

Doyle, Gillis, 69

Dull Knife (Cheyenne chief), 157; 1866 treaty signed by, 140

Dutch (Cherokee war chief), xiii, 37, 40, 52

Dye, William McE. (Maj.), 160, 162

Eagle Drinking (Noconi Comanche chief), 128

Eagle's Feather (Plume, Otoe chief), 94

Eagle's Head (Arapaho chief), 94

Edmunds, Newton (Gov.), 178; treaty commissioner role of, 138

Edwards, Ninian (Gov.), treaty commissioner role of, 15

Eighteenth U.S. Infantry, 141–42

Eldredge, J. C., peace efforts of, 63–65

Elliott, Joel (Maj.), 145, 166; death of, 168; Medicine Lodge treaty debunked by, 148

Elliott, W. L. (Lt.), wife of, 90
Ellsworth, Henry W., Pawnee treaty conducted by, 44
Ellsworth, Kansas, 145
Emory, William (Col.), Indian Territory withdrawal made by, 115–16
Eshcatarpa (the Bad Chief, Pawnee), 16
Essequeta Apache Indians, 74
Etla, (Kiowa woman), 111
Evans, A. W. (Col.), 168
Evans, John (Gov.), 113, 126

Faithful Partisan (Arapaho chief), 95
Fannin, James W., 58
Fayel, William, 145
Fetterman, William (Capt.). See Fetterman Massacre
Fetterman Massacre, 142
Fifth U.S. Cavalry, 169
Fighting Bear (Sioux chief), 96
Fillmore, Millard (President), visited by Indians, 95
Fire Heart (Saone Sioux chief), council of with Atkinson, 21
Fire Prairie (Missouri), 1808 treaty site at, 28–29
First Regiment of Dragoons, 36, 87
First U.S. Cavalry, 107–08
First U.S. Infantry, 17
Fitzpatrick, Thomas, 86, 95, 97, 102–04, 126, 133, 149; Arapaho widow of, 125; commissioner activities of, 89; death of, 194; delegation to Washington led by, 94; treaties initiated by, 100–101
Florida, 70, 171; Seminole wars of, 62
Fool Chief (Kansa chief), complaint of, 27
Ford, John S. (Capt.), 82; at Spring Creek council, 79
Ford County, Kansas, 82
Forsyth, George A. (Maj.), 165–66
Fort Gibson treaty council, 42–44
Fort Laramie treaty councils: 1851 council, 87; 1866 council, 140; 1867 council, 145; 1868 council, 160
Forts: Abraham Lincoln, 178; Arbuckle, 82, 115, 129; Atkinson, 16–18, 100–102, 104; Bascom, 166, 168; Berthold, 160; Bridger, 86, 157; C. F. Smith, 142, 154, 160–61; Caddo, 76; Chadbourne, 81; Cobb, 84,
108, 115, 118, 129, 165, 168; Concho, 170; Cottonwood, 135–36; Dodge, 119; Ellis, 178; Ellsworth, 131; Fetterman, 156, 161, 173–74, 178; Gates, 78; Gibson, 34, 36–38, 41–44, 47–50, 53–54, 56, 58, 62, 70, 118, 122; Graham, 79–80; Griffin, 169–70; Harker, 145; Hays, 144; Kearny (Nebraska), 94, 96, 106; Kiowa (Kioway), 19–20; Laramie, 82, 86–87, 95, 100, 103, 106, 116, 126, 128, 131, 133, 137, 140, 142–45, 147, 153–58, 160–62, 165–66, 172–74; Larned, 107, 113; Leavenworth, 44, 143; Lookout, 19; Lyon, 113, 151, 158, 166; Mandan, 24; Mann, 100; Marion, 171; Martin Scott, 78–79; McPherson, 135; Osage (Fort Clark), establishment of, 28, 30–31; Phil Kearny (Wyoming), 142, 154–55, 160; Randall, 138, 157; Reno (Wyoming), 142, 160; Rice, 144, 162, treaty council at, 158–60; Richardson, 169; Riley, 143; Robinson, 176; Scott, 122; Sedgwick, 134; Shaw, 174; Sill, 168–71; Smith, 116, 129, 122–23; St. Vrain, 100, 103, 106; Sully, 124, 139, 172; Supply, 167, 170; Towson, 58, 115; Union (New Mexico), 170; Union (North Dakota), 88, 93; Wallace, 144; Washita, 120; Wise, treaty council at, 109–10; Worth, 78, 81; Zarah, 1866 council at, 130–32
Fourth U.S. Cavalry, 170
Fox Indians, 1815 treaty of, 15; removal of, 33
Fredericksburg, Texas, 78, 125, 128
Fremont, John C. (Capt.), California march of, 86
French, 5, 10, 28; Missouri population of, 27
Friday (Arapaho chief), 94
fur trade, 15–16, 24

Gall (Co-kam-i-ya-ya, Man that Goes in the Middle, Sioux chief), 158, 160, 174
Galveston, Texas, 68, 72
Gatesville, Texas, 78
Georgetown, Texas, 128
Georgia, xii; Cherokee treaty overridden by, 9
Geren, Charles E., 158
Germain family, 171
German immigrants, 56, 72, 79, 125; Comanche treaty made by, 78; killed by Indians, 77

Gerry, Elbridge, 113
Gibbon, John (Gen.), 178
Goliad, Texas, 58
Goose (Assiniboine chief), 94
Grand Pawnee Indians, 1819 treaty of, 16
Grant, Ulysses S. (President), 158, 160–61, 164, 173, 176; edict of to abandon forts, 160; failure of peace policy, 179; Indian Bureau placed under Quakers by, 11, 169; Indian delegation met by, 170; new Cheyenne/Arapaho reservation assigned by, 168
Grattan Massacre, 133
Grattan, John (Lt.), 133
Great Osage Indians, 20–21; annuity awarded to, 32
Greenwood, A. B. (Commissioner), Fort Wise council held by, 108–10
Grey Head (Cheyenne chief), 147
Groesbeck, Texas, 58
Gros Ventre Indians, 23, 44, 88, 93; Indian treaties with, 187
Guernsey, Oran, 138
Guerrier, Edward, 150

Hagan, William T., 153
Hall, S. F., 145
Hancock, Winfield Scott (Maj. Gen.), 119, 143–44, 147, 150
Handful of Blood (Arikara chief), 22
Harlan, James (Sec. of Int.), 138–39
Harney, William S. (Gen.), 125, 133–34, 144, 146–47, 150, 155, 157–58, 160–62, 170, 172; role of as treaty commissioner, 125
Harrison, Charley, 121
Harry, Jack (Delaware), 72–73
Harvey, Thomas, 33
Hayes, Jack (Capt.), Texas Ranger forays led by, 61
He-ka-too (Hi-ka-toa, the Dry Man, Quapaw chief), speech of, 53
Henderson, John B. (Sen.), 144, 146, 150, 152, 156, 161; fallacious promise of, 11; treaty role of criticized, 148
Hennessey, Pat, murder of, 170
Hicks, Elijah (Cherokee jurist), 69–71; treaty dispute mediated by, 72
High-backed Wolf (Cheyenne chief), 21; murder of, 44

Hillsboro, Texas, 68, 78
Hindman, Samuel D. (Rev.), 160, 162
Hockley, William, 63
Hoish (Honey Eaters, Comanche) Indians, 55, 61, 64
Holmes, T. H. (Lt.), 37
Honore, Joseph Tesson, 94
Hopewell, South Carolina, treaty of, 5
Horse Creek Treaty (1851), 87, 102. See also, Treaty of Fort Laramie
Horse Back (Comanche chief), 125
Horsman, Reginald, xiv
Houston, John Charles, 130
Houston, Sam, 59, 62–63, 76; called "friend of Red man," 65; 1844 council attended by, 67–68; Indian disturbance abated by, 77; peace efforts of, 58, 62, 66; reverses Lamar Indian policies, 61
Howland, John, 145
Huerfano River, 109
Hunkpapa Sioux, 139, 157, 160; peace mission of, 22
Hunter, David (Capt.), 38
Huntsville, Texas, 170

Ichacoly (the Wolf, Comanche chief), 52
Indian affairs, resurgence of military influence in, 154
Indian Appropriation Bill, 171
Indian Bureau (Department), 10, 17, 82, 177; support of Sherman's war edict, 165
Indian lands, demise of, 181; invasion of, 179
Indian oratory, as a native skill, 5–6
Indian Peace Commission (1819), 16
Indian Peace Commission (1825), 17
Indian Removal Bill, 9
Indian Territory, 13, 33–34, 36–37, 42, 47–49, 55, 58–59, 61–62, 65, 69, 73, 80–84, 98–99, 118, 120, 122–25, 128, 131; Civil War impoverishment of, 116; designation of, 4, 129–30, 134, 143, 148, 153, 156–57, 163, 165–66, 168–71, 174; immigrant tribes of, 118; strategic position of, 115
Indian treaties, 48; American model of, 1; British pattern of, 1, 4; categories of, 3–4; conduct of, 2; Congressional curtailing of, 4; end of treaty system, 180; evolution of, 7; formalities of, 7; historical

value of documents, xv–xvi, 182; national, legalistic, and moral effects of, 3; protocol of, 5; rationales regarding, xv; structural flaw of system, 183; translation problems of, 10; use of in tribal removal, 4

Indian tribes: considered as separate nations, 13; ends sought in making treaties, 2; land titles of, xiii

Ioni Indians, 65, 67, 74, 117, 129, 187; Texas treaty with, 62

Iowa Indians, 25, 33, 96; 1815 treaty of, 15

Iron Shirt (Plains Apache chief), 125

Iroquois Indians, 23

Irving, Washington, 37; prairie tour of, 34

Irwin, W. R., 130

Jacksboro, Texas, 169

Jackson, Andrew (President), 91; attitude of regarding Indian treaties, xii; role in Indian removal, 4; as supporter of states' rights regarding U.S. treaties, 9

Jacob (Caddo chief), 111

Jacobs, William R., xi

James, Thomas, 99

Jefferson, Thomas (President), 27; hopes for Indian integration, 184; Indian trade views of, 28

Jefferson Barracks, Missouri, 36

Jerome Commission, 171

Johnson, Andrew (President), 144, 164–65; peace commission appointed by, 138, impeachment trial of, 156

Jones, Horace, 120

Jose Maria (Anadarko chief), 62–63

Jutan (Otoe chief), 44

Ka-hi-ke-tung-ka (Osage chief), 120

Kansa (Kaw) Indians, 15, 35, 98, 122; 1825 pact of, 32–33; removal of, 31; treaties with, 187–88

Kansas, 11, 31, 35, 47, 82, 98, 100–101, 107–8, 115, 120–22, 124–27, 129–31, 135, 143, 145–46, 151, 153–54, 161–62, 165–66, 168–69, 171; Kansa homeland of, 33; loyalist Indians retreat to, 118; Osage range of, 27; removal of tribes to, 33; statehood of, 144

Kansas City, Kansas, 101, 108

Kansas City, Missouri, 28, 112

Kansas Pacific Railroad, 131–32, 150

Kansas River, 33

Kaskaskia Indians, removal of, 33

Kataka Indians, 54–55

Katumse (Comanche chief), 81

Ke-chi-ka-rogue (Stubborn, Tawakoni chief), 63; speech of, 64

Kearny, Stephen W. (Maj.), 36, 86; service of with Yellowstone Expedition, 18

Keim, DeB. Randolph, 168

Kendall, George, 73; Comanche Peak signing described by, 75

Kennerly, George F., 23

Ki-he-kay-tungah (Osage Indian), 48

Kichai (Keechi) Indians, 63, 65, 68, 72, 74, 81, 129; Civil War refuge of, 120; Indian treaties of, 188; Texas treaty of, 58, 62; treaty with South signed by, 117

Kickapoo Indians, 33, 74, 120; 1815 treaty with, 15

Kicking Bird (Kiowa chief), 125, 128, 184

Kidder, Lyman (Lt.), massacre of, 144

Kikehahki Pawnee Indians, Pike expedition hosted by, 14

Killough family, massacre of, 58

Kingman, Samuel A., Little Arkansas treaty chronicled by, 125; Little Arkansas treaty opinion of, 129

Kiowa Indians, 35, 37, 41, 43–44, 48–49, 51–53, 55, 86, 98–104, 107–8, 111–12, 119, 123, 127–28, 145, 148–49, 152, 161, 167–68, 170, 172, 184; attendance at Fort Gibson council, 42, 54; depredations of, 113, 118, 122, 169; at Little Arkansas council, 125; at Medicine Lodge council, 146–47; Parker's Fort raided by, 58; reservation assigned to, 128; traders attacked by, 36; treaties of, 188; treaty with South signed by, 118

Kiowa/Comanche agent, 125; Washington delegation of, 8

Kiowa/Comanche village, attacked by Cheyenne/Arapaho force, 99

Knapp, George (Col.), 86

Kosharoka (He Who Marries His Wife Twice), 47, speech of, 52

Kotsoteka (Cochetaka, Buffalo Eaters) Comanches, 55, 61, 82, 117, 130

La Chanier (Osage) band, 30
La Framboise, Franc, 160, 162
Lakota Indians, xvi
Lamar, Mirabeau, anti-Indian actions of, 59
Lawrence, Kansas, 122, 124
Lea, L. (Commissioner), 95
Lean Bear (Cheyenne chief), 110–11, 183; death of, 113
Leased District, Texas Indians removal to, 83, 117, 123
Leavenworth, Henry (Col.), 37, 125; battle with Arikaras, 17; injury and death of, 38; prairie expedition of, 36–39
Leavenworth, Jesse, at Fort Zarah council, 130
Lee, Francis (Capt.), 49
Lee, Robert E. (Gen.), surrender of, 122
Leeper, Matthew, 119–20
Left Hand (Arapaho chief), 110
Lewis, J. O., Indian sketches of, 25
Lewis, M. G., 70, 72, 74; appointment of as Indian commissioner, 69–70; escorts Indians to Washington, 76
Lewis, Meriwether, 14, 28; harsh demands of, 30; treaty revised by, 29
Lewis and Clark Expedition, 24; as first official contact, 1
Lincoln, Abraham (President), 113, 127, 183; meeting with Indian delegation, 111–12; Fort Wise treaty proclaimed by, 110
Lincoln, Mrs. (Mary Todd), 112
Linney (Shawnee chief), 62
Lipan Apache Indians, 57–59, 67–71, 73–75, 80; treaties with, 188–89
Lisa, Manuel, 30
Little Arkansas River, 120, 126, 129
Little Bear (Cheyenne chief), 130
Little Big Man (Sioux leader), 176
Little Bighorn River, 142, 178
Little Chief (Cheyenne chief), 94
Little Heart (Kiowa), 111
Little Osage Indians, 28–30, 32, 120–21
Little Owl. See Blah-at-sah-ah-kak-che
Little Raven (Arapaho chief), 108, 110, 125, 130; speech of, 151; treaty views of, 126
Little River, 37, 48–49, 56
Little Robe (Cheyenne chief), 125
Little Robe Creek, 82
Little Shield (Cheyenne chief), 157

Little Thunder (Brulé chief), village of attacked, 133
Little Wolf (Cheyenne chief), 110, 157; Fort Reno destroyed by, 161
Llano River, 77–80
Lockhart, Matilda, Comanche return of, 60
Lodge Trail Ridge, 142
Lone Wolf (Kiowa), 111, 125, 184, capture of, 168
Long, Stephen H. (Maj.), meeting with Pawnees, 32, 34
Long Hair (Crow chief), 23
Louisiana Purchase, xiii, 28; Western exploration of, 12; importance of, 27; Indian removal potential of, 4
Loup River, 34–35
Lowe, Percival G., 102; Fort Laramie council described by, 91

Mackenzie, Ranald (Col.), 164, 170
Madison, James (President), 4, 15
Maman-ti (Kiowa leader), 184
Man-Afraid-of-His-Horses (Sioux chief), 140, 158
Mandan Indians, 16, 22–23, 88, 93; treaties of, 189
Manifest Destiny, 86, 138
"Manifest Falsehood," 146
Many, James B. (Col.), prairie incursion of, 34
Manypenny, George W. (Commissioner), 96, 168, 178
Martin, Gabriel (Judge), 36
Martin, Matthew, captivity of, 36; rescue of, 40
Mason, Richard Barnes (Maj.), 18, 36; treaty site selected by, 48–49
Mathews, H. M., 155
Mathewson, Buffalo Bill, 129
Maynadier, Henry W. (Col.), role as treaty commissioner, 140–41
McClaren, Robert N., role as treaty commissioner, 140
McCullough, Ben (Capt.), 60
McCusker, Philip, report of on Indian death march, 129
McDaniel, Caroline, 128
McDaniel, Rebecca Jane, 128
McIntosh, Chilly, 42, 44, 72, 117

McIntosh, Roly (Creek chief), 42, 44, 53–54

McKenney, Thomas L., *12;* speaks to land titles, 31–32; treaty efforts of, 26

McNair, Alexander, treaty assignments of, 31

McPhail, Leonard (Asst. Surgeon), 50

Medicine Arrow (Cheyenne chief), 152

Medicine Lodge Creek, 150, treaty council at, 145–46

Medicine Man (Cheyenne chief), 157

Melton, David (Cherokee chief), 52

Menominee Indians, 25–26, 33

Mexican War, 69, 78, 100

Mexico, xiii, 14, 55, 57–58, 73, 78, 80, 102; captives of, 74, 80; Comanche treaty with, 63; Comanche war with, 66; Indian raiding in, 56, 59, 77–79, 104, 118–19; tribal peace with sought, 52

Michigan Territory, 11, 25–26

Miles, John D., poor-quality beef for Indians accepted by, 11

Miles, Nelson (Gen.), 164, 170, 178

Millar, Robert, 107

Miniconjou Sioux, 134, 139, 157

Minnesota uprising, 134

Mission Creek, Kansas, as site of 1846 Kansa treaty, 33

Mississippi River, xii, 4, 12, 15, 25, 27, 30–31, 34, 76

Missouri, 27, 30–33, 35–36, 47, 97–98, 118; legislature of, 35; Osage land titles of ceded to U.S., 31

Missouri Fur Company, post of, 17

Missouri Indians, 1825 treaty with, 24

Missouri River, 14, 16–20, 22, 24, 28, 30, 37, 53, 85–86, 88, 92–93, 122, 138, 140, 144, 157–58, 162, 172, 175, 178; as crucial fur trade route, 15; military posts on, 15; Sioux reservation on, 173

Missouri Territory, 15; 1821 admission to Union, 31

Mitchell, David D., 86–88, 91–93; delegation led to Washington by, 94; speech of, 85, 90; treaty commissioner activities of, 89

Mitchell, Robert B. (Brig. Gen.), council with Sioux held by, 135–36

Modoc Indians, General Canby killed by, 171

Monroe, James (President), 15

Montana, 17, 142–42, 155–56, 160, 172, 174–75, 177–78

Moo-wa-tuh (Spirit Talker, Comanche chief), at San Antonio peace council, 60

Moosh-o-la-tu-bee (Mush-la-Tabee, Man Killer, Choctaw chief), role of in Fort Gibson peace talks, 44

Mooers, John (Dr.), 166

Moore, John H. (Col.), 59; Comanche camp attacked by, 60–61

Mormons, caravan of, 133; family of attacked, 124

Mountain Tail (Crow chief), 93

Muscalero Apache Indians, at 1846 council, 74

Murphy, Thomas, treaty commissioner role of, 125, 129; treaty council arranged by, 145

Muscogee (Creek) Indians, 53

Musha-la-Tabbee (Creek chief), 53

Na-as-to-wa (Tawakoni chief), 72

Nah-ish-to-wah (Lame Arm, Waco chief), 63

Nancy (Wichita interpreter), 75

Navajo Indians, 157

Nebraska, 14, 18, 87, 94, 106, 134, 156, 169, 174; Indian problems of, 96, 155

Neches River, 59

Neighbors, Robert S., 73, 77, 79, 81; Comanche-German treaty worked out by, 78; solution to Texas Indian problem sought by, 83

Neosho River, 31, 33, 98

Neva (Arapaho chief), 111

New Mexico, 35, 97, 102, 109, 116, 157, 166, 170

New Orleans, 70, 76

New York City, 112, 173; Indian visits to, 7

New York Indians, 121–22; removal of, 33

Nineteenth Kansas Volunteer Regiment, 168

Niobrara River, 136, 162

Nokoni (No-co-nee, People in a Circle) Comanches, 61, 117, 128, 130

Noisy Pawnee Indians, 1819 treaty of, 16

Noon-ah (People of the desert) Comanches, 61

North, Frank J. (Capt.), Pawnee scout commanded by, 136

North Canadian River, 55, 117, 166, 168; tribal conference on, 101

North Fork of Red River, 40, 64

North Fork Town (Indian Territory), 117

North Platte, Nebraska, 156

North Platte River, 106, 126, 174

Northern Arapaho Indians, 137–38, 156–58; treaties of, 189

Northern Cheyenne Indians, 137–38, 140–41, 145, 154, 156, 167, 169, 175, 177–78; Fort Reno destroyed by, 161; treaties of, 189

Northern Pacific Railroad, 175

Northrop, Lucius B. (Maj.), 55

O'Fallon, Benjamin (Maj.), 16–20, 23–24

Oceola (Seminole chief), 171

Ogallala, Nebraska, 133

Oglala Sioux, 87, 93, 134, 137, 139–41, 144, 154, 157, 172, 176; Atkinson council with, 20–21

Oklahoma, 4, 27–28, 30–31, 49, 128–29, 169

Old Owl (Mo-pe-chu-co-pe, Comanche chief), at Council Springs, 67, 73, 75, 78; death of, 78

Old Bark (Bear's Feather, Cheyenne chief), 92

"Olive Branchers," 124, 144

Omaha Indians, 15, 24, 44, 134, 144, 156, 158, 160; treaties of, 189

One Horn (Sioux chief), 94

100th meridian, 82, 130

103rd meridian, 175

Opothle Yahola: as pro-Union leader, 117; retreat to Kansas, 118

Oregon Trail, 85–86, 96–97, 134

Osage Indians, 27–28, 30, 32–33, 37, 41, 47, 50, 53–55, 58, 64, 70, 118, 121–22, 125, 127; attack on Kiowas, 43; effects of smallpox epidemic on, 33; 1808 treaty, 28; 1815 treaty, 15; 1818 treaty, 31; 1822 and 1825 treaties, 31, 98; 1835 treaty, 47–48; Kansas reservation area of, 32; removal of, 31; scouts of, 167; treaties, 189–90; war with Cherokees, 31. *See also* Big Hill Osages, Great Osages, La Chanier Osages, Little Osages

Osage River, 28, 30, 32

Otoe Indians, 43–44, 94, 96; captive girl of, 20; 1819 council, *21;* 1825 treaty, 24

Ottawa Indians, 1825 treaty of, 25

Otter Creek, 157

Otter-tail Lake, 26

Over the Buttes (Comanche chief), 125

Overland Mail Route, 112

Pa-la-ne-ona-pe (Man Who Was Struck by the Ree, Yankton chief), 138

Pacific, trade route to, 15, 85

Pahaucah (Pah-hah-uca, Pah-hah-yuco, the Amorous Man, Comanche chief), 64, 68, 72, 75; desire for peace, 80; mourns death of son, 66; presence at 1846 council, 74; Texas peace commission hosted by, 65

Painted Bear (Sioux leader), 90

Palmer, George H. (Lt.): tells of Red Cloud's resistance, 154; views offered by, 155

Palo Duro Canyon, battle of, 170

Panic of 1819, 16

Panic of 1873, 175

Para-saw-a-man-oo (Ten Bears, Comanche chief), 103

Parker, Cynthia Ann, capture of, 58; rescue refused by, 74

Parker, Commissioner Ely, 122, 173

Parker, John, 74; capture of, 58

Pawhuska (White Hair, Osage chief), treaty signed by, 120

Pawnee Indians, 14, 17, 35, 44–45, 54–55, 58, 86, 94–96, 98, 134, 165; council, 32; council with Dodge, 44; depredations of, 15; 1819 treaty of, 16; 1825 treaty of, 24; 1833 treaty of, 44; Loup River council of, 34; scouts of, 136–37, 169; treaties of, 190

Pawnee Fork, 107, 143

Pawnee Killer (Sioux chief), 144

Pawnee Pict (Wichita) Indians, 43

Peace commission of 1867, 144–45

Peneteka Comanches, 79–80; treaty of with South, 117

Penn, William, peace policy of, 144

Peoria Indians, removal of, 33

Perryman, Benjamin (Creek chief), 44

Philadelphia, Pennsylvania, Indian visits to, 7

Piankeshaw Indians, 33, 55; 1815 treaty of, 15

Pierre, South Dakota, 20
Pike, Albert, pacts with Indian Territory tribes initiated by, 116–118; report of, 120
Pike, Zebulon (Lt.), visit of to Pawnee village, 14
Placido (Tonkawa chief), death of, 120
Plains (Prairie) Apache Indians, 35, 48, 52, 54, 99–102, 107, 127–28, 161, 170; at Little Arkansas treaty council, 125; at Medicine Lodge, 146–47; treaties of, 188
Plains Indians, 70, 85–86, 123, 184; councils and treaties with, xi; depredations by, 97; dire needs of, 129; immigration onto lands of, 31; limited control of war societies, 12; as problems to U.S. commerce, 35; resolution of conflicts with, 87; U.S. relations with, 114; warring as societal custom of, 169
Platte Bridge, 125, 137
Platte River (Valley), 44–45, 54, 86–87, 93, 98, 100, 103, 106, 127–28, 131, 133–37, 140–41, 143, 147, 152–55, 160–63, 165, 170, 172, 174; Indian problems along, 97
Platte Trail (Route), 106, 113, 124, 133–34, 136–37, 145, 155
Plum Creek, battle of, 60
Po-char-na-quar-hip. See Buffalo Hump
Pohebits Quasho (Iron Jacket, Comanche), killing of, 82
Poinsett, Joel (Sec. of War), 54
Polk, James (President), 76–77
Ponca Indians, 18, 134, 162; council of, 19–20; treaties of, 190; treaty of 1865, 162
Poor Bear (Plains Apache chief), 111, 125
Port Lavaca, Texas, 60
Portage des Sioux, Indian treaty site of, 15, 30–31
Pottawatomie Indians, 33, 96; 1815 treaty of, 15; 1825 treaty of, 25
Powder River, 141, 154–55, 158, 172, 176
Prairie-du-chien, Wisconsin, Indian treaty site of, 25
Pratt, Richard H. (Lt.), 171
Price, Monroe E., xi
Price, William (Col.), 170
Prickled Forehead (Comanche), 111
Prucha, Francis Paul, xi; and U.S. Indian policy, xii

Purgatoire River, 35, 109
Pushmataha, (Choctaw chief), 91; Washington burial of, 113

Quakers, 144, 168, 170, 179; Indian affairs assigned to, 11, 169
Quapaw Indians, 51, 53, 79; alignment of with South, 118; Texas removal of, 81

Rector, Elias, 117
Red Cloud, 140, 145, 155, 157–58, 159, 160, 162, 174; Bozeman attacked by, 141; Fort Phil Kearny destroyed by, 161; message sent by, 157; speech of 172–73; treaty gifts rejected by, 141; visit to Washington by, 183; white intrusion resisted by, 154
Red Cloud Agency, 178
Red Fork of Brazos, 70
Red Leaf (Sioux chief), 140
Red Plume (Sioux chief), 95
Red River, 36–38, 40–41, 47, 58, 64, 70, 76, 79–82, 86, 115–17
Red River War, 170–71
Red Skin (Sioux chief), 94
Reed, Henry, role of as treaty commissioner, 138
Republic of Texas, 56, 58, 61, 69; Indian dividing line of, 68; Indian problems of, 12; Indian relations of, xii; treaty-making efforts of, xi. See also Texas
Republican River, 14, 113, 151, 166
Reynolds, Milton, 145–46
Riley, Bennett (Maj.), 23, 35, 98
Rio Grande, 68, 77
Roasting Ear (Delaware chief), 62
Rocky Mountains, 44, 93, 98, 100, 106
Rogers, John (Cherokee chief), 52; at Fort Gibson council, 42–43; Washington burial of, 113
Rogers, John (Texas agent), initiates Comanche treaty, 80
Rollins, John R., 73, 78–79; at 1846 council, 73; death of, 80; treaty expedition of, 79; treaty with Comanches sought by, 79
Roman Nose (Cheyenne war leader), 143, 147, 152; speech of, 130
Rosebud battle, 167

Ross, John (Cherokee chief), 9, 116, 118; challenge of to leadership, 123
Running Bear (Sioux), 140
Rusk, Thomas (Gen.), Texas Cherokees defeated by, 59

Sac and Fox Indians, 121
Sac Indians, 33, 96, 121; 1816 treaty of, 15; 1825 treaty of, 25
Saline River, 165, 168
Salt Plains, 66, 70, 130
San Antonio, Texas, 56–57, 61, 78; Courthouse Massacre at, 60, 64–65, 68, 73
San Jacinto, battle of, 58
San Saba mission, 68
San Saba River, 59, 79–80
Sanaco (Comanche chief), 81
Sanborn, John R. (Gen.), 127, 156–58, 161; treaty commissioner role of, 125, 144
Sanchez, Lewis, 75
Sand Creek Massacre, 114, 122, 126, 131, 158, 167, 183; effect on Plains tribes, 144; fear of repeat of, 143
Sans Arc Sioux, 139, 157, 160
Santa Anna (Comanche chief), 68, 73, 75–76, 78; death of, 78–79
Santa Fe, New Mexico, 97–98, 112; trade with, 35
Santa Fe Expedition of 1871, 73
Santa Fe Trail (Road), 54, 85, 98, 100, 106–8, 127–28, 168; depredations on, 119, 124; effect on Kansa tribe, 33; Indian raids along, 97; opening and development of, 35
Santee Sioux, 157, 160
Saone Sioux, 20–21
Satank (Kiowa chief), 103, 125, 128; arrest of, 168–69; family of captured, 107; peace efforts of, 99–100; speech of, 143, 169
Satanta (Kiowa chief), 125, 170, 184; anger of at killing of buffalo, 146; at Medicine Lodge, 152; role of at Medicine Lodge, 147–48; visit to Fort Larned, 145
Schermerhorn, Rev. John F., as Jackson treaty commissioner, 9
Schoolcraft, Henry, criticism of interpreters by, 10; treaty presence of, 25
Schurz, Carl (Sec. of Int.), 177
Seawell, Washington (Lt.), 51

Second U.S. Dragoons, 79; Texas Indian campaign of, 80
Secondeye (Delaware Indian), 61, 63
Sedgwick, John (Maj.), command of, 106–8
Sells, Elijah, 122
Seminole Indians, 4, 37, 70, 78, 116–18, 130, 171; ceded lands of, 123; Civil War position of, 117; loyalists of retreat to Kansas, 118; scouts of, 70; Texas removal of, 81
Seneca Indians, 43, 47, 51, 53; alignment with South, 118
Seventeenth Illinois troops, 123
Seventh Iowa Cavalry, 136
Seventh U.S. Cavalry, 143–45, 166, 168, 173; defeat of, 178
Seventh U.S. Infantry, 36–38, 49, 51
Shaking Hand (Comanche chief), 130
Sharitarish (Pawnee chief), 14
Shave Head, 110
Shaw, Jim (Delaware leader), 61, 63–64, 75
Shawnee Indians, 74; alignment of with South, 117–118; Civil War refuge of, 120; Council Springs treaty, 67; removal of, 33; Texas removal of, 81; Texas treaty with, 58, 62; Wichita agency attacked by, 120
Shellman (Sioux chief), 94
Sheridan, Phil (Gen.), 157, 163–69, 172–73, 175–76; replaces Hancock, 153; Yellowstone campaign of, 177
Sherman, William T. (Gen.), 135, 155–57, 161–62, 171–73; abrogation of Sioux treaty recommended by, 176; denounces peace effort, 145; frontier fort tour of, 169; opts for war, 164–65; rejoins peace commission, 154; role as treaty commissioner, 144
Shirley, John, property of destroyed by Comanches, 119
Shone-ta-sah-ba. See Black Dog
Shoshone Indians, 55, 87, 157; at 1851 Fort Laramie council, 88
Sibley, George C., Osage treaty criticized by, 30
Sibley, Henry H. (Gen.), role as treaty commissioner, 138; Sioux campaign of, 134
Silver Broach (Toshowa, Comanche chief), 125, 147; speech of at Medicine Lodge, 148

Singing Bird (Otoe woman), 94
Sioux, xvi, 15, 17, 20, 44, 86–87, 92–93, 96,
103–4, 113, 124, 133–34, 137–38, 140, 142,
145, 154–58, 161, 165, 172–76, 178, 183; at
Fort Laramie council, 88; Atkinson's
meeting of, 19; council ceremony of
described, 135; council of, 135–36; 1866
agreement of, 141; removal of to
reservation, 162; treaties of, 190–91; treaty
procedure of, 90. *See also Sioux tribes by
name*
Sioux of St. Peter's River Indians, 1815
treaty of, 15
Sioux of the Lake Indians, 1815 treaty of, 15
Sitting Bull, 158, 174, 178, 184; refusal to sign
treaty, 160
Sixth U.S. Infantry, 15, 17
Skullyville, Indian Territory, 56
slaves, 69, 73; escape of to Mexico, 80
Slemmer, A. J. (Brig. Gen.), 158
smallpox epidemic, 78; Indian decimation
from, 33
Smith, Edward P. (Commissioner), 176
Smith, Jedediah, death of, 35, 100
Smith, John Simpson, 10, 90, 94, 110–11,
130, 149, 151–52, 166; at Little Arkansas
treaty, 125; at Treaty of Fort Wise, 109
Smith, Thomas J., 62
Smoky Hill River, 113, 130, 132, 135, 151;
railroad and stage line along, 131
Snake Indians, 87, 157
Society of Friends (Quakers), 169
Society of German Noblemen, Texas land
grant to, 77
Solomon River, 107, 168; settlements on
raided, 165
South (Confederacy), 36; immigrant tribes
from, 129; rebellion of, 134; treaty
affiliations with Indian Territory tribes,
116, 134
South Dakota, 17, 20, 175
South Park (Colorado), fur trade of, 35, 98
South Platte River, 98, 103, 106–7, 144
Southern Arapaho Indians, 11, 156, 168;
treaties of, 192
Southern Cheyenne Indians, 11, 98, 156,
165, 168; treaties of, 192
Southern Plains tribes, relocation of, 12; talk
with, 124

Spain (Spaniards, Spanish), xiii, 10, 28, 35,
52, 57–58, 102; northern advance of, 36;
Osage meeting with, 28
Spaniard (The), 38, 40; attends Fort Gibson
council, 42–43
Spotted Tail (Shan-tag-a-lisk, Brulé chief),
140–41, 156, 174; dog feast hosted by, 155;
speech of, 133, 135–36; Washington visit
of, 173
Spotted Wolf (Arapaho chief), 111
Spring Creek, 59, 79
St. Augustine, Florida, 171
St. Louis, Missouri, 15–18, 24, 29, 31, 36, 86,
95, 101, 108, 138, 144–45, 170; site of 1825
Osage treaty, 31
Standing Buffalo (Oglala chief), 20
Standing Elk (Sioux), 140
Standing-in-the-Water (Cheyenne), 111;
death of, 114
Stanley, David S. (Col.), 175
Stanley, Henry M., 145, 150, 152, 155; treaty
criticism by, 148
Stanley, John Mix, Comanche portraits
painted by, 66
Steele, James (Gen.), treaty commissioner
role of, 125
Steen, Enoch (Lt.), 37
Stem, Jesse, 80
Stinking Saddle Cloth (Kiowa chief), 125
Stokes, Montford (Commissioner), 37, 44,
48, 52–54; Fort Gibson council attended
by, 42; opening remarks of at council, 51
Storm (Arapaho chief), 94, 108, 110, 125
Stuart, J.E.B. (Lt.), Kiowas pursued by, 107
Stumbling Bear (Kiowa chief), 184
Sturgis, Samuel D. (Capt.), 108
Suhtai Cheyenne band, 183
Sully, Alfred (Brig. Gen.), 157; Indian
Territory campaign of, 166; Sioux
campaign of, 134
Sumner, Edwin V. (Capt.), 36, 38, 110;
Cheyenne campaign of, 106–07
surveyors, massacre of, 78, 170

Ta-ka-ta-couche (Black Bird, Kiowa chief),
arrives at Fort Gibson, 54
Tabaquenna (Ta-we-que-nah, Big Eagle,
Comanche chief), 41; threatened by
Camp Mason troops, 43, 49, 55, 64

Tahlequah, 116, 118, 120–21
Tahuacaro (Tawakaro) Indians, treaty with South signed by, 54, 117, 129
Taime, Kiowa medicine bag, 43
Tall Bear (Cheyenne chief), 110
Tall Bull (Cheyenne chief), 131, 143, 147, 152; Carr attacks camp of, 168; death of, 169
Tappan, Samuel, role of as treaty commissioner, 144, 157, 161
Tarrant, E. H., 65
Tawakaro Indians. *See* Tahuacaro Indians
Tawakoni Indians, 62–65, 68, 79, 81; at Bird's Fort, 65; at Comanche Peak, 72; at Council Springs, 1844, 67; at 1846 council, 74; Civil War refuge of, 120; treaties of, 192
Taylor, Dorcas, 128
Taylor, Edward B., 141; role of as treaty commissioner, 138, 140
Taylor, James F., 145
Taylor, N. G. (Commissioner), 161–62; Black Kettle interview of, 149; service with peace commission, 144, 154
Taylor, Gen. Zachary, 73
Te-nay-wash (People in the Timber) Comanches, 61
Tehuacana Creek, 66; Texas peace council held on, 62–64
Ten Bears (Para-saw-a-man-oo, Comanche chief), 103, 111, 125, 130, 148; speech at Medicine Lodge, 147–48
Tenth U.S. Infantry, 108
Terrell, G. W. (Gen.), 62, 65
Terry, Alfred H. (Gen.), 157–58, 161, 177–78; role as treaty commissioner, 144
Teton River (Bad River), 19–20, 22
Teton Sioux Indians, 19–20; 1815 treaty with, 15
Texas, xiii, 11, 27, 41, 48, 54–55, 57–58, 60–61, 63, 70–71, 73, 78, 80–81, 98, 104, 107, 118–20, 125, 128, 130, 169, 170; army of, 59; battles with Comanches, 60; campaign to punish Comanches, 59; captive Waco girls held by, 63; Cherokee treaty rejected by, 59; Comanche hatred for, 62; Confederate forces of, 116; depredations in, 79, 83–84; 1843 Council Springs meeting, 67; frontier forts of, 81; German land grant of, 72; Indian campaign of, 80; Indian delegation's visit to Washington, 76–77; Indian dividing line promoted by, 68, 75, 77, 79–80; Indian relations of, 57, 74; jurisdiction over public domain retained by, 77; Kiowa raids into, 118–19; line of Ranger camps established by, 78; pact with Comanches, 59; peace commission to Comanches, 65; peace commission party of, 62; peace efforts of, 65; responsibility for tribes denied by, 81; statehood of, 68–69; Texas Rangers attack Comanche camp, 59; tribal relocation of, 83; troops of, 117; U.S. help requested by, 82. *See also* Texas Mounted Volunteers, Texas Panhandle, Texas Rangers
Texas Mounted Volunteers, 79–80
Texas Panhandle, 35–36, 128, 130, 168–70
Texas Rangers, 73, *83*; battle with Comanches, 60; camps of, 78; Comanche camp attacked by, 82
Third U.S. Infantry, 166
Thirty-eighth U.S. Infantry, 145
Thomas, Eleasar (Rev.), 171
Throckmorton, James W. (Gen.), 122
Thunderfire (Sioux), 140
Tiche-toche-cha (Kiowa chief), role of at Fort Gibson council, 42–44
To-to-lis (Seneca chief), role of at Fort Gibson council, 42
Tohawson (Kiowa chief), 103, 125; speech of, 17–28, 104
Tongue River, 138
Tonkawa Indians, 74–75, 81–82; cannibalism suspected of, 120; scouts of, 59, 82; Texas treaty with, 58; treaty with South, 117; U.S. treaties, 192–93
Torrey, Thomas, 63
Torrey's trading house No. 2, 62, 77
Toyash (Tow-y-ash, Taovaya) Indians, 10, 36. *See also* Wichita Indians
Treaties with the Confederacy, 116–118
treaty making, 11; evolvement of, 13; flaws in, 10; litigations evolving from, xi; methods of bribery employed in, 9; role of interpreters in, 10; social and religious factors of, xiv; spread of techniques onto Plains, xv; value as tool of conquest, 2–4

Treaty of Bird's Fort, Texas (1843), 65

Treaty of Camp Holmes, Indian Territory (1835), 49–54, 66

Treaty of Comanche Peak, Texas (1846), 71–75, 78–80

Treaty of Council Grove, Kansas (1825), 98

Treaty of Council Springs, Texas (1844), 66–68

Treaty of Council Springs, Texas (1845), 68

Treaty of Fort Atkinson, Kansas (1835) 101–4; rejection of, 112

Treaty of Fort Laramie (Horse Creek, Nebraska, 1851), 85–91, 101, 103, 133, 138–39; Cheyenne/Arapaho region defined by, 98; failure of, 96, 104; Indian view of, 126–27; territorial assignments of, 106–09; tribal assistance promised by, 138

Treaty of Fort Laramie, Wyoming, (1866), 160; value of denounced, 142

Treaty of Fort Laramie/Fort Rice, North Dakota, (1868), 157, 160, 162–65, 174–79, 184

Treaty of Fort Osage, Missouri, adjunct of entered into, 31; contest of by Osage faction, 29; stipulations of, 28–29

Treaty of Fort Smith/Washington, D.C., 122–23, 129

Treaty of Fort Wise, Colorado, 108–11; challenged by Cheyennes, 113

Treaty of Guadalupe Hidalgo, Mexico, 78; captives returned by, 80

Treaty of the Little Arkansas (Kansas), 125–26, 130, 183

Treaty of Medicine Lodge (Kansas), 11, 152, 161, 164–65, 168, 175, 183; falsity and effects of, 153

Treaty of New Echota, Georgia, (1835), Jackson manipulation of, 9

Treaty of Spring Creek (San Saba), Texas (1850), 79

Treaty of Tehuacana Creek, Texas (1843), 62

Tribal agreements, as substitute for treaties, 4

Trinity River, 59, 63, 65, 70, 78

Twain, Mark, 134

Twiggs, David (Gen.), 82; Alamo headquarters of, *83*

Two Bears (Sioux chief), 158

Two Kettle Sioux, 138–39, 157, 160

U.S. Capitol, 76, 112; Indian tours of, 7

U.S. Congress, 9, 16, 79, 129, 139, 161–62, 169, 176, 179–80; abandonment of treaty system, xvi; annuity agreement altered by, 96; fault of in Indian affairs, 182; Indian Peace Commission approved by, 17; parsimony in fulfilling treaty commitments, 11; Plains Indian treaty effort approved by, 48; promise of tribal protection, 6; role in treaty making, 2; Santa Fe Trail protection sought of, 35; Sioux title to Black Hills abrogated by, 178; stoppage of Sioux subsistence by, 175; treaty council funded by, 108; Treaty of Fort Atkinson rejected by, 112; treaty making ceased by, xi. *See also* U.S. Senate

U.S. Dragoons, 42, 49, 86, 91

U.S. Government, 12, 112, 125, 140; failure of regarding treaty promises, 11; goals in treaty making, 2; transportation and settlement concerns of, 111

U.S. House of Representatives, 180; treaty system ended by, 164, 171

U.S. Indian Bureau, 116

U.S. Indian policy, xi; attitude of officials toward, xii; criticism of, 105; evolution of, 164; innovation in, 171; legalities and ethics of, xii; spread of onto Plains, xv

U.S. Interior Department, 155

U.S. military, 83, 106, 115, 131, 142, 153; dominance in Indian affairs reestablished, 171; escort for Platte Trail provided by, 134; inability to guard Santa Fe Trail, 35; Indian policy control sought by, xiv; influence on Indian policy, xiv; lack of protection for Texas frontier by, 77; move to control Indian affairs defeated, 169; power of, 17; role as tribal protector, 11; Texas use of, 82; used to awe Indians, 7

U.S. Mounted Rangers, 34

U.S. Naval Yard, 76, 95, 173

U.S. Senate, 75, 110, 164; amends 1853 pact, 104; considers 1861 treaty, 141; failure to appropriate annuities, 77; treaty approval of, 10; treaty left unratified by, 48; treaty revisions made by, 78, 130. *See also* U.S. Congress, U.S. Government, U.S. House of Representatives

U.S. treaty commissioners, 3; behavior of, 8; techniques of, 5; use of interpreters by, 10

U.S. War Department, 23, 179, 155

Union (United States), 15–16, 120–22

United States, 1, 15–16, 24, 26, 30–31, 33, 47, 52, 56, 62, 64, 69, 74, 76, 79, 81, 91, 93, 97–98, 100, 102, 105, 109–10, 116–17, 121, 126–27, 139–40, 142–43, 156–58, 161–62, 173–74, 177–78, 180, 184; agreement to remove Texas Indians, 83; attitude toward Indian tribes, xiv; Comanche expedition approved by, 36; Creek/Seminole lands purchased by, 123; effect of treaty making on Plains Indian wars, xi; and 1825 friendship treaties, 19; and exploration beyond Mississippi River, 12; and Fort Laramie treaty commitments, 94; and Indian relations, xii, 165; and Indian removal, 34; Indian sovereignty recognized by, xiii; jurisdiction over Texas public domain released by, 77; "least attention" given to peaceful tribes, 129; military might of, 8; officials of opt for punishment of Indians, 133; pacts modeled after British, 1; peace commissions of, 123; and post-Civil War treaties, 118, 123; proprietary control of Western lands, 27; rationales for conquest, xv; responsibility for Texas Indians assumed by, 81; sovereignty over prairie tribes, 75; strategies of influencing tribal leaders, 7; Texas Indian problems taken up by, 68; Texas treaties sponsored by, 80; title to Pawnee lands won by, 44; treaty method of, 2, 181; treaty promises of, 146; treaty system ended by, 171; treaty system flaws of, 2; treaty violations of, 179; use of military might by, 153. See also U.S. Congress, U.S. Government, U.S. House of Representatives. U.S. Senate, Union

Upper Brazos Reservations, 81

Upper Platte and Arkansas Agency, 86, 100

Ute Indians, 151

Uvalde Canyon (Texas), battle of, 61

Van Buren, Martin (President), role in Indian removal, 4

Van Camp, Cornelius (Lt.), death of, 82

Van Dorn, Earl (Maj.), 128; Comanches attacked by, 82

Verdigris River, dissident Osages move to, 30–32; Rebel massacre on, 121

Vial, Pierre, New Mexico route opened by, 3; peace efforts of, 57

Victoria, Texas, 60

Virginia, 5; governor of, 109

Wabasha (the Leaf, Sioux chief), 25

Waco, Texas, 71

Waco Indians, 39, 41, 48, 54, 63, 68, 75, 79, 129; at Bird's Fort, 65; at Comanche Peak council, 72; at Council Springs, 1844, 67; at Council Springs, 1846, 74; captive girls of, 63; Texas treaty with, 62; treaty of with South, 117; U.S. treaties of, 193

Walker, Commissioner Francis A., 1, 170

Wan-na-sah-tah (Who Walks With His Toes Turned Out, Cheyenne chief), 92

Wap-pe-ton (the Little, Yankton chief), 26

War Bonnet (Cheyenne chief), 111; death of, 114

Ward, Artemus, 134

Ward, Nancy (Cherokee war-woman), speech of, 5

Ward, Seth, 158

Ware, Eugene (Capt.), 134

Warren's trading post, 64

Washbourne, Josiah H., 70

Washington, D.C., 7, 15, 48, 55, 75–77, 96, 102–3, 109–13, 129, 136, 145, 149, 155–156, 173–174, 183; Comanche-Kiowa delegation visit postponed, 56; deputation to, 55; 1851 delegation to, 94; 1872 delegation to, 170; 1873 visit of Kiowas, 8; Fort Smith council moved to, 123; Osage delegation to, 29

Washington-on-the-Brazos, 63, 66

Washita River, 37–38, 73–74, 83, 122, 148, 167

Watchful Elk (Sioux chief), 94

Watie, Stand (Cherokee rebel leader), forces of, 118

Watson, Daniel G., peace mission of, 66

We-ter-ra-shah-ro (Wichita chief), 40; Fort Gibson council attended by, 42–43; speech of, 41

Wea Indians, relocation of, 33

Webbers Falls, Indian Territory, 56

Weichell, Maria, rescue of, 169
Westport, Missouri, 35, 97
Wheeling, West Virginia, 76
Wheelock, Thompson B. (Lt.), Leavenworth Expedition chronicled by, 42
Whipple, Henry B. (Bishop), 1, 178; treaty incident cited by, 8; view of U.S. treaty system, 2
White, A. S., 157
White Antelope (Cheyenne chief), 94–95, 110, 113; at Fort Wise council, 109; death of, 114
White Bear (Hunkpapa Sioux chief), 22
White Bull (Kiowa chief), 111
White Crow (Cheyenne chief), 157
White (Great) Father, xiii, 92, 41, 43, 47, 52–53, 75, 90–92, 95, 104, 108, 126, 130–32, 136, 143, 160, 173; Kiowas reject offer of, 148; love for expressed, 6, 41, 43; wishes of invoked, 90
White Hair (Pawhuska, Osage chief), 28–29; band of, 120; 1825 delegation led by, 31
White House, 76, 95, 112, 160, 176; Indian visits to, 7
White Paint Creek, 18
White River, 174; council site at mouth of, 19
White Wolf (Pawnee chief), 14
Whitfield, J. W., 104
Wichita, Kansas, 125
Wichita Agency, 117–19, 170; creation of 83–84
Wichita Indians, 37–38, 40–41, 48, 51–55, 64, 68, 99, 123, 129; Camp Holmes treaty attended by, 49; captive interpreter of, 48; Civil War refuge of, 120; Comanche Peak attended by, 72; 1846 council attended by, 74; Fort Smith council attended by, 123; mourning of, 50; peace council at village of, 41; Texas treaty with, 62; treaty of with South, 117; U.S. treaties of, 193; village of attacked, 82, 128
Wichita Mountains, 34, 37, 39–40, 64, 80, 82, 168
Wild Cat (Seminole chief), 78; aid of to peace delegation, 70
Williams, L. H. (Col.), 73; peace mission of, 66
Wilmarth, Margaret, interpreter role of, 125
Wilson, Peter, agent at Fort Kiowa, 19
Winnebago Indians, 1816 treaty of, 15; 1825 treaty of, 25; 1827 treaty of, 26
Wistar, Thomas, 122; role as treaty commissioner, 140
Wolf Creek, 55, 99, 166
Wulea-boo (Shaved Head, Comanche chief), 103
Wynkoop, Edward W. (Maj.), 106, 145; clash avoided by, 143; expedition to Republican River, 113; threatened by Roman Nose, 147
Wyoming, 86, 137, 141, 155–57, 160, 172, 174–75, 177–78
Yamparica Comanches (Yam-pa-ric-co, Hamparika, Root Diggers), 55, 61, 74, 117, 130
Yankton Agency, 138
Yankton Sioux Indians: Atkinson meeting with, 19–20; 1825 treaty of, 25–26, 87, 138
Yanktonai Sioux Indians, 138–39, 157–58; Atkinson meeting with, 19–20
Yellow Buffalo (Kiowa), 111; Washington burial of, 112–13
Yellowstone Expedition, 16, 21, 24; military-scientific effort of, 15; operations of, 17–18
Yellowstone River, 24, 157–58, 177–78; fort ordered for, 15
Young Man Afraid of His Horse, 176